The **DAD** Manual

Published in September 2007
Reprinted 2009, 2010, 2013 (twice), 2014 and 2016

A catalogue record for this book is available
from the British Library

ISBN 978 0 85733 806 8

Library of Congress control no. 2007934588

Published by Haynes Publishing,
Sparkford, Yeovil, Somerset BA22 7JJ, UK
Tel: 01963 440635
Int. tel: +44 1963 440635
Website: www.haynes.co.uk

Haynes North America Inc.
861 Lawrence Drive, Newbury Park,
California 91320, USA

Printed and bound in the USA

The **DAD** Manual

HOW TO BE A BRILLIANT FATHER

Contents

6 How to be a brilliant father

10 Making toys

Stilts	12
Bows and arrows	14
Targets	16
Clothes peg catapult	17
Periscope	18
Pizza plane	20
Balsa glider	22
Kite	24

26 Simple fun

Fun with a magnifying glass	28
Making animals from paper	30
Making animals from papier mâché	32
Making a treasure chest	34
Taking things apart	38

40 Skills

Riding a bike: getting started	42
Riding a bike: fixing problems	44
Skateboarding: getting started	48
Skateboarding: essential tricks	50
Tying knots	52
Juggling basics	56

58 Sports basics

Football	60
Cricket	62
Rugby	64
Tennis	66
French cricket	68
Badminton	68
Rounders	69
Table tennis	69

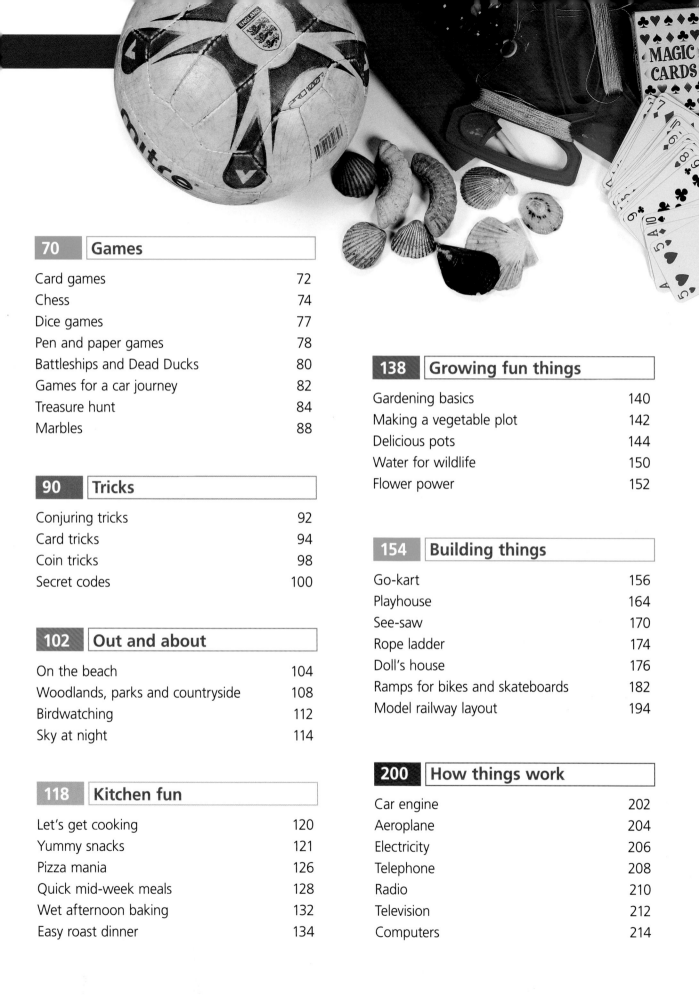

70	**Games**	
Card games		72
Chess		74
Dice games		77
Pen and paper games		78
Battleships and Dead Ducks		80
Games for a car journey		82
Treasure hunt		84
Marbles		88

90	**Tricks**	
Conjuring tricks		92
Card tricks		94
Coin tricks		98
Secret codes		100

102	**Out and about**	
On the beach		104
Woodlands, parks and countryside		108
Birdwatching		112
Sky at night		114

118	**Kitchen fun**	
Let's get cooking		120
Yummy snacks		121
Pizza mania		126
Quick mid-week meals		128
Wet afternoon baking		132
Easy roast dinner		134

138	**Growing fun things**	
Gardening basics		140
Making a vegetable plot		142
Delicious pots		144
Water for wildlife		150
Flower power		152

154	**Building things**	
Go-kart		156
Playhouse		164
See-saw		170
Rope ladder		174
Doll's house		176
Ramps for bikes and skateboards		182
Model railway layout		194

200	**How things work**	
Car engine		202
Aeroplane		204
Electricity		206
Telephone		208
Radio		210
Television		212
Computers		214

How to be a brilliant father

Most of us don't normally do brilliant things. Most of us won't be brilliant sportsmen or have brilliant careers. Which is great for our children, because high fliers tend to lack what's most needed to be a brilliant Dad – enough time, and a clear focus on your child.

Fifty years from now, most of the people who are famous today will have been forgotten. But you won't be forgotten by your children. You're in a great place to create brilliant memories with them, and have a lot of fun doing it!

If being a brilliant Dad isn't about being brilliant or doing things brilliantly, what is it about? It's about expressing your love in different ways. Partly by having enough time for your son or daughter; partly by sharing their interests; and partly by sharing activities, doing things with them and for them. That's where this book can help.

The activities included here are interesting and fun. Underneath there's also quite serious, very valuable stuff. For example, sports and other games will help build your child's confidence. Making things together will develop their talking and interpretive skills, as well as their dexterity. Which may sound surprisingly serious when you thought you were simply having fun!

Dads are a vital male role model for children – but you don't need to do 'masculine' things. For example, some people think of cooking as Mum's domain. It isn't, and Dads can have a lot of fun cooking with their children. Equally, we hope that many Mums will find the activities in this book useful and fun.

Activities for life

Some activities here can help develop resilience – especially valuable for girls, who often rely heavily on friendship groups that can turn sour. You and your child can learn to win games, and, just as important, to cope with losing and to enjoy other people's success.

From around the age of eight, boys in particular are often worried about not measuring up to their peers. Get them involved in a wide variety of activities: find some they're really good at and you'll give a great boost to their self confidence – especially if they're not good at football.

Share the things you like doing. Do the things your children like doing. There's lots of information in this book that can encourage long-term interests. From about seven years old, girls and boys are like sponges, absorbing interesting ideas and knowledge, picking up skills. From about eight, boys in particular start to want to become great experts in accumulating facts and becoming real experts in various subjects, from football to *Star Wars*. You'll soon see their interests widening – the *Dad Manual* will help.

Girls often develop interests that Dads don't find too absorbing. They tend to be more interested in being with friends than doing things with friends, but you still have a great role to play. Watch out for opportunities. Making things with your daughter and sharing her interests can provide great happy times, however much she seems to go in a separate direction.

Similarly, by the time they're teenagers most kids have, of course, developed their own interests, quite possibly in very different worlds. But if you've shared knowledge all through their early lives there's a better chance that they'll keep sharing it with you.

Making things for and with your children

Ask people for some of their fondest childhood memories and you'll probably find it was when they did and made things with their Dad.

Right into their teenage years, your children will be quite proud to say 'My Dad made it'. From about five, they may also be more proud to say 'I made it with my Dad'. And best of all, from about seven onwards they'll be extra proud to say 'I made it' – and you can be proud too. (Never mind if you put a lot of work into it as well – just let them have the glory!)

You don't have to be perfect

Brilliant Dads aren't perfect. For example, you don't have to be amazingly patient. But try to allow extra time for things, for children to catch on or get the knack of things. They're less likely to learn to persevere at something if their Dad's always in a hurry or gets really annoyed when things go wrong.

Take your time. Slow and fiddly jobs can mean comfortable conversations. Time talking with your child is never wasted, even if there are other things you want to be getting on with.

Allocate more time for them to help or do it, and allow extra time so that if (or when) someone makes a mistake – or possibly make a complete mess of something – you have time to put things right.

You don't have to do too much

Some brilliant Dads do go into their sheds, do loads for their children and spend ages on projects. But it's not essential, because time making things with, rather than for, children is probably time better spent.

When adults make things, they often set high standards. If you're making something with children you may want to think about this. Don't shut the shed door and lock yourself away for hours to make the perfect kite – a wobbly one that two of you make together will be much better.

From the age of eight or nine children need encouragement to see what they really can do on their own. They also need to understand that they aren't yet old enough to do some things that they want to. Let them make mistakes – but step in if the mistakes start getting too drastic.

Some brilliant Dads develop a useful knack: they keep children occupied for a long time while investing only a little time themselves. But it's not easy. Think about what your child can do, and how they'll stick at it. For example, make papier mâché together once and after that you may find your children can do it alone, keeping them occupied for a lot of time with little adult input.

Positive criticism

Consciously or unconsciously, many brilliant Dads use positive criticism. It's a valuable technique, but because we're all used to negative criticism it's a skill that takes a bit of learning.

Positive criticism is when you assess something and work out the good points as well as the bad points. You talk about things without putting anyone down. Instead of criticising the way something looks, you can ask why it looks that way. Instead of pointing out that something is being done wrong, you say 'If you do it this way it may be easier'. Instead of criticising faults, you pick out the good points, and phrase your comments regarding the bad points in such a way that your child is free to disagree amicably (which teenagers will certainly want to do!).

Here are some examples:
- Your child says 'Look at the horse I made, Dad.' Saying 'That doesn't look anything like a horse,' isn't as good as 'I love the tail.'
- Or your child says 'Look at my car, Dad.' Saying 'But it's only got three wheels,' isn't as good as 'What an interesting model, tell me how it works.'

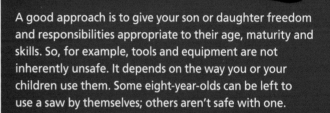

Praise and encouragement

Your child (in fact, most of us) will really thrive on a mixture of praise, encouragement and positive criticism.

What's the difference between praise and encouragement? Most parents praise their children for doing things well, and that's fine as far as it goes. But if you only receive praise, it can make you dependent on the person giving it. You're relying on what they think: and that doesn't build up your self-confidence. That way it's their judgement that tells you how well you're doing, not yours.

By contrast, encouragement rather than praise can help your children become more self-confident. Encouragement provides messages of support. It can come from positive statements seen as independent of the person making them. For example, you can use 'I' statements, where it shows it's your opinion, not some unarguable fact, and you can focus on something specific.

For example, you could say 'That was a good tackle,' but it's more encouraging to say 'I thought that was a good tackle because you surprised the striker at just the right moment.' This says to your child: 'I'm good at tackling not because my Dad says so but because my timing is good.'

You could say, 'Well done, that's a lovely picture,' but it's more encouraging to say 'I like the way you coloured that so neatly,' because that means (1) 'Dad likes what I'm doing,' and (2) 'I'm good at colouring neatly.'

With practice you'll find it easy to come up with various good phrases that will really encourage your children.

It's time to get started

We hope you'll get a lot from this book. Some of the activities have been great favourites with Dads and children for many years. Others will be new to you. But being a brilliant Dad is about doing lots of different things with your children, and sharing their interests and activities. Whether you have half an hour or a whole weekend, turn the pages here and you'll find something that will be fun for both you and your child.

Safety

Some people believe in protecting their children from all danger. Others believe that it's better to expose their children to some danger. Overall, most people would agree that safety depends on the child, the activity and the situation.

A good approach is to give your son or daughter freedom and responsibilities appropriate to their age, maturity and skills. So, for example, tools and equipment are not inherently unsafe. It depends on the way you or your children use them. Some eight-year-olds can be left to use a saw by themselves; others aren't safe with one.

Some good basic rules include the following:
- Explain things properly, and explain them again.
- Show the risks, know the risks, and keep them controlled.
- Do things and enjoy them: don't let small risks put you off.
- Don't use or do something in such a way that it causes undue risk.

COMMON SENSE?

Safety is often a matter of what adults would call common sense, but you need to remember that even common sense has to be explained and learned. And children have a remarkable ability to do the unexpected.

You'll see some safety rules on several pages in the *Dad Manual*. It's sometimes worth making a point by showing what the danger can really mean. If you give children the appropriate freedom, they may well still hurt themselves. For example, allow them the freedom to use a knife unattended and a child may cut his or her finger – which may mean greater safety long term, as they're not so likely to do it again!

We talk about safety in numbers, yet there's also danger in numbers. You need to increase supervision when there are more children around. Activities on a one-to-one basis are easy to watch, and one adult to two children is usually fine; but one to three or more can mean problems. It depends on the activity. For example, a group of five kids throwing beanbags is probably safe enough. A group of five kids with bows and arrows probably isn't.

Making toys

Stilts 12

Bows & arrows 14

Targets 16

Clothes peg catapult 17

Periscope 18

Pizza plane 20

Balsa glider 22

Kite 24

Stilts

Children absolutely love 'stilting'. Like learning to ride a bike, they'll need help to stay upright at first, but it doesn't take them long to get the knack of 'walking tall'.

You will need:

- Drill stand and mains-powered drill
- Drill bits
- Battery-powered screwdriver
- Smoothing plane
- Clamps/cramps
- Carpenter's square
- Countersink
- Tenon-saw
- Stanley knife
- Chisel
- Adjustable spanner
- Bradawl
- Expanding rule
- Wood glue
- Glasspaper
- Masking tape
- Timber and plywood as per cutting list
- 4 M10 x 75mm zinc-plated coach bolts

If you're making the stilts for a young child you may need to reduce the size of the timbers. This is because the tops of the stilts need to be shaped into handles, and the dimensions given in the cutting list are rather big for small hands.

You need to be selective at the timber yard and make sure you choose knot-free wood for the uprights, otherwise a knot will almost certainly turn up just where you want to drill a hole for the footrests.

These stilts have adjustable footrests fitted to the uprights by coach bolts, for which holes are bored at intervals. All that it's necessary to do to adjust the footrest is to remove the coach bolts, move the footrest up or down the upright and re-fix the coach bolts.

Cutting list

- Legs – cut 2 @ 1,830 x 44 x 38mm (timber)
- Footrests – cut 4 @ 152 x 102 x 12mm (plywood)
- Footrest cores – cut 2 @ 108 x 44 x 38mm (timber)

1 **A** The uprights are longer than necessary to allow for two offcuts which will form part of the footrest. Clamp or tape both uprights together. Mark the length of the legs, and then the two short footrest stubs.

B Saw the legs to length.

C Next cut the footrest stubs to length and put them to one side. Note the use of a cutting block in this picture.

2 With the leg uprights taped or clamped together, mark the positions for the footrests, ensuring that the spacing intervals are equal. Mark across both legs using a carpenter's square. You don't have to drill the coach bolt holes yet – that comes later.

3 Each footrest is actually a wooden 'sandwich', consisting of a timber filling between two pieces of plywood.

4 Squirt plenty of glue on both sides of the timber filling.

5 Next put the sandwich together and drive in screws from both sides. Be aware that when timber is sandwiched with glue like this the pieces have a tendency to slide, so be careful that they don't slip out of place while you're screwing the blocks together.

6 A Clamp the footrest to the bench and, using a tenon-saw, cut off the hatched area (take the dimensions from the plan).

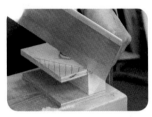

B When the first side is cut, turn the footrest over and cut the other side.

C Wrap a piece of glasspaper around a waste block and work over the footrest to remove all the sharp corners. Remember, children's ankles and legs will be in contact with the footrests, and if you don't do a good job then scratches will result.

7 A Take one of the footrests and align its top edge with one of the spaced lines that you drew in Step 2. Fit a cramp to hold the footrest to the leg and

mark the two holes that need to be drilled. Bore holes in the footrest and leg using the correct size drill for the bolt. This is a job best done in a drill stand, which ensures accurate alignment of both pieces so that the bolt will go in without sticking.

B Once the first pair of holes has been bored, move the footrest along to align with the next pencil line, and mark and drill the next pair of holes. Repeat the process until you've bored as many holes as you need.

8 A Secure the footrests in place using galvanised coach bolts. The square shank at the top, just below the rounded head, will grip in the timber when the bolt is fastened on the other side.

B Tighten the nuts using a small adjustable spanner.

9 The completed stilts with both footrests fitted. To prevent the bottoms of the legs becoming ragged, use a plane to chamfer all four edges. You should also make sure that the tops of the legs are nicely rounded off. If you intend to paint the stilts it's not a bad idea to leave the areas where the footrests go paint-free. Paint inevitably makes the legs thicker, and the footrests will spoil the paintwork when they're adjusted up and down.

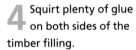
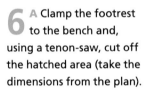

Bows & arrows

The simplest bows and arrows will keep children happy for a while. Just find a thin branch, tie on some string and you can get going. But old wood tends to be brittle; young wood needs to be cut off the tree, and this may not make you popular with the wood's owners.

You will need:

- 2 x 2.4m pieces of stripwood about 30mm wide x 5mm thick
- Small saw
- Drill
- Pencil
- Knife
- String
- Sandpaper
- Flexible wood glue – PVA or similar
- Material for the grip (eg an offcut from tennis or badminton binding, a strip of leather, cloth or towelling, duct tape)

The bow

If you are fortunate enough to know a source of yew, holly, apple or ash, these can all provide good springy branches. Most people, however, will need to settle instead on what's available from a DIY shop or timber merchant, but since this sort of wood isn't intended for bending like a bow it will need some strengthening.

This bow is simple to make, and children can help.

If you're in a hurry, you can glue the strips immediately, drill holes at one end of the longest piece, and cut notches at the other. Put in some string and you're ready to shoot! However, if your son or daughter can be patient, spending a little more time on construction will probably make the bow last longer.

The measurements here are for a bow 1m long. Your bow should be up to about the height of your child's eyes, so you may need to adjust the measurements accordingly.

1 Cut four pieces of stripwood: 2 x 1,000mm; 2 x 300mm. Pencil a line 350mm along one of the 1,000mm lengths. Put the two 1,000mm pieces together, and place the 300mm pieces on top, lined up to the mark.

2 Drill a small hole through all four pieces at the mid point, *ie* 150mm along the 300mm lengths. This doesn't have to be very precise.

3 Lay out the four pieces and get some glue ready. Spread glue generously on one side of every piece.

4 Stick the pieces together, with the 300mm strips on the outside and the two 1,000mm strips in the middle. Using a small screw in the drill hole made at step 3, screw the four pieces together and line them up.

5 Take about 2.5m of string and tie it around and back along the full length of the bow. Cutting a notch at either end, or drilling a hole and threading the string, may make it easier to keep it in position. Pull the string firmly, making a good curve in the wood, and knot it. How much you can safely bend it will depend on the quality of the wood.

6 Use clamps or constrictor knots (page 55) all along the bow to hold the wood strips tightly together. Leave to dry. Cut off any string and remove any clamps. Trim the wood with a craft knife to shape the handle.

7 Drill holes at each end and cut notches at one end.

8 Wrap binding material around the handle and fix with glue, tape or staples.

9 Taking a new piece of string, tie a figure-of-eight stopper knot (see page 53) and thread the string through the hole at the bottom of the bow; then make a bowline (see page 54) to go round the top. The bowline should be slipped off when the bow is put away after use, in order to release the tension.

The arrow

Use 5–6mm dowel or thin bamboo. Make sure they're reasonably straight pieces. You can also try thin branches from trees after stripping off the bark. Whatever you use, the arrows should be about 100mm longer than the archer's arm.

To shoot well, an arrow needs (a) to be straight, (b) to have some weight at the front, (c) to have flights at the back, and (d) to have a notch at the end. Make the notch with a knife or file.

You'll need to experiment with various weights. Try using pieces of Blu Tack, metal pen-caps, quantities of duct tape, screws, and so on. If you cut a slit at the front you can experiment with thin pieces of metal.

Arrowheads – try using a pen cap, a screw or a drill bit bound on with duct tape, or a bottle top bent and hammered onto the dowel.

Finding good feathers for the flights can be very difficult. Turkey, swan and goose feathers are good; most other feathers are too weak to be functional but may look good, so will please a child. If you're lucky enough to find some good feathers:

1 Remove the fluffy bits by gripping firmly and pulling toward the quill point.

2 Cut the quill in half, and trim off some feather.

3 Glue or bind them to the arrow with thread. The flights should be applied in threes, positioned at equal distances round the shaft. One flight (usually a different colour) should be at right angles to the notch.

You can make flights from feathers, pizza bases or thick paper, glued onto the dowel.

Targets

To encourage target practice, you need good targets. Biscuit tin lids make a good noise and move when they're hit. Another possibility is shooting into a wastepaper basket or bin. You can make this competitive by awarding points for each 'hit'.

1 For catapults. You want to imagine firing boulders into a castle. This is a very simple target to make, using corrugated cardboard and kitchen paper rolls.

2 Skull and crossbones target, made from corrugated cardboard and aluminium foil. Hits make a satisfying noise!

3 How do you know for sure where you hit the target? This target catches the bullets, which means that competitors can work out who scored what. It's made from corrugated cardboard, wood and a yoghurt pot.

4 Three-in-a-row target, made from corrugated cardboard and yoghurt pots.

Shooting safely

In most real archery, it's usual to pull back the string to touch the archer's cheek. However, that may be too much of a strain for the wood we're using. Pulling back to the shoulder will probably provide enough force to shoot an arrow a reasonable distance.

Children can hold the arrow between forefinger and thumb, but if they do there's a greater risk of slipping and shooting it off in the wrong direction. Holding the arrow between forefinger and second finger is safer. Avoid allowing the lower fingers to curl around the string.

To shoot, stand side on to the target and turn your head to look at it. Draw back the bowstring with the arrow notched on it, close one eye and look along the arrow to take aim. The arm holding the bow should be still and shouldn't move until after you've released the arrow.

IMPORTANT – SAFETY RULES

Even very makeshift bows and arrows can be dangerous. It's worth telling children four very strict rules, and adding extra ones depending on circumstances:

- Never point a bow with an arrow at someone, even if it's not ready to fire

- Never shoot an arrow if anyone is in front of you, even if to one side

- Always point your bow down when you have an arrow ready, unless you're about to shoot

- Never shoot anywhere unless you can see where the arrow is likely to go (ie no shooting over walls, over cliffs or rocks etc where you can't see)

These rules are equally valid for catapults, crossbows, air guns etc. Teach children the important basic rules and they'll be safer dealing with more dangerous things as they grow up.

Clothes peg catapult

This is ideal to make with even very young children. Some children aged about 7 or more can make this entirely by themselves.

You will need:

- Wooden clothes peg with spring
- Wooden lolly stick or small flat piece of wood
- Small block of balsa or other wood about 70mm x 30mm x 20m
- Larger block of balsa or other wood about 150mm x 50mm x 30mm
- Small jam jar lid
- Glue – epoxy resin, strong wood glue or hot gun glue

1 Cut the two pieces of wood. Glue the smaller piece on top of the larger, roughly in the middle. Glue the clothes peg on top.

2 Glue the jam jar lid to the lolly stick, with about 20mm sticking out at one end and more at the other.

3 Glue the lolly stick to the clothes peg so that the tin lid is 10mm or more away from the peg.

4 You're ready to fire hazelnuts, Maltesers, dried beans and suchlike indoors, small stones and marbles outdoors.

How to make a peashooter

WHAT YOU'LL NEED

A4 sheet of paper; masking tape or sellotape; suitable projectiles – dried peas, small balls of dampened tissues, peanuts, Smarties etc

You can make peashooters in minutes and they provide a great deal of fun. When they get soggy just make new ones.

- Roll up the sheet of paper widthwise around a pencil.
- Tape it to the diameter you want – you need to allow 2mm more than the size of your bullets.
- You're ready to shoot!

As regards shooting technique, you can get good results by simply blowing with a 'whooshing' action; but you can get even better results using another technique. Anyone who's been taught to play the recorder should recognise it. Put the tip of your tongue over the end of the peashooter. Start to blow and build up pressure, then with a kind of tutting action with your tongue, let the air out in a precise blast.

Periscope

Children like periscopes because you can look over walls, round corners and over people's heads with them. They're great for spying on people, and you can imagine you're in a submarine or in a World War One trench.

You will need:

- Pieces of corrugated cardboard
- Duct tape or masking tape
- Glue (a hot glue gun is ideal)
- 2 pieces of mirror glass, about 180mm x 140mm

(You can often pick up mirrors cheaply in charity shops, and picture-framing shops can cut small pieces at a low cost.)

1 Wrap tape around any edges of the mirror glass that are sharp and could cut fingers.

2 Mark out and cut pieces A, B, C, D, E and F. as shown below.

This periscope is quick to make and uses corrugated cardboard. The same design can be made from wood but will be substantially heavier. Adjust the dimensions to reflect the size of the cardboard and mirrors that are available.

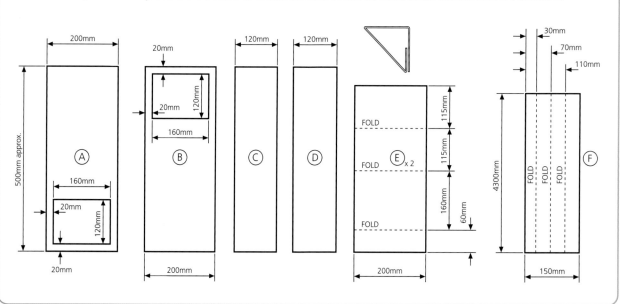

Budding artists can finish off their periscopes with some camouflage painting.

3 On the lines for folding, cut slightly into one side and fold the two E pieces and glue or tape them to form two triangular-sectioned units. Viewed side on, they should each make a right-angled triangle, with the long side as close to 45° as possible.

4 Using tape or glue, fix the two mirrors as shown.

5 Tape panels A–D together to create a long box.

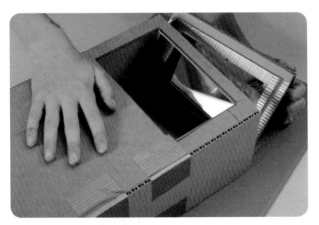

6 Fit the two mirror units in at top and bottom. Secure them in place with tape at top and bottom.

7 Fold piece F and glue and/or tape it to the back of the periscope to make the handle.

Pizza plane

The packaging of many ready-to-cook pizzas includes a thin disc of expanded polystyrene, and this ultra-light material is great for making a simple glider. The design shown here is very simple to measure out, cut and assemble. Once you've made it once or twice with a child of about 11, they can probably go into production alone – so long as they're safe to leave alone with a sharp knife.

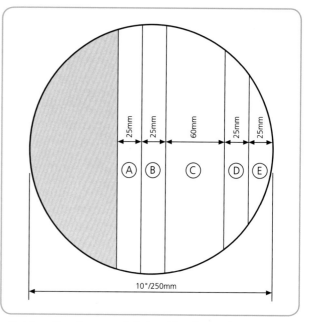

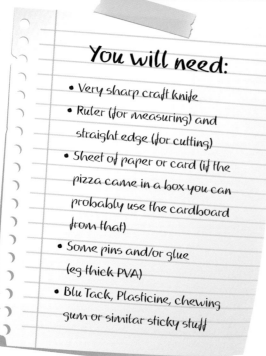

You will need:

- Very sharp craft knife
- Ruler (for measuring) and straight edge (for cutting)
- Sheet of paper or card (if the pizza came in a box you can probably use the cardboard from that)
- Some pins and/or glue (eg thick PVA)
- Blu Tack, Plasticine, chewing gum or similar sticky stuff

1 Place the disc on a slightly wider sheet of card or paper and draw round it. Mark out guidelines on the paper as shown in the diagram. The measurements here are for a 10in/250mm circle. Some pizzas come on 9in or 12in circles: if you're using one of these, scale the pattern down or up accordingly, reducing by 10 per cent or increasing by 20 per cent.

2 Tape the disk to the card.

3 Using the straight edge, cut across carefully to make the strips, as marked. (Keep the offcuts to one side, for replacement parts.)

4 Taking the two fuselage pieces (A and B), stick or pin them together.

5 Slot the tail piece (E) between the two fuselage pieces and glue or pin it in position.

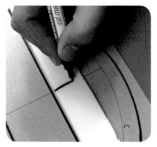

6 Mark centre lines on the wing (C) and tail (D).

7 Place wing on top of the fuselage with pins or glue, and the tail piece in position underneath the fuselage.

8 Wrap a blob of sticky stuff round the nose and you're ready for your first trial flight. If the plane dives too soon, reduce the weight on the nose. If it climbs then stalls, add a bit of extra weight. Keep experimenting. You should be able to achieve a flight of more than 10m with a slow gentle launch motion. Children can try launching while standing on a chair, if you're there to keep an eye on them and they can be trusted not to fall off.

Once you've achieved good results with the basic design described here, you can experiment with different wing and tail proportions, and different wing angles. Instead of simply fixing the tailpiece underneath, try slotting it in halfway up the fuselage.

Classic paper dart

This version of a classic design takes just a little paper-folding skill. You get a good stable dart which flies very well, and it only take 9 folds.

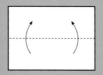

1 Take an A4 sheet of paper. Fold it in half lengthways, and open out.

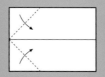

2 Fold the top corners in, to line up along the centre crease as accurately as possible.

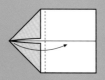

3 Fold the top down to touch a point 20–30mm from the bottom of the crease. Turn paper over.

4 Fold the two corners into the middle crease, leaving a small triangle showing.

5 Fold the small triangle upwards (it stops the flap coming loose in flight).

6 Turn paper over, and fold in half with the small triangle on the outside.

7 Fold one upper flap to the bottom edge, as accurately as possible.

8 Turn over and repeat for the other upper flap.

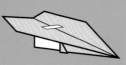

9 Open out both wings. Put a small piece of tape across the top of the wings for more stable flight.

Balsa glider

This model is simple enough for many children aged 11+ to make, if they're reasonably accurate at measuring and marking, and safe with a very sharp knife. You need just one sheet of balsa, which will still leave you with sufficient left over for spare parts in case of breakages or cutting mistakes. Use a thickish weight of balsa, which is easier to cut and less prone to splitting. The downside is that the glider will then be on the heavy side. Once your child has gained confidence, it's worth experimenting with thinner balsa for longer flights.

You will need:

- A sheet of 2mm balsa measuring 75 x 790mm
- Very sharp craft knife or scalpel
- Ruler
- Pencil or markers
- Straight edge for cutting
- Balsa cement
- Pins
- Blu Tack, Plasticine, chewing gum or similar sticky stuff

1 Mark up the balsa sheet as in the diagram. Cut out all the pieces.

2 If you want, decorate the fuselage, wing and tail pieces with markers.

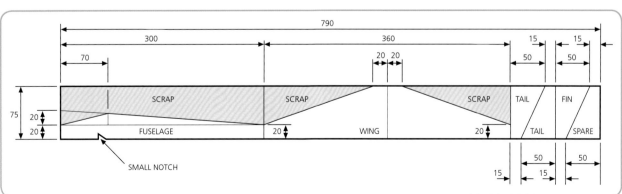

3 Glue the tail pieces onto the fuselage along the guideline running parallel to the base, at right angles and as accurately as possible. Glue the tail fin onto the back, in line with the fuselage and also as accurately as possible.

4 Glue the wing under the fuselage, as square as possible to the fuselage.

5 Fix some Blu Tack or other sticky stuff firmly onto the nose. You're now ready for a trial flight. Find the glider's centre of balance by lightly holding it under the fuselage between forefinger and thumb. It should balance on your finger at around the midpoint, under the wing. Adjust the sticky stuff to improve the balance if necessary. Then try to fly it.

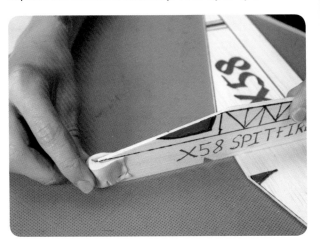

Launch tips

A long gentle level throw will be more effective than a sudden launch (children tend to chuck gliders upwards). Note that you may have to keep adjusting the blob of sticky stuff for different types of flight. Also, this glider will fly well upside down as well as the right way up!

Launching with an elastic band works well at a slight angle, up to 20–30°. Children love shooting at higher angles – the results can be spectacular, but things can also get out of control.

The plane can fly a long way, so only fly it in a large garden or open space.

If experimenting away from your own home, bring some spare ready-cut pieces, glue and a craft knife to be ready for instant repairs.

Kite

You can get loads of different kites from shops these days, but making your own is something else. Your children will love it. This kite is easy to make, and quick too. It should take you about half an hour, or, if the children help, a bit longer.

You will need:

- Sheet of heavy-duty polythene or a large, heavy-duty rubbish/rubble bag, big enough to provide a usable piece 1m square
- 2 x 1m lengths of 5–6mm dowel or thin bamboo
- About 1.3m of thin string to make the kite, and 30m or so to fly it
- Strong sticky tape, ideally duct tape or elephant tape
- Ruler
- Sharp craft knife or pair of scissors
- Something to use as a guide for cutting out circles – eg a tin can

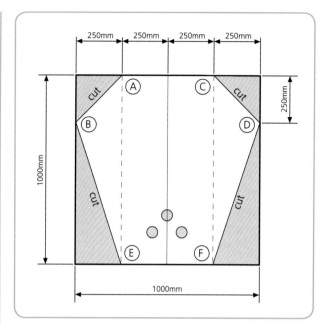

1 Cut a 1m square of polythene. If the piece you've got can't stretch to a full metre, scale down all the sizes given here in proportion. Fold the sheet in half to make a crease down the middle. Fold the sides over to the middle and make two further folds. Turn the top corners over to the first crease to make creases A–B and C–D. Fold the bottom corners up to make creases from E–B and F–D. Cut off all four triangles.

2 Lay the sheet flat, and tape the dowels along lines A–E and C–F, at the top, bottom and roughly in the middle. 100mm pieces of duct tape will be just right. Any young helpers can cut the tape ready, and help with the fixing. Put a small piece of tape on the wing corners; make a hole about 10–20mm from the edge on each side. Tie a length of about 1.3m of string at corners B and D. Cut out three holes – you can mark these out by eye, but it's easier to cut round a tin can, tin lid or something similar.

3 Attach the string to a longer line, at least 30m, and go and find a large field.

Up and away?

There's little that makes a dad feel more useless than not getting a kite up. Here are a few tips to make sure it flies.

LAUNCHING

Running with a kite to try to launch it is fun, but doesn't work well. Instead, check the wind direction carefully, hold the kite into the wind at arm's length, and release.

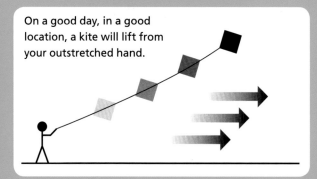

On a good day, in a good location, a kite will lift from your outstretched hand.

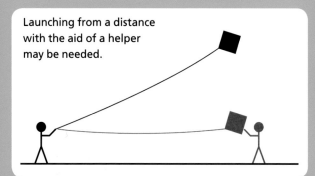

Launching from a distance with the aid of a helper may be needed.

If that doesn't work, get a helper to stand about 5m from you, ready to throw the kite smoothly – *ie* not chuck it – into the air. Feed some line onto the ground, but hold it taut to the kite. You walk slowly backwards, still holding line taut but ready to let it out quickly. If that doesn't work, try a different spot – or another day.

WIND DIRECTION

Stand with your back to the wind. Make sure the kite is headed directly into the wind, otherwise it won't lift properly.

Clouds tell you the wind direction high above, but lower down it may be quite different. You can get your children to check it at ground level in various ways:

throwing grass up in the air; licking their forefinger and telling you which side feels cold (explain to them that's where the wind is coming from); holding up a strip of paper or ribbon; looking at the way nearby trees are moving; observing smoke from a fire or chimney (this can also give an idea of wind speed).

WIND SPEED AND LIFT

A kite relies on wind for lift and stability, but it's the effect caused by things on the ground that's critical to successful flying. Terrain, buildings and trees all affect ground-level winds – for example, even a light breeze can be turbulent when passing over an uneven landscape; but choose your launch site well and you can enjoy the extra lift it provides.

Air is more turbulent in the first 15m or so above the ground, but from about 30m upwards it's more stable, so if your kite gets that high it should stay there. Wind speed also tends to be greater at higher altitude. It can also change direction, so be ready to move around. Make sure there's plenty of room behind you so that you can walk backwards to give your kite more lift.

It's best to keep your kite well out in the open where the ground is even and the wind steady. Beaches, edges of lakes, large fields, wide open spaces – are all good. Watch out for pylons, power cables, washing lines, trees, helicopters, as none of them agree with kites...

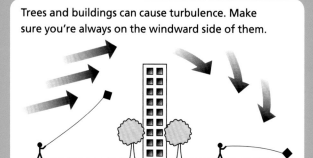

Trees and buildings can cause turbulence. Make sure you're always on the windward side of them.

On a hill, there's extra lift on the windward side. On the leeward side turbulence makes flying difficult.

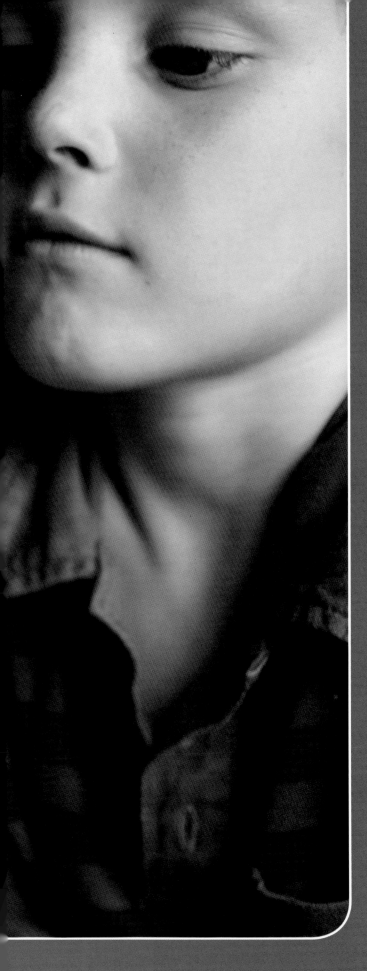

Simple fun

**Fun with a
magnifying glass**   28

**Making animals
from paper**   30

**Making animals
from papier mâché**   32

Making a treasure chest   34

Taking things apart   38

Fun with a magnifying glass

It's fun spending time playing around with magnifying glasses. Here are a few activities you can try.

CHOOSING A MAGNIFYING GLASS

You can pick up cheap plastic magnifying glasses, but it's worth paying a little more for a good glass one. Plastic magnifying glasses tend not to magnify so well, and produce a cloudy or distorted image.

Really good magnifying glasses aren't cheap, so it's worth looking out for them in junk shops. As well as the classic Sherlock Holmes variety (A, B), look out for other types, such as folding ones (C). Linen counters (D, E) hold the lens in exactly the right position to provide a sharp, highly magnified image. A watchmaker's eyeglass (F), held right against the face, also gives a very sharp image. A loupe (G) is used by photographers and designers to check the quality of pictures, and can be very powerful. It has a transparent ring of plastic around it so that it can hold things like insects in place for very close scrutiny. A cheap bug viewer (H) does this too, but provides a poor image: a magnifying glass over a jam jar can do a much better job. Multi-lens units (I) provide a lot of fun but usually not very sharp images.

A light bulb on your hand

Hold the magnifying glass under a light in which the bulb isn't covered – for example, under a standard lamp. Move the magnifying glass between your hand and the lamp, and at about 15cm you'll project a sharp picture of the bulb on your hand. You can both see it and feel its warmth.

Hole burning

Most of us have done it, and it's so satisfying for any child. Simply wait for some good bright sunlight, move the magnifying glass so as to focus the rays onto a piece of wood or paper, and wait.

It's a good idea to wear sunglasses, as the concentrated bright light can hurt your eyes. It's also easier to focus the light better.

Getting a lot of smoke is one thing, but it's surprisingly hard to set anything on fire. If you want to be successful, try focussing the light on the edge of some newspapers, or where there's a large area of solid black (the printing ink can encourage burning). You could try using some dried grass, or focus the light on the head of a match for a very satisfying instant explosive burning.

You can also try burning shapes and letters onto wood, melting holes in candles, or melting and distorting plastic (though extra care is required here, since many plastics give off toxic fumes, or burst into flame suddenly).

IMPORTANT – SAFETY RULES

It's vital that you always emphasise the dangers of playing with fire, and make sure that your children understand it must never be done unless a responsible adult is present. Playing with fire is under no circumstances an indoor activity!

Close encounters

A good magnifying glass is a valuable tool for looking at many things that will surprise children when they see them close up.

What things can you look at? A feather, a leaf, a flower, mould on old food, wood, your finger, eye or ear, spiders, ants and other insects, photographs printed in newspapers and books, postage stamps, banknotes, a rusty nail, a coin, a pen nib, string, fabrics and jewellery – the possibilities are endless.

Some things look more exciting and interesting if you shine a torch across them at a low angle to highlight the different textures and details.

'Australian' television

You will need:

Sheet of tracing paper or greaseproof paper; old cardboard box; knife; tape; a room with a window

In opposite sides of the box, cut out two rectangles slightly smaller than the sheet of tracing paper. Tape the paper over one of them. Set the box with its open side towards a window, then hold your magnifying glass in front of it, moving it round until you get a clear picture on the tracing paper – the view through the window (the image will be upside down). This may be improved if you draw the curtains slightly.

Young would-be TV stars can dance in front of the lens and appear on the screen...upside down. It may seem silly and simple, but capturing images this way is what started scientists on the path to inventing photography.

Fun with magnets
Paperclip races

You will need:
2 small magnets; some large paperclips; corrugated cardboard, at least 300mm x 450mm, for the racetrack; 4 strips of corrugated cardboard about 300mm x 50mm, to make feet; marker pens; 2 wood or plastic rods, a little longer than the width of the racetrack; tape or glue

Draw a racetrack on the cardboard. Make triangular section feet for the racetrack by folding and gluing the cardboard strips. Tape or glue the magnets to the rods.

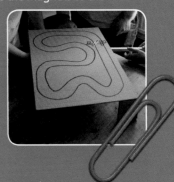

Place the paperclips on the start line, one per player. The players move their 'cars' by holding the magnets underneath the paper. If your magnets are strong enough, they may even be able to race small metal toy cars.

Magnetic fishing

You will need:
Cardboard; thick paper; paperclips; 2–4 small magnets; 2–4 wooden rods (dowel, bamboo or similar) about 4mm in diameter and 30mm long; knife and scissors; thick thread or thin string

Make a square or octagonal tube from the cardboard, 20mm or more tall and about 250mm wide. Cut out about 20 card or paper fish-shapes in assorted sizes, and decorate them – to add an element of competition you can write numbers on the fish to add up for final scores. Fix a paperclip onto the mouth end of each fish.

Make the fishing rods by sticking a magnet onto a length of thread and tying the thread to the rod. To start fishing, just lower your fishing magnet into the pond and see what it catches. You're not meant to peep, but most children can't resist.

Making animals from paper

It can be great fun making animals out of various materials with your children. Don't be put off by thinking that you have to be artistic or creative. You can produce models that will delight your child, whatever skills you have. You don't need to be able to draw, you don't need to work accurately. Even if your animal looks nothing like the real thing, it'll probably be a great success.

THE SECRET FOR SUCCESS

As adults, we tend to have quite precise pictures in our minds. Children think differently. To make an animal successfully, your model doesn't have to be accurate: it just needs to show one or two of the animal's most distinctive characteristics. The most memorable thing about a toucan, for instance, is its enormous beak, so a few bits of cardboard can do the job fine. And a vital thing about sheep is that they are white and woolly.

Making a sheep

You will need:

Two sheets A4 white paper; pencil; craft knife; a safety match

1 Draw a rough, wiggly oval to fill most of the sheet, and a sheep's head and legs. Don't worry too much about what a sheep looks like. Any blob with a head and feet will be OK.

2 Lightly draw small, long, thin, horizontal oblongs all over the sheep's body, about 30–40mm wide, 8–10mm high.

3 Cut the tops, bottoms and left-hand sides of the oblongs with a knife, but leave all the right-hand sides uncut.

4 Show your young assistant how to curl the paper, by rolling it around the match.

5 When you have finished puting curls all over the sheep, glue it onto another piece of paper.

Making a toucan

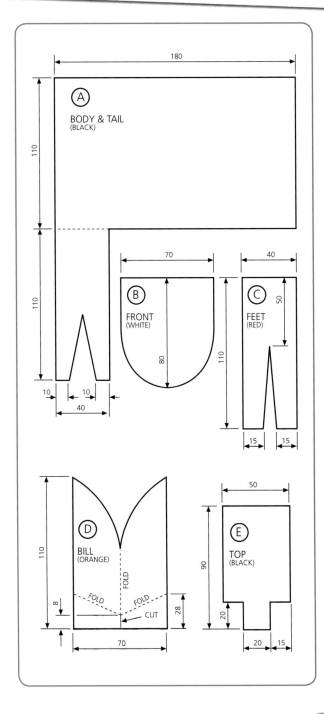

A
BODY & TAIL
(BLACK)

180

110

110

10 10
40

B
FRONT
(WHITE)

70

80

C
FEET
(RED)

40

50

110

15 15

D
BILL
(ORANGE)

110

8

FOLD FOLD FOLD
CUT

70

E
TOP
(BLACK)

50

90

28

20

20 15

1 Cut out the five shapes.

2 Roll piece A around the tube and glue it down.

3 Bend and glue piece B at the top, around piece A.

4 Glue piece C, which makes the feet, and stick it in the tube, about half way in. Curl the paper sticking out.

5 Fold piece D: put glue on the tabs and a little dab on the top front of the beak.

6 Stick the beak in place. Making a hole with scissors or a needle, push in two split pins as eyes (or draw eyes with a marker).

7 Glue the small tab of piece E on the inside front of the tube, and fold the top down. To finish, you may want to add some Blu Tack, sticky stuff or some other weight to make sure the toucan perches comfortably on a shelf without falling over.

Making animals from papier mâché

It's excellent to have a go at papier mâché (it's a French term – pronounced pappya mashay). You can achieve good results quite quickly, and then if they stick at it (sometimes they will, literally), your children can get better and better, with more and more imaginative applications. Once they're hooked, help them look up specialist books and craft magazines for lots of creative ideas. Here are two projects as an introduction...

You will need:

- Scrap paper or newspaper
- Wallpaper paste or PVA glue
- Cling film
- A small mixing bowl
- A bucket or large bowl to mix glue and paper
- A small piece of corrugated cardboard
- Masking tape
- Pencil
- Scissors or craft knife
- Paints, brushes and jam jars

Tortoise

This model makes use of two papier mâché techniques. Both are great for making a mess and getting sticky, which always adds to the fun of making things together.

1 Choose a small bowl to be the mould for your tortoise. Wrap it outside with cling film and put it on a plate.

2 Pour some glue into a mixing bowl, and add a little water if necessary to make it a creamy consistency. Tear the paper into strips measuring about 20 x 80mm and drop some of them into the bowl, allowing them to get thoroughly soaked.

3 Lay the strips in different directions all over the bowl. Add more glue, using a paintbrush. Keep tearing and adding strips until you have a good thickness of paper (about 6 or more layers) over the mould. Children can get bored with this after a while, so be prepared to take over from them. It does not help to turn a fun job into an awful chore!

4 Leave to dry in a warm dry place (this may take two or three days) then remove from the mould. It may be easier first cutting a bit round the edge of the papier mâché.

Trim the edges and cut off about 2–3cm at each end to make space for the legs, tail and head. Remove the cling film.

5 To make the head, legs and tail, make papier mâché sausages in the same way as for the Loch Ness Monster project described on the right. Make four sausages for the legs, a larger one for the head, and a slightly conical one for the tail.

6 When dry, paint all the parts, adding some PVA glue to the paint. Wash brushes thrououghly after use, as the glue is very hard to wash out when dry.

7 Cut a bit off the front and back of the shell to make space for the legs, tail and head. Cut a cardboard base about 1–3cm smaller diameter than the shell, and glue down the legs, tail and head.

8 To finish, tape or glue the shell to the base and legs, or leave loose.

Loch Ness Monster

This is very easy to do, even for very young children.

1 Cut or tear the newspaper into very small pieces – aim for pieces less than 10 x 30mm. (If you have a paper shredder, that's ideal: shred sheets from about half a newspaper). Mix some PVA glue with water, to make it like thin double cream in consistency. Soak the paper in glue and squeeze and knead it to make a soggy mass.

2 Make four sausage shapes, about 20–40mm thick and 120–200mm long.

3 Bend the two longest pieces to make semicircles: press them down so they stand and leave to dry on a plate or board.

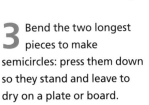

4 Shape the other bits into a head and tail. For the head, either just press the end firmly with your fingers to make a suitable shape, or else make it as complicated as you like by adding extra bits of papier mâché. Stand with the middle pieces and leave to dry in a warm dry place. Next day, or when dry (it may take several days), paint to finish.

Making a treasure chest

Making a treasure chest, and the treasures to go in it, can occupy children for hours on many a wet afternoon and keep them quietly absorbed at weekends. You and your children can enjoy devising more and more interesting things to include, and improvising ways to make them.

You will need:

- A shoebox
- Masking tape or duct tape
- PVA glue or glue gun
- A brush for glue
- Corrugated cardboard
- Spray-paint or other paints
- Paintbrushes
- Split pins (optional)

Making the chest

If the shoebox you use to make your chest has a separate lid, cut off the back edge of the lid and use tape to create a kind of hinge. You now have a hinged shoebox.

1 Paint the outside of the shoe box the colour of your choice and leave to dry.

2 Using a craft knife, cut about 6 strips of cardboard, about 30mm x 300mm, and other shapes if you want to experiment with clasps, handles etc.

3 Paint the long pieces black, other pieces gold, silver or other colours.

4 Glue the long black pieces, bend them round the box's edges and glue again.

5 If you've made handles, fix them with strips of corrugated cardboard: squeeze the cardboard in the middle so that it can make a good curve and hold the handles.

6 If you've been adventurous and made a clasp or catch or a padlock, fix them in place.

7 If you have some, decorate the box with split pins. Make a holes with a bradawl, skewer, or – more fun for youngsters – a hand drill.

Making treasure

This is an opportunity for you and your children to think up some great ideas and some clever solutions.

MONEY
Gold ingots can be made out of smarty tubes or small cardboard containers filled with something heavy. Or how about simply polishing up some 1p and 2p coins to make them really shiny, and making a little cloth bag for them?

JEWELLERY
You can make necklaces and jewels in various ways. Use paper rolls or pasta, coloured with gold and silver spray paints; wrap small things up in silver foil; use polished stones or other shiny things from home, such as scrunched up milk bottle tops or sweet wrappers. You can make a silver bracelet using a thin piece of cardboard covered with silver foil.

What about weapons?

No home with children aged between 7–11 should be without some pirate weapons!

DEVILISH DAGGER

Make a small dagger from cutting gluing and shaping balsa wood with a knife.

SWORDS AND SCIMITARS

Corrugated cardboard is perfect for these. You can cut out shapes quickly, gluing or taping together a couple of layers. They won't necessarily last long, particularly if battles are fierce, but they can easily be replaced. If you use wood there's a far greater risk of painful accidents.

FLINTLOCK PISTOL

You can improvise a good-looking pistol from wood and cardboard.

TELESCOPE

The two essential things about a telescope are (a) that you can look down it, and (b) that it slides open and shut like a telescope should. You can make one from cardboard tubes of slightly different diameters, or by rolling thin cardboard. There are various way of achieving the telescopic movement, and though in cardboard it probably won't last long it'll hopefully last long enough.

PIRATE'S HOOK

This will prove popular with young pirates who want to scare people. It uses a bit of a metal or plastic coat hanger, one end of a fizzy drinks bottle and a lot of duct tape. Simply cut through the fizzy drinks bottle just below the shoulder (discard the bottom bit), and cut the curved hook off the hanger, leaving about 30mm of stem. Stick the stem through the top of the drinks bottle and wind a lot of tape around the hook and the bottle. Paint over if you like. You use the hook by holding onto the portion of stem covered by the bottle.

Gruesome relics

Children, especially boys, often like gruesome and scary things, so here are some to consider for the treasure chest.

BONES

Select a few real ones from the Sunday roast – just boil them to remove any remaining meat or gristle, scratch on a few marks to make them even scarier, and rub in some dark wax or shoe polish.

BLOODY CLOTHES

Find an old white shirt or handkerchief, sprinkle liberally with ketchup or red ink and leave to dry.

BOTTLE OF POISON OR BOTTLE OF SCENT

Find a clear small bottle, for example a scent bottle or food colouring bottle. Mix up a vivid coloured potion from water and food colouring. If you have any, add almond flavouring and explain to your child that cyanide, one of the nastiest poisons, tastes and smells of bitter almonds (it really does). Pour it into the bottle. Don't forget to put a label on it saying 'POISON', complete with a skull and crossbones.

To change this into a bottle of precious or magic perfume from Aladdin's cave, make a lighter-coloured concoction, maybe in a delicate pink, and find some strong cheap scent from the back of the bathroom cupboard. Add a few drops and tie some pretty ribbons round the bottle. A special magic message on a label will finish it off nicely.

POTIONS AND POWDERS

Let your children's imaginations roam free if you fancy exploring the exciting world of magic potions or medicines.

All you need are some small jars, labels, and a bit of inspiration. Make up some stories: tangy curry powders can magic you to India in your mind; powdered cumin smells of stale sweat so can be 'pretend' powdered hair; oatmeal can stand in for ground up bones; old cooked spaghetti stained green makes a good supply of wicked worms…in fact the more you look at the kitchen cupboard, the more ideas you and your child can have. Don't forget to label the jars dramatically.

Magnetic Indian rope trick

This is interesting and intriguing for most of us, especially boys and girls under 13 (older ones may 'know it all' from school).

You will need:

A table; a strong magnet; thin thread; paperclip; ruler; some books; tape

Though you can work out a special stand if you want to, this improvised version does the trick fast.

Tie or tape the magnet to the end of the ruler. Then put the ruler on a pile of books, with the magnet hanging over the edge, and add another book or weight on top to hold the ruler in place.

Tie a length of thread to the paperclip – the thread should be just long enough that when you tape the other end to the table it leaves a small gap between the paperclip and the magnet. The force of the magnet should keep the paperclip apparently floating in the air, which looks mystifying.

Now you can experiment to find out what affects the magnetic field – *eg* paper, fingers, plastic, a feather, cardboard, metal foil, a coin, a nail, etc.

Taking things apart

A good rule is that if it ain't broke, don't fix it. Another good rule, especially for dads, is that if it is broken, and you can't mend it, don't throw it away – take it apart. It's a great opportunity for you and your children to investigate the insides of everyday pieces of equipment. So next time someone ruins the toaster by trying to get a piece of toast out with a fork, wait until your anger has subsided and then take it apart.

You will need:

- Small screwdrivers
- Blunt chisel or large screwdriver
- Wire cutters and/or metal snips
- Small torch
- Jam jar lid for small screws
- Yoghurt or margarine pot for components
- A bin for discarded pieces

If you've been given one of those toolcases that contain every size and shape of screwdriver imaginable, now's your chance to try out some of the ones you've never used before.

Let your children do as much as possible. The aim of taking things apart is simply to find out how to dismantle them and what's inside – without breaking anything if possible, but by forcing something with a screwdriver or old chisel if you need to. Take it at a relaxed and easy pace, since there's no need to take care or worry about putting anything back together again when you're done!

There are lots of treasures to be rescued and interesting bits to be stored away for model making later. You may be able to identify certain electronic components as you go along, and you may discover what the cogs and belts do. If there's a motor or coil with copper wire it'll prove immensely attractive to a child, who'll enjoy just unwinding the wire. Loudspeakers are a good source of strong magnets. Homemade spaceships look really good with genuine circuit boards stuck on them; homemade robots look realistic bedecked with multicoloured wires and connectors; and at the very least you may end up with some very useful small screws of the sort that can easily get lost from other equipment and are very hard to replace.

Though you'll be able to recognise and identify some of the pieces, don't make it an engineering or electronics lesson – unless your child is keen to pick up knowledge. You can both simply enjoy wondering what the various wonderful bits do.

Items in the home that are very rewarding to take apart include kitchen and bathroom scales, old clocks, clockwork kitchen timers, CD players, MP3 players, scanners, loudspeakers, toasters, vacuum cleaners, video players, computer keyboards, lawn mowers and hair dryers.

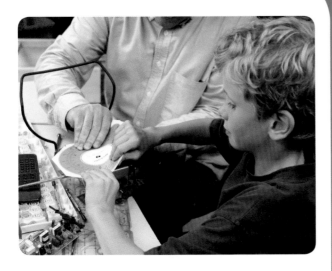

Here are a few electronic components you might spot. They all appear in assorted shapes and sizes.

Heat sinks are small metal walls, sometimes with fins, that dissipate heat. They act a bit like a radiator, only by cooling things down rather than by spreading heat.

Resistors control currents and voltages. They're called resistors because they resist a current and reduce it to the correct amount. They're colour-coded to indicate their resistance value, which is measured in Ohms.

Capacitors store an electric charge and release it when it's required. They can even-out varying DC (direct current) supplies by acting as a reservoir of charge. They also allow AC (alternating current) signals to pass but block DC (constant) signals.

Transistors enable very small currents to control much larger ones. The process is called amplification, which most people recognise in terms of sound: in a radio, for example, they amplify a tiny signal – received via an aerial – into a loud sound.

Transformers step up or step down the AC voltage – for example, taking 100v in and putting 50v out. They're basically coils of wire, which can sometimes be fun to unwind when you're taking things apart.

Diodes allow electricity to flow in only one direction. They're the electrical equivalent of a valve.

Rheostats vary the current, for example to control the brightness of a lamp or the volume of a radio.

Cotton-reel tank

This crawls along slowly and can climb over some obstacles. It's very easy to make, and fun to play with again and again.

You will need:

Cotton reel; short rubber band; 2 used wooden matches; slice of candle or a tap washer

To get a slice of candle, cut it crossways using a fine saw or a bread knife. Make a hole in the slice with a drill bit, penknife or hot kebab stick.

Cut one match in half and put the rubber band round it. Push the rest of the rubber band through the cotton reel and the slice of candle using either a match or something like a knitting needle or kebab stick. Fix the half-match with a bit of tape. Then loop the free end of the rubber band round the full-length match, to hold it in position.

If you use a tap washer instead of a slice of candle you may need to roughen the surface with a knife or file, to stop the match slipping.

To set the tank moving, turn the long match round enough times to get powered up – but not too many, as this will snap the rubber band.

If the tank slips on the terrain, roughen the edges or cut notches with a craft knife.

This tank can climb some obstacles. Try it on slight slopes of corrugated cardboard, or old pieces of cloth or vinyl spread over books or piles of magazines.

Skills

**Riding a bike:
getting started** 42

**Riding a bike:
fixing problems** 44

**Skateboarding:
getting started** 48

**Skateboarding:
essential tricks** 50

Tying knots 52

Juggling basics 56

Riding a bike: getting started

Learning to ride a bike is a major milestone for most kids, and for many is their first taste of independence. Initially it can be daunting, frustrating and downright scary, for both parent and child. It will take time and determination to discover a sense of balance and to master the bike's controls, and for many children it will be the biggest challenge they've undertaken so far. Once they have the knack of balancing, however, the sense of achievement and the sheer exhilaration of those first unaided rides is something that few will ever forget.

Buy the right bike

Most kids start out as toddlers on a tiny, but heavy, inexpensive single-speed bike fitted with stabilisers. These are great fun, but should really be regarded as garden or driveway toys only. They are *not* very suitable for learning to ride, which is only realistic on a bike that can be properly adjusted to fit the rider, and which has real tyres with inner tubes. Gears aren't essential, and may even prove a distraction early on.

The dilemma is that children will quickly outgrow their first real bike, and it's tempting to buy something inexpensive with this in mind. However, what they really need to give them a good start is a good-quality, lightweight bike. If you have a growing family you may be able to justify buying a better bike that can be handed down. Alternatively, ask around the local bike shops, which may have taken something suitable in part-exchange. Bike shops are unlikely to waste time and space on a poor-quality bike, so you may well pick up a bargain this way.

Once you've obtained a bike, start out by removing any stabilisers that may be fitted. If you don't, your child will continue to use the bike as a glorified tricycle, and will never begin to develop a sense of balance. You should also set it up so that it fits the rider, who needs to sit fairly upright, be able to reach the ground with both feet, and shouldn't be stretching to reach the handlebars. Also check that they can reach the brake levers easily – many levers can be adjusted for reach, or you may be able to fit new levers that can be adjusted. Again, a good bike shop will be a great source of advice and help here.

Preparations

Generations of parents have spent hours jogging behind a wobbling child who's struggling to achieve balance. Other than the problem of parental backache, this method works fine for many kids. You just need to pick a large open space (a recreation ground is good, and provides a relatively soft landing if they take a tumble). Persistence is the key – once you can feel that they're more or less balancing unaided you can begin to let go of the saddle for increasing intervals until they take off on their own. The problem for some children is that there are actually several things that need to be learnt, and it's hard to do all of them at once. Just consider what the young rider has to learn:

■ How to operate the front and rear brakes.
■ That you don't actually steer a bike by turning the handlebars – even though it seems like you do.
■ How to master pedalling and possibly gear changing, too.

This really is a lot to take on board, so it may work better if you tackle these skills one at a time. The hardest thing to master is balance, and, incidentally, steering. So it's this you should concentrate on first – once it clicks with the young rider, the rest follows easily.

Start by removing all non-essential complications by unscrewing the pedals. You'll need a fairly thin-jawed spanner to do this – it fits on the flats where the pedal attaches to the crank arms. The right-hand pedal has a normal right-hand thread, so is unscrewed by turning it anti-clockwise. The left-hand pedal, though, has a left-hand thread, so must be unscrewed by turning it clockwise. Remove both pedals and put them safely away with the stabilisers. Now lower the saddle so that the rider can put both feet flat on the ground easily. This isn't the right setting for normal riding, but it renders the centre of gravity lower and so makes the rider feel a lot more secure and in control.

You've just created a modern version of the Draisine or Hobby Horse (also known as a 'pushbike' – a term still used to describe bicycles today – because the rider sat astride and pushed it along with their legs). Although this device was invented nearly 200 years ago and is pretty much forgotten, it's still a great way to learn how to balance, and our version has the advantage that it can be converted back to a bicycle once this has been achieved.

Where to start

You can do a few basic exercises just about anywhere, because the bike doesn't even need to move. Get the child seated and comfortable, with the bike upright. Get them to lift their feet just off the ground to sense how the bike begins to fall one way or the other. The nearer to the point of balance, the longer they'll be able to keep their feet off the ground. This does two things. Firstly, the child begins to get a sense of balance – the point at which the bike doesn't quite fall one way or the other. Of course, this doesn't last; as soon as there's the slightest imbalance, gravity pulls both bike and rider off balance quite quickly; but it does give a hint of what balance *feels* like, and this is important. Secondly, the child gets to feel the weight of the bike and how easy it is to support and recover when it starts to fall. Try to make this fun – get your own bike out and see who can balance the longest.

The next step is to find a really good place to practise. Ideally it needs to be a large, quiet area of smooth tarmac, like a private car park or a school playground. Alternatively, try to find an especially quiet road or a long driveway. Avoid anywhere with heavy traffic or a lot of obstructions – you'll both want to be able to concentrate on the business in hand.

Make sure your child is wearing a cycle helmet and gloves (if they fall they'll instinctively use their hands to save themselves), and if they have skateboard knee and elbow pads these can also be useful to fend of minor scrapes and bruises.

Get your child to push themselves along with their feet. This should be done slowly at first, and you can also try getting them to use the brakes to stop the bike. Gradually build up speed, until they can manage a second or so with their feet clear of the ground. Combining this with the static balancing practice described above should eventually result in short bouts of coasting, during which they're effectively balancing. With encouragement, your child should soon be whizzing along with both feet clear of the ground. Don't be too quick in refitting the pedals, though – let the child have fun and gain confidence without the extra complication of pedalling.

Once they're ready, refit the pedals (remember that the left-hand pedal has a left-hand thread, so don't mix them up!). You'll also need to raise the saddle so that their legs are not quite straight when the pedal is at the lowest point. Do this progressively, though, because it will feel precarious at first. You may need to compromise on the saddle height to make sure the rider can touch the ground with their toes on both sides. Early attempts at combining pedalling with balancing are going to be wobbly, so make sure there's plenty of unobstructed space for this. Once confidence begins to grow, try to convince your young rider to practise riding slowly by telling them that anyone can ride fast, but only really skilled riders can do it slowly.

There will still be much to learn about road safety, signalling and so on, but once the basic skills are there training can move onto quiet country roads, where experience and encouragement will help them to become safe, confident riders. It's also well worth looking out for cycling proficiency courses run by local authorities, often in conjunction with schools.

Riding a bike: fixing problems

Cycling is great fun, superb exercise and provides many kids with their first taste of independence. Bikes can go wrong, however, so it is good to know how to fix the most common problems as they crop up. A bit of preventative maintenance will also minimize the trauma of a roadside breakdown.

Punctures

REMOVING WHEELS

Slacken or detach the brake cable so that the tyre can pass easily between the brake pads. Where the wheel is held by a quick-release lever, turn the lever through 180° and then unscrew it by a couple of turns. Where nuts secure the wheel use a spanner on each side, turning the nuts anti-clockwise to release it.

The front wheel can now be removed after lifting the bike slightly to allow it to drop free.

Rear wheels are more complicated. On three-speed bikes you need to release the gear cable – the knurled lockring will allow you to fit it in the correct position during installation. Lift the back of the bike and wiggle the wheel free. On bikes with derailleurs, move the wheel forward to help disentangle the chain from the sprockets. If you're not familiar with derailleurs it's worth making a quick sketch or taking a photo with a digital camera or phone. This will help you figure out how the chain is routed around the sprockets and derailleur pulleys when you refit the wheel.

REMOVING THE TYRE

Where fitted, remove the dust cap and knurled retainer ring from the tyre valve. Release any remaining pressure from the tube if it isn't already flat. With Presta valves, unscrew the small locknut and depress the valve. With Schraeder (car-type) valves, depress the valve pin. On older bikes with Woods valves, unscrew the knurled ring and remove the valve insert.

Squeeze the tyre together so that the tyre beads drop into the recessed well at the centre of the rim – this makes it easier to remove.

Hook a tyre lever under the tyre bead, roughly opposite the valve. Make sure that you don't trap the inner tube between the lever and the bead. Lever the edge of the tyre over the rim, and hook the lever onto a spoke to retain it.

Repeat using a second lever a few inches further round the rim, then work the second lever around the rim until one side of the tyre is free. Push the valve out of the rim and then remove the tube.

FIXING THE PUNCTURE

Locate the puncture by adding a little air to the tube. If you can't spot the hole easily, hold the tube under water so that the stream of bubbles helps to locate it. Dry the tube and mark the position of the hole. Feel around the inside of the tyre and remove any object sticking through it.

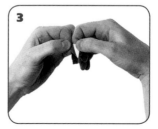

Clean and dry the area around the puncture, and roughen the surface using abrasive paper. Apply a thin film of rubber solution, using your finger to spread it evenly. Leave this to dry for about five minutes.

Peel off the foil backing from a patch, and press the patch evenly onto the touch-dry solution. Use your fingernail or a tyre lever to smooth down the patch and remove any air bubbles. Remove any backing paper without peeling off the patch. Use chalk dust around the repair to stop it sticking to the tyre.

FITTING THE TYRE

Add just enough air to the tube to make it round. Place it into the tyre and thread the valve through the rim. Work the tyre bead onto the rim by hand, making sure it sits down into the rim well. If necessary, use a lever to ease the last few inches of bead onto the rim. Inflate to the recommended pressure, checking that the tyre beads pop out on the edge of the rim and that the tyre is fitted evenly.

FITTING THE WHEEL

Reverse the removal procedure, making sure that the chain is fitted correctly. On derailleur bikes, loop the chain around the smallest sprocket and pull the wheel spindle back into the frame drop-outs. Check that the wheel is aligned properly before you secure the wheel nuts or quick-release lever. On three-speed bikes, fit the gear cable in the same position as before. You'll also need to check that the wheel is in line with the frame, and that the chain tension is correct – there should be just slight up-and-down play. On all types of bike, reconnect and adjust the brakes. Check that everything works properly before handing the bike over to your child.

HOW TO AVOID PUNCTURES

- Keep tyres correctly inflated – soft tyres puncture easily.
- Check tyres for cracks or embedded objects regularly, and replace if damaged.
- Buy puncture-resistant tyres – they cost more but are well worth the extra.

Sizing & adjustment

Your child's bike needs to be the right size if they're to learn to ride safely. It may be tempting to buy a bike that's a bit too big, to allow a bit of 'growing room', but this isn't a good idea – the bike will be too much of a stretch, and will be hard for them to control. It's best to choose something the right size and then trade it in when they need to move up to a bigger bike. Note that many bike shops will offer this option, but if you buy through mail order or on the internet you'll have to dispose of the old bike yourself.

Kids come in all shapes and sizes, but bikes can be very approximately categorised by wheel size as follows:

14in	Up to 5 years old
16in	5–8 years old
20in	8–11 years old
24in	11 years to late teens

When buying a bike, check that it fits the child properly. The saddle should be set as high as possible while still letting the rider touch the ground with the toes of both feet, though while learning it could be set a little lower to help build confidence. The ideal position for easy pedalling is for the leg to be very slightly bent when the pedal is at its lowest point. If the saddle is too low it makes pedalling very much harder.

The handlebars should be set quite high so that the child isn't hunched forwards. This aids control and forward vision. Most bikes have quill stems that can be moved up or down after slackening a central bolt. Don't raise the stem above the maximum height marking, and check that you're not stretching any cables. Make sure that you tighten the bolt firmly after checking that the bars are at right angles to the front wheel. (A few kids' bikes use a different steering stem arrangement that's less easy to adjust – if you run into problems ask your local bike shop, which may be able to adjust or change the headset for you.)

Gears

STURMEY ARCHER HUB GEARS

Hub gears are operated by a cable that pulls a selector rod in and out of the hub to select them. If you're having gearchange problems, check that the cable is adjusted correctly: select second gear, then look through the inspection hole in the wheel nut where the gearchange chain enters the hub – the chain is attached to a rod, and when second gear is selected the shoulder on the rod should be aligned with the end of the axle. If it isn't, adjust the cable until it is. Try the gears by riding the bike, and make any necessary small corrections until all three gears operate correctly.

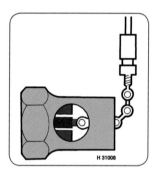

DERAILLEUR GEARS

These look a lot more complicated than they really are; the derailleur simply drags the chain from one sprocket to another to change gear, and also maintains the correct chain tension while doing so. The main trick with derailleurs is to keep everything clean and well lubricated (this includes the

gearchange cables), and not to fiddle with the adjustment screws. These are used to set the limits of travel, preventing the derailleur from flinging the chain off either end of the sprockets. There's normally no need to change these settings unless the bike has been dropped or somebody has tried moving the screws.

REAR DERAILLEURS

The most common problem with derailleur systems is incorrect indexing, in which the gears don't shift cleanly. Most derailleur systems, even on the cheapest bikes, use indexed gears, in which the shifter on the handlebar determines the precise position of the derailleur, and in time wear and cable stretch may require slight adjustment to the indexing. This is done using the cable adjuster at the shifter or derailleur end (some bikes have an adjuster at both ends – you can use either).

You may find that the derailleur doesn't shift far enough, leaving the chain grinding away on the side of the sprocket. To correct this, turn the cable adjuster a quarter turn

anti-clockwise and recheck the shifting, repeating as necessary until you get a clean shift. If the derailleur shifts too far, try screwing in the adjuster a quarter turn at a time and rechecking the shifting.

If you have problems with the chain shifting beyond either the smallest (high) gear or biggest (low) gear sprockets, you may need to correct the relevant adjuster. You'll find the two screws close together on the derailleur, and they're normally marked 'H' and 'L' (if unmarked a little experimentation may be required). If the chain is falling off the smallest gear, turn the 'H' screw clockwise by a half turn, and check to see if this has fixed the problem.

If the chain shifts past the largest gear, turn the 'L' screw clockwise until it isn't quite possible to shift into lowest gear, then back the screw off until it just shifts cleanly. There's a third screw on most derailleurs, known as the 'B' screw. You shouldn't mess with this one either, but if somebody *has* been twiddling it, note that it should be set so that the top jockey wheel just clears the biggest sprocket when bottom gear is selected.

Another thing to note is that jumping gears are typical symptoms of a worn chain and sprockets; fitting a new chain and rear cassette will almost always fix it. You can check the chain by pulling it away from the chainring – if it pulls away easily, leaving a gap between it and the chainring teeth, it needs replacing. If you're uncertain about this ask for advice at your bike shop.

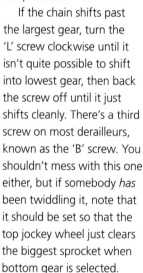

FRONT DERAILLEURS

These are fitted on bikes with more than one chainring, and do pretty much the same job as the rear derailleur. It too has 'H' and 'L' stop screws to prevent overshifting. If the chain throws off the big ring, tighten the 'H' screw a quarter turn at a time until the problem is resolved. If the chain falls off the smallest sprocket, use the 'L' screw to correct it, again turning the screw a quarter turn at a time and rechecking.

For more detailed information on the various gear systems and shifter types, see Haynes's *The Bike Book* or enlist the help of a professional mechanic.

Brakes

There's not too much to go wrong with brakes, but they're a vital safety feature so always take care when working on them. If in any doubt, get expert assistance from a good bike shop. Once again, Haynes's *The Bike Book* covers brakes in far greater detail than is possible here.

PADS

Most kids' bikes will be fitted with cantilever or Vee brakes. Over time the pads will wear down – they usually have a wear indicator in the form of slots or a lip on the pad surface, and should be replaced when this is reached. The pads are fixed to the operating arm by a clamp arrangement (cantilever) or by a nut and shaped washers (Vee brake) and are easy to remove for cleaning or examination. Make a careful note of where everything goes, though! This is also a good time to check that the brake arm moves smoothly. Use a Teflon-based lubricant on the pivots, or remove and grease them.

Recondition part-worn pads by carefully rubbing the braking surface flat on some abrasive paper – the brakes can't be adjusted if the pads are ridged or unevenly worn.

Once resurfaced and clean, loosely reassemble the pads. They should be positioned a few millimetres from the rim, with the front edge of the pad set closer than the rear to avoid brake squeal. Ideally, the front should be 1mm from the rim surface and the rear edge 2mm. Use a piece of thick card at the back of the pad as a gauge

when positioning them. Once set correctly, tighten the nut or clamp to secure the pad.

Move the brake arm to check that the pad contacts the rim at the front edge first. It should also align with the rim, and should not contact the tyre at any point. Check that both pads contact the rim simultaneously. On some bikes you may be able to adjust the bias by turning a small screw on the brake arm.

CABLES

Check the cables regularly, looking for signs of fraying or corrosion. If you spot any, the cable must be replaced immediately. It's a good idea to take the bike or the cable with you to the bike shop when buying new cables – that way you can be sure the new one is going to fit correctly. Cable replacement is generally straightforward, but make sure that the brakes are adjusted correctly afterwards (see above).

FAULT DIAGNOSIS

Problem	Cause	Solution
Squealing	Pads not toeing-in correctly	Adjust (see 'Pads' above)
	Grease or dirt on the rims	Clean and degrease
Grabbing or pulsing	Wheel buckled or out-of-true	Adjust (see Haynes's *The Bike Book*) or replace wheel
Stiff operation	Dirty or corroded cables/pivots	Clean and lubricate
	Frayed cables	Replace immediately
Excessive lever travel	Poor adjustment	Adjust

DECK

WHEEL

BEARING

TRUCK

Skateboarding: getting started

Skateboarding is a superb activity for burning off physical and nervous energy, and occupying boys especially from ages 8 to 18+.
They probably won't want much help from you, but it helps if you know a bit about it ...

The parts of a skateboard

The wooden part is called the deck; the front is the nose, the back is the tail. There's usually a slight curve from side to side, which is called the concave. The deck is covered with griptape, rather like sandpaper. This stops people slipping too much but also, unfortunately, wears down shoes at a surprisingly fast rate.

The metal units underneath, with axles, are called the trucks. The wheels are held onto the axles with bearings and hexagonal nuts. The trucks each have a kingpin with rubber bushes. This allows some play between the truck and deck, and this flexibility is important for smooth turning. You can adjust the kingpin for more or less flexing, using a hexagonal key. The trucks are fixed to the deck with bolts, usually adjustable with a hexagonal key or a Phillips screwdriver. These bolts are a useful guide in positioning the feet.

Sandwiched between the deck and the trucks are usually risers, plastic pieces which cushion some of the impact as the board hits the ground.

Choosing a board and accessories

Younger children find full-size skateboards rather large and heavy. However, small skateboards are generally not very good, and are more difficult to ride than full-size ones. You can buy pro mini-skateboards, but they're hard to find. However, children can cope with a full-size skateboard from about the age of eight, and many do so earlier.

To start off, a child's first skateboard only needs to be 'good enough', not high quality. Only after gaining a bit of experience, by the age of ten or eleven, will your child genuinely get something out of having better equipment.

COMPLETE SET-UP OR SEPARATE PARTS?

A skateboard with all its bits is called a complete set-up. Buying a complete set-up can be very economical: a package deal of deck, trucks and wheels will typically do a good job and cost less than buying separately. However, you should get one from a specialist skateboard shop rather than a general toy or sports shop, as you can get better advice there and good value, if not the cheapest kit. Complete set-ups from non-specialist shops can be cheap but very disappointing.

DECKS

Decks vary in size and shape, which are a matter of personal preference. Blanks – unprinted decks available from most skateboard shops – represent very good value and can be surprisingly good quality. Decks printed with great designs tend to cost much more, and the latest design isn't a guarantee of great riding quality.

TRUCKS

Trucks can be very expensive, but generally the more expensive ones are the toughest, designed for older, heavier skateboarders who'll give their boards and trucks a lot of punishment. Go for the cheaper ones at first. After your child has progressed, consider buying more expensive ones. Their design, kingpins and bushing may feel better than cheaper trucks.

BEARINGS

Good bearings are important for a comfortable ride and speed, but it's not essential for beginners to buy higher spec bearings. One measure of quality is 'ABEC' – the higher ratings, such as ABEC7s, cost considerably more but don't greatly affect performance.

WHEELS

Wheels are another matter of personal preference. For riding ramps, 53–55mm wheels are generally reckoned to be best; for street skateboarding, 53mm and under. So 52–54mm are ideal for all-round use.

Thinner, smaller wheels tend to feel rougher and grittier, whereas wider, larger wheels feel firmer. Until your beginner has become experienced there's no need to choose expensive wheels. However, some set-ups come with poor quality rubber or composite wheels: it is well worth replacing them with low price urethane wheels. It's tempting to be seduced into buying smart ones, often with impressive printed designs, but they're costly. The differences are often merely cosmetic, or only appreciated by experienced skateboarders; they're simply a waste of money as far as novices are concerned.

SKATEBOARDING SHOES

Unfortunately, it really does help to have good skateboarding shoes – and there's a price tag that goes with them. They provide good cushioning and ankle support, will provide some protection, and they make it easier to do some tricks. Cheap skateboarding shoes aren't a waste of money for beginners, as they're less likely to receive as much hard wear. However, cheap or not-so-cheap shoes not specifically designed for skateboarding may well fall apart much quicker.

Skateboard safety

Skateboarding is dangerous – but not very dangerous. Many more youngsters end up in hospital accident and emergency departments every week because of football injuries than those resulting from skateboarding.

Some safety gear is a good idea, but it's not essential. It depends on the risks you want to take. Wrist-guards are a good idea, however, because one of the most common skateboard injuries is broken or twisted wrists.

Younger skateboarders will be happy to wear a helmet as they feel they look cool and will make them feel safe. Even older skateboarders tolerate them because they don't hinder them much. All indoor skateboard parks insist on helmets being worn, because that's what their insurance companies insist on, but the reality is that skateboarders sustain relatively few head injuries. This is partly because few of their tricks result in a head-first fall. Rollerblading and BMX biking are much more prone to head injuries.

Full protection – kneepads, elbow pads, wrist-guards and helmets – are a very good idea if your child starts riding vertical ramps.

For safety, one of the best things to learn is how to do a good bail: this means stepping off and running alongside the board as a trick starts to go wrong. You can see this happening in any skate park. It's a great skill that any new skateboarder needs to learn.

Every skateboarder has his fair share of falls. It's useful to learn to fall on hands and knees, as this can take the impact better. Falling on the back or sides can be much more dangerous.

Skateboarding: essential tricks

How to ollie

It's important to learn to ollie, as it's the building block of most tricks.

1 Stand with front foot behind the front bolts, and the other foot with the heel off the board and the toes pointing forward on the tail.

2 Bend down at the knees and push down hard with the back foot.

3 Just as the tail of the board hits the ground, jump up, and as you jump let the front foot slide up – don't force it as it will come up naturally.

4 Aim to have both feet level.

5 Land with both feet flat on the bolts.

Fifty-fifty grind

You may want to apply candle wax or skate wax to the edge of a grind box to make the grind easier.

1 First, ollie up to land with both trucks touching the coping of a ledge or the edge of a grind box.

2 Keep your weight centred and keep well balanced as you grind along the metal.

3 To get out of the grind, treat the next move as the start of an ollie, pressing down on the tail and lifting the front foot. Lean back a little on the tail, but not too much; be careful to stay parallel to the metal. Keep your weight in the middle of the body and your feet roughly parallel, at right angles to the deck. Lift the leading foot a little and bend the back leg a little – don't keep your legs straight or rigid: aim to keep them relaxed.

4 Land as squarely as you can and be ready to move straight ahead or make a turn.

Doing a kickflip

Kickflips are harder than ollies and require even more practice. They take a while to master, and it's very difficult to be really consistent in landing a kickflip.

1 Take the same starting position as an ollie, but with the front foot further from the bolts, towards the middle of the board and pointing out at about 45°.

2 Bend down as with an ollie, and kick the front foot forwards and also slightly towards the side, depending on the concave, to start the board turning.

3 Aim to catch the board with both feet and land squarely on the bolts. Alternatively, it can be easier to catch the board with one foot first and then a split second later with the other.

Tying knots

Children often expect their dads to do 'simple' things like tie things together, put ropes on trees for swinging from, make rope ladders and so on. Boys in particular like to knot things together. It's been going on for millennia.

In this chapter we'll look at some very useful knots, old and new. All you need is some nice flexible rope – avoid the hard blue plastic type available in most hardware shops. Go for flexible material like dressing gown cord. Braided cord is very good to work with, and thicknesses between about 4mm to 8mm produce very satisfying knots. An easy alternative is shoelaces – use long ones with a round rather than flat section – but the knots will be rather small.

It'll also be useful to have something to help loosen a knot. It's very frustrating to deal with a knot that's jammed solid, and children find it particularly difficult to undo knots. You might spot a marlinspike – a tool specifically designed for working with ropes – in a shop, or find a penknife that includes one. A good substitute is a crochet needle or thick knitting needle, cut to about 100mm.

HOW TO STOP ROPE FROM FRAYING

It's annoying and frustrating to work with rope that's fraying. One simple way to stop fraying is to use a constrictor knot (described below). If the rope you're using is made from synthetic materials you can often stop it from fraying by holding the end over a candle or cigarette lighter flame for a few seconds and melting the end. However, you should never let children do this unsupervised: some rope can catch fire astonishingly quickly, and there's always a risk of very hot melting plastic dripping onto them or the floor.

INTERESTING TERMINOLOGY

Technically, anything thicker than 10mm is called a rope. Thinner stuff (yes, 'stuff' is the correct term for these materials) is called braided cord, cord, string or twine. A rope that's made of three strands is called a hawser, while one that's made of several filaments covered in braid is called a sheath and core (or, in climbing, a kernmantel).

Rope or cord suited to a particular purpose is called a line – eg a bowline for holding a sail at the bow of a boat.

Knots that join two ropes together are called bends; knots that attach a rope to a rail, post, ring or another rope are hitches; and a knot in the middle of a rope is usually called a stopper. A stopper can also be at the end of a rope, to stop it slipping through your hands or a pulley.

A U-shape in the rope is called a bight, so a knot made in the middle of a rope and not requiring a free end is 'made in the bight'. This can be very useful, for example when you have a lot of rope and don't want to spend time finding one end, or when you want to put several knots into one rope.

IMPORTANT – SAFETY RULES

Playing with knots is generally safe enough, but playing at tying people up is not. It's extremely important to explain this to children. Even tying string round a finger for fun can be dangerous, as it can stop circulation. And make no mistake, if misused any knot – and particularly the constrictor knot described further on – can be very dangerous indeed.

Basic knots to start with

OVERHAND KNOT
A good stopper, very easy to knot but difficult to undo if it's been pulled hard.

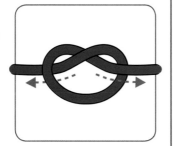

FIGURE-OF-EIGHT KNOT
This is a better stopper because it's easier to untie after use. Good for putting on a rope for climbing (it provides something to grip) and for a rope intended for use in a tug-of-war.

CONTINUOUS FIGURES-OF-EIGHT
There seems to be a little bit of magic in this one. You set up a coil of rope, pull it gently, and hey presto – if you're lucky you get a nice row of figure-of-eight knots. There's a bit of history too. Figures-of-eight knots used to be put in at regular intervals on ropes – typically every yard (about 1m), for sometimes hundreds of yards, since multiple knotting saved a lot of time. The knots were used for various purposes: for example, to check water depth, or a ship's speed – even today speed at sea is measured in 'knots'.

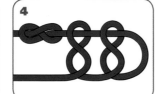

Tying two ropes together: bends

REEF KNOT
Probably one of the oldest, most well known knots, but not a good one! Its major disadvantages are that it jams solid when put under strain and isn't very good for joining ropes of different thicknesses.

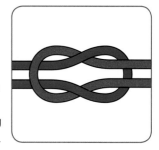

SIMPLE SIMON BEND
This is much better than the reef knot and almost as easy to learn. It can join two lines of the same or different thicknesses very easily and securely. It's a relatively new knot, one of a generation developed in the 1980s.

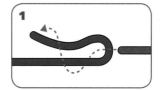
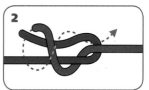

OPEN SESAME BEND
Better still, how about a knot that ties two ropes together firmly, and comes free again easily? This knot is easier than it looks. It's made of two overhand knots, intertwined, and will hold two lines together very securely. Then pull at the short ends, and hey presto – or open sesame – and the knot becomes easy to untie. It's a classic new knot, invented in 1993.

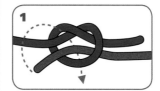
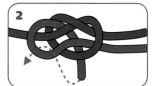
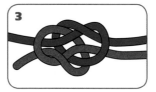

Knots to hold things up: hitches

CLOVE HITCH

This can be made – and undone – quickly. As long as the weight is pulling at right angles to the knot, it holds well, but don't rely on it if it's being pulled from side to side.

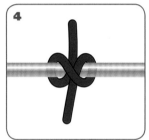

OSSEL HITCH

Simple and very reliable, this knot is better than the clove hitch. It holds brilliantly when tugged in any direction, so is good for things like a monkey swing. (It's called an ossel after an old term for a cord between fishing nets and hauling-in ropes.)

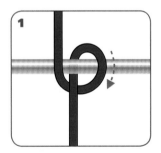

Tying over a post

BOWLINE

Pronounced bo-lin, this is a classic and easy way to make a fixed loop at the end of a piece of string or rope to put round a post or rail.

MOORING HITCH

A knot quickly tied 'in the bight' (ie from a loop in the middle of a rope) and slipped over a post or mooring. This takes a little practice, but isn't difficult. There's something a bit magical about the way it comes together.

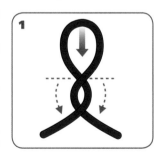
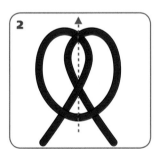
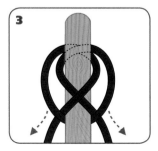

CARRICK BEND

This is a tough, serious working knot, but it isn't hard to tie. It can hold together enormous ropes and cables that are sometimes thicker than a tree – you may see it used, for instance, aboard a ferry or liner. It's a clever solution to this challenging problem, as it doesn't require the ropes to bend much. You'll see how good it is if you use it to join medium or thick pieces of rope. It might prove handy when you're doing some heavy towing and want to link two thick ropes together.

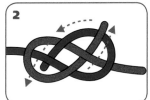
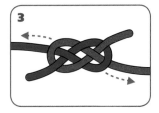

Tying really tightly

CONSTRICTOR KNOT

This is a great knot for tying something extremely tightly, so tightly that if you ever want to undo it you'll probably have to cut it. This is a very old knot that's probably been in use for thousands of years. It will hold wood together as tightly as a clamp.

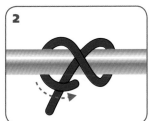
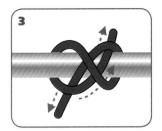
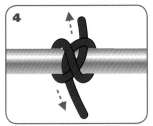

A decorative knot Carrick mat

This takes a bit of practice, but is very satisfying to complete. It can be purely for decoration, or can be used as a beer mat or table mat. It could provide a solution to several Christmas presents!

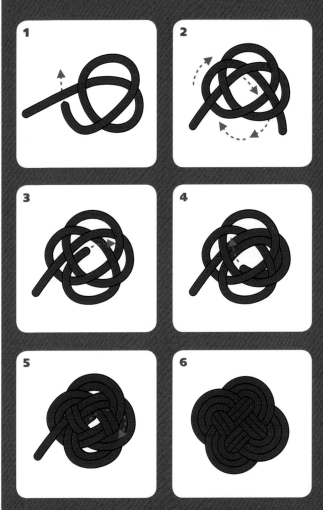

A Carrick mat involves a kind of weaving. Once you've established the pattern from stages 1–3 it works easily: the rope goes round side by side with the strand on its left so that you end up with the pattern having three strands throughout. Finish it off by cutting the rope, tucking it in and either tying, stitching or gluing it underneath. Alternatively you can make a loop so that the mat can be hung as a decoration.

Juggling basics

Juggling takes a lot of practice. It's the kind of thing you go back to again and again, and eventually you may get the knack. And it's one of those rare activities that's fun when you can do it, and still fun when you can't.

Generally children aren't very good at persevering with things, but they often do with juggling. For children having a go at it with their parents, it's particularly enjoyable, because they'll enjoy the adults' misery if they fail but will derive great delight from bragging to friends that 'my dad (or mum) can juggle' if they succeed.

Few children under seven can manage to juggle: they don't usually have the necessary co-ordination. However, once children are good at throwing and catching they may also make good headway with juggling.

WHAT TO USE

Juggling balls, which are slightly squishy, are perfect, and are available in sizes suited to small hands. Alternatively you can make own bean bags filled with lentils or rice. You may find juggling with two or three different colours is easier than same-coloured or identical multicoloured balls. Tennis balls aren't very good – they're too large for most people to hold a pair comfortably in one hand, and they bounce or roll away if dropped, so that you'll end up wasting a lot of time chasing after them.

Getting started

At first, kneel when you're practising. That way you won't have to keep bending down to pick up dropped balls. If possible, position yourself with a wall less than a metre in front of you: this will help you throw vertically, and will stop balls from flying too far.

1 Start off by juggling just one ball. Aim to achieve an even arc (as below), gently throwing the ball from left to right and right to left. This isn't kids' stuff. Even professionals often start their practice sessions using just one ball, perfecting the arc and the rhythm between their hands.

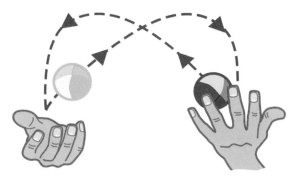

2 Next try two-ball juggling. Make a pattern as shown above, starting with the right hand, over to the left, keeping the balls rising to eye level. Practise with two different coloured balls. From time to time change the hand you start with.

3 Then move on to three-ball juggling. Hold two balls in one hand, one in the other. Start by throwing up a ball from the hand that's holding two: throw up the outer ball – that's the one closer to your fingertips. Then start the three-ball pattern whilst counting 'one, two, three' steadily out loud as you throw and – hopefully – catch each of the three balls one after another on an even beat.

Aim for an even tempo, and focus on getting rid of the ball, not hanging onto it. Aim to get the arc going well first, achieving a pattern as shown below. And don't worry about dropping the balls. If you keep practising long enough you'll find that catching becomes a simple action, providing you keep the rhythm even and the arc regular as you throw the balls.

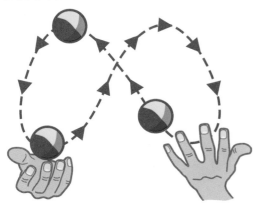

Throwing 3 balls between 2 people

This is a good exercise, and it's easier than solo juggling as you only have to think about one hand. It's also a lot of fun.

Two people stand side by side, their inside arms behind their backs. If there's a big difference in height, one person may want to kneel. You can start off by throwing two balls from side to side as if you were a single juggler.

For three-ball juggling, person A holds two balls in their free hand; person B holds one ball. Person A starts by throwing the outermost ball (the one nearer their fingertips) in an arc to the other person's hand. When this ball is at its peak, person B throws through an arc to person A's hand, counting 'one, two, three' as for solo three-ball juggling.

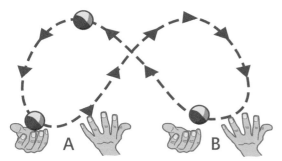

Round-the-clock juggling

This isn't really juggling, but is an enjoyable group activity that improves people's throwing and catching skills. It looks good too. The aim of the game is to get the next person to catch from your throw, and to learn to throw in an arc. You need at least five players and at least three balls – tennis balls, light foam balls, or juggling balls.

Form a circle, with the players about 2m apart. The first person throws a ball to the right, in an arc, and the person on the right catches it and throws it on. After completing the circle a couple of times and establishing a rhythm (which will take a while with younger children) another ball is added to the circle, so players have to switch quickly from throwing to catching.

You can then add another ball, either in the same direction or even going the other way. With practice, the group may be able to keep up continuous throwing and catching for several minutes.

Sports Basics

Football   **60**

Cricket   **62**

Rugby   **64**

Tennis   **66**

French cricket   **68**

Badminton   **68**

Rounders   **69**

Table tennis   **69**

Football

Football is often referred to as 'The Beautiful Game' and is by far and away the most popular sport in the world. Children love it and having a kick about with Dad is a time-honoured tradition. Much of its delight is derived from its sheer simplicity – even the clumsiest of children, or indeed dads, can kick a ball around.

THE RULES

Football is an 11-a-side game played on a rectangular pitch with a netted goalpost at each end. The aim of the game is to score more goals than the opposing team. The ten field players on each side are only allowed to use their feet, head or body to move the ball forward. Only the goalkeeper is allowed to handle the ball, and only within the penalty area that's marked out in front of the goal.

Football is relatively simple and has fewer rules than many other sports, making it very easy to learn. However, one rule that does cause confusion is 'offside'. This states that if a player passes to a team-mate who has fewer than two defenders, including the goalkeeper, between them and the goal-line then offside is called, resulting in a free kick being awarded to the opposing team.

SCORING

A football game consists of two halves of 45 minutes and the team that scores the most goals wins. If the same number of goals have been scored by both sides then the match is drawn.

In certain knockout competitions, where there has to be a winner, the game can run into 30 minutes of extra time, arranged in two 15-minute halves. If there's still no winner the penalty shoot-out takes place, with the team that scores the most goals from a set amount of penalty kicks winning.

LEARNING THE GAME

It couldn't be easier to have a go; all you need is a football, a dad and a child or two. If your child hasn't played before, start with a simple passing game, kicking the ball around to get the feel of it. Next you can find some goalposts – just use a couple of jumpers – and act as goalie while you see how many goals your child can score, making sure to let a few in accidentally to encourage them. Kids love scoring goals, especially against Dad!

Most neighbourhoods have their fair share of football-mad children so try getting together with some other families and having a semi-organised game in the local park. Just be careful that overly competitive dads don't turn it into a game for themselves.

TAKING IT FURTHER

Football is played in every school in the land, so finding somewhere to play isn't hard. Even the smallest villages may have a football club so there's also plenty of opportunity outside school. In addition, the FA and many professional clubs run coaching clinics and have open days that help children learn the game.

FURTHER INFORMATION

www.thefa.com – Official site of the Football Association, the game's governing body.

POSITIONS

Football is a flowing game without the rigidity of most other team sports, but players still have positions in goal, defence, midfield or attack.

DEFENCE

If your child is good at dispossessing others of the ball then defence could be right for them. Defenders are there to stop the opposition from threatening the goal and to move the ball away from danger. This isn't the most glamorous position on the field, so if your child shows defensive aptitude then you'll need to do your best to encourage it by letting them tackle you.

MIDFIELD

Midfielders have a linking role and must be able to both attack and defend. It's perhaps the most influential position on the field and midfielders must be unselfish and able to distribute the ball well, ensuring that it's passed up the field accurately and safely to the attackers.

ATTACK

Attackers, also known as strikers and centre forwards, are the finishers of a football team. Their job is to slot the ball in the back of the net. This is the most exciting position on the pitch and every child wants to score goals.

A good striker must have excellent vision and ball control, and must be able to react quickly and place the ball accurately. The dad of any budding striker must be prepared to spend long hours in goal being peppered by shots!

GOALKEEPERS

Goalkeepers must be able to read the game well and be good at catching and parrying the ball. They must also have a hefty kick, as goal kicks are often used to restart the game. If your child shows aptitude at goalkeeping then practise by testing them with different kinds of shots – slow ones, fast ones, high ones and low ones. Encourage them to advance towards the ball: this narrows the angle, making it more difficult for an attacker to shoot.

REFEREE

It could be that your child is more interested in the laws of the game than actually kicking a ball about; if so they may be destined to become a referee. There is a shortage of referees in amateur football at the moment, so any budding refs should be nurtured.

Cricket

Cricket is a wonderful game beloved of young and old alike. It also has one of the most complicated and archaic set of rules in the sporting world. These continue to confuse people who've played the game for 30 years, so trying to explain them to a child is always going to be difficult. Don't worry, the basic premise of cricket couldn't be simpler: defend a set of stumps with a bat.

THE RULES

Cricket is a bat and ball game played by two teams of 11 players. One team bats whilst the other team fields. At the start of the game, the batting side sends out two batters who stand at either end of a pitch and face deliveries from the other team's bowlers, who're trying to hit the batter's stumps. The batters score points ('runs') by hitting the ball and then running between the two sets of stumps (see 'Scoring'). The fielders are arranged across the pitch to try and catch any wayward balls and to prevent runs being scored. Batters are out when their stumps are hit or a ball they've hit is caught. Play continues until all bar one are out, and the teams then swap.

There are various different versions of the game, which can last anything from a couple of hours to five days. However, the object is always the same: score more runs than the other side.

LEARNING THE GAME

All you need to start with is a bat and a tennis ball. It's probably not advisable to use a cricket ball at first, since they're heavy and very hard and are difficult for smaller children to play with. They can also do considerable damage to people and property if whacked in the wrong direction by an over-enthusiastic child.

Take your bat and ball to an open stretch of land. Playing in the garden will probably result in your neighbours becoming fed up retrieving your ball, so a park or playing field is probably better. Stumps are inexpensive and not absolutely necessary – a tree stump or even a couple of water bottles can serve just as well.

SCORING

A game of cricket is played over a set period. In amateur cricket this is usually according to the number of 'overs' bowled. An over involves six balls being bowled from the same end of the pitch, so a 20-over game means that each side faces 20 overs of six balls to score as many runs as possible. However, if one side loses all their wickets then they're out, regardless of the amount of overs that have been bowled.

A run is scored when a batter successfully runs between both wickets (both batters run simultaneously, so will end up changing ends on an odd number of runs). If the ball is hit past the boundary of the cricket field this is automatically worth four runs; if it reaches the boundary without first hitting the ground it's worth six runs

Team scores are normally recorded in terms of the number of runs scored for the number of wickets lost. For example 253 for 5 means the batting team has scored 253 runs for the loss of five wickets.

TAKING IT FURTHER

Many primary schools don't play organised cricket games, as the game is confusing for very small children and is time consuming. However, most secondary schools teach the game and school cricket is of a high standard in both state and private sectors.

Many schools and clubs play a version of the game called Kwik Cricket, which uses lightweight plastic equipment and has much simpler rules than the adult game.

FURTHER INFORMATION

www.ecb.co.uk – Official site of the England and Wales Cricket Board.

BATTING

Children love to hit balls, so batting will immediately appeal to them. Start by bowling some gentle underarm balls to your child, making sure that the ball hits the ground before it reaches them. The correct stance is important: the bat should be held at a slight vertical angle so that it rests just behind the back foot. Encourage them to defend their stumps rather than just swinging at the ball wildly.

If your child is good at batting start to vary the way you bowl at them. Leave some balls long and some short so that they have to defend their wicket in different ways.

BOWLING

Children mostly just want to bat, but bowling skills should be nurtured wherever possible (reward good balls by getting 'out' on purpose). Bowling is easier if you start with underarm throws, but if your child intends to play cricket at school or a club then they'll need to learn how to bowl overarm. This involves bringing the ball past the ear with a straight arm before releasing it. There's a wide and wonderful array of different bowling actions that all have a different style, but forget about that for the time being – it's something that they'll develop later on.

The most important aspects of bowling are line and length, the line being the direction of the ball and the length being how far it travels before it bounces. Try rubbing a patch in the ground so that your child has something to aim at, and let them bowl at the stumps to see how often they can hit them.

FIELDING

Children generally don't enjoy fielding and are usually itching to get into bat or at least to bowl a few balls. Yet it's a central tenet of the game and should be given proper attention. Play a fielding game by hitting or throwing the ball towards your child, varying where you send it so that they have to run for it.

Rugby

The laws of rugby can be very complicated, but you don't need to worry too much about the more in-depth rules or the scoring system to start with. All your child should be concerned with is learning how to run with the ball, kick and catch.

THE RULES

Rugby is a 15-a-side (or sometimes seven-a-side) team game played with an oval-shaped ball. The basic aim is to attack the opposition's goal-line, the goals being marked by a pair of tall H-shaped posts at each end of the pitch. Players advance by either carrying or kicking the ball forward, and score points by touching the ball down beyond the opposition's goal line (called a 'try') or by kicking it over the horizontal goal post.

There are actually two versions of rugby, called rugby union and rugby league, each with a different set of rules, but if your child expresses an interest in learning rugby don't worry about whether to teach union or league. They're basically the same, and if your child wants to take it further then which version they actually play will probably depend on the area of the country you live in.

LEARNING THE GAME

Take a ball out into the garden or park and have some fun! Do a bit of running and passing with your child – ball-handling is the most important aspect of the game and your aim should be to make them comfortable passing and receiving the ball.

Encourage them to run in front and pass the ball back to you and then do the same to them; forward passes are illegal in rugby, so young players need to learn this as soon as possible.

SCORING

Both versions of rugby are played over two halves of 40 minutes. Draws are rare but extra time can be played in competitions where a winner is required.

The scoring system differs between the two versions of the game. In rugby union, a try is worth five points and the kick that follows each try, called a conversion, is worth two. The other methods of scoring are drop goals and penalty kicks, and are both worth three points. In rugby league a try is worth four points, a conversion two, a penalty two, and a drop goal just one.

TAKING IT FURTHER

If your child enjoys your impromptu games and wants to take it further then encourage them to join a local club. Few primary schools, particularly in the state sector, teach the sport so your local rugby club is your best bet. Find out if they have a 'mini-rugby' section where youngsters can play a children's version of the game.

If you're worried about them being hurt, touch rugby is a game in its own right and there are many clubs across the country.

FURTHER INFORMATION

www.rfu.com – Official site of the Rugby Football Union.
www.barla.org.uk – Official site of the British Amateur Rugby League Association.

KICKING

Kicking is another key aspect of the game. As well as kicking for points, kicks are also used to gain territory. Children will enjoy playing a kicking game, so try some gentle kicks that they can catch easily, and then encourage them to kick the ball back. Have a competition to see who can kick it the highest, and make sure they win!

To practise kicking for points, dig a little hole in the ground with your heel and place the point of the ball in it so that it's standing up. Then let your child kick it at a target. If you have rugby posts nearby, fine, if not try a tree or something similar. They're unlikely to hit it, so have a little contest to see who can get the nearest.

TACKLING

Tackling is a central feature of the game and is how teams defend against attacking players. When a player is tackled to the ground they have to release the ball. In rugby circles there's some debate over the amount of contact that should take place and at what age. Some suggest that tackling should be taught as young as possible, but others think that it can discourage children.

Dads should start with touch rugby, so that when the ball-carrier is touched by a rival player they have to release the ball. Try a game of one-on-one; give your child the ball and encourage them to try and run past without you touching them. This will teach them to change direction and speed to try and get past you, which are essential skills in the real game.

If you want to bring tackling in then let them tackle you. They'll undoubtedly enjoy getting Dad dirty! If they manage to wrap themselves around you, go down and release the ball.

If your child doesn't like getting dirty or you're worried about the safety aspects of tackling then just carry on with touch rugby.

POSITIONS

If your child begins to show a particular aptitude for the game then it's time to think about which position they may want to play in. A rugby team is split into 'forwards' and 'backs': forwards are the ball winners, competing to win the ball for the backs, whose main job is to advance the ball towards the opposition's goal-line. If your child likes getting dirty and scrabbling about in the mud then they should be in the forwards. If they're quick and nimble and enjoy running with the ball they're probably better suited to the backs.

Tennis

Tennis is the most popular racket game in the world. It's played on a specially marked court with a low net across the middle. The basic aim of the game is to hit the ball over the net in such a way that your opponent cannot return it.

THE RULES

Each game begins with a service: the server hits the ball from behind the baseline into the service area diagonally opposite. The other player must return the ball after it has bounced once and before it bounces a second time; thereafter the ball must be returned after one bounce or before it has hit the ground at all. A 'rally' continues until one player fails to return the ball, hits it so that it lands outside the marked-out court area, or hits it into the net.

LEARNING THE GAME

Tennis is an easy game to play and is ideal for children. At first you don't need a tennis court, or even a net. Just buy or borrow a couple of cheap rackets and then hit a tennis ball back and forth on a patch of concrete, or in the garden if the ground is very firm. This will teach your child the basics of the game before you try it on a court.

When you progress to a court ignore the markings at first – it can be hard enough for children to hit the ball over the net at all, without worrying about whether it's in or out. Serve underarm and see how many times you can hit it back and forth before one of you hits the net or misses.

SCORING

The scoring system in tennis is confusing. To win a match a player has to win a certain number of 'sets'. Each set is made up of a certain number of games, and each game is made up of a certain number of points. Most amateur tennis matches comprise three sets.

At the start of each game both players have a score of 0, known as 'love' in tennis. After that the first point scored is worth fifteen, the next takes this total to thirty, and the third takes it to forty. The server's score always comes first, so if the score is 15–40 it means that the server has won one point to their opponent's three. If the score is tied at 40–40 the score is called 'deuce'. One player then has to go two points clear to win the game: if a player wins one point at this stage it's called 'advantage'; if they win the next they've won the game, but if they lose it then the score returns to deuce.

When a player wins six games they win the 'set' – unless their opponent has won as many as five games. In that situation the player with six games must win one more, to take the set by seven games to five, since a set can only be won by being at least two games ahead. To prevent things going on for too long a final game, called a tie-break, is played if the score reaches six games each. In a tie-break each point is worth just one and the first player to reach six wins. If the score reaches six points each, then one player has to win by two clear points – *eg* 8–6.

TAKING IT FURTHER

Grassroots tennis is actively encouraged in this country and there are tennis clubs in most towns and villages. There's a special junior version of tennis called short tennis, which has the same rules but uses a smaller court, lighter rackets, and large foam balls.

FURTHER INFORMATION

www.lta.org.uk – Website of the Lawn Tennis Association, the governing body of the game in Britain.

TENNIS COURTS

Tennis courts can be outdoors or indoors, and can have a variety of surfaces.

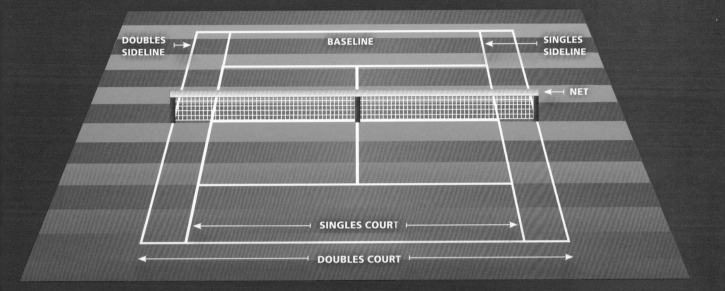

SERVING

The serve is the shot that starts each game. To begin with you should both serve underarm, as this is easier to execute and to return. However, if your child likes tennis and wants to play competitively then they'll need to master the overarm serve.

The correct position for serving is with the legs shoulder-width apart, in a sideways stance behind the baseline. The ball is then tossed in the air and struck whilst above the head, and the ball must land in the diagonally opposite service box without hitting the net.

Overarm service is very difficult to master, so a dad needs plenty of patience when teaching it. Be prepared for long hours on the other side of the court acting as a target.

THE FOREHAND

This is the most important shot in tennis and is used the most frequently; as such, your child should concentrate on mastering this first. To return a ball well you need to stand face on to the net and take the racket back as soon as the ball leaves your opponent's racket. Then transfer your weight to your back foot and bring the racket through in a smooth motion to connect with the ball, transferring your weight to your front foot as you do so. Children will find it easier to hit a falling ball, one that's reached the top of its arc after bouncing and is coming back down.

THE BACKHAND

The other most commonly used shot, the backhand, is more difficult to master as it involves returning the ball with the racket stretched across the body. Beginners tend to miss a lot of backhands, so encourage your child to watch the ball intently and return it with a firmer grip than a forehand.

It's worthwhile taking the time to specifically practise backhands each time you play. If your child lacks confidence with this shot then they may avoid it and try to play everything with a forehand.

OTHER SHOTS

A multitude of other shots are used in tennis. The volley involves hitting the ball before it bounces, and is often used to smash high shots into your opponent's half of the court so that they have no hope of returning them. The lob is an underarm shot used to hit the ball long and high over your opponent's head. A drop shot is used if your opponent is a long way back, and involves lightly tapping the ball over the net in the hope that they won't be able to cover the ground in time to return it.

Just concentrate on the forehand and backhand at first, but as children get more proficient at the game you should encourage them to extend their repertoire of shots. This will increase their skill levels and makes the game more exciting.

French cricket

In this fun version of real cricket a ball is bowled underarm at the legs of another player, which take the place of cricket stumps. The delight of the game is that all you need in order to play it is a tennis ball and a bat or a tennis racket.

You can play it with any number of people right down to just two. One player bats and the rest field. The aim of the game is for the bowler to hit the legs of the batter with the ball. Nominate a player to bowl first, and after the ball has been hit the next ball is bowled by whichever fielder collects it, and from where they're standing.

The batter is bowled out when their legs are hit below the knee, and can also be caught out in the same way as normal cricket. Whoever gets the batter out takes their place.

You can play two different versions of the game dependent on whether the batter is allowed to turn to face the ball or not. If playing with young children it's probably best to always let them face the ball, as they'll find it difficult to hit it when it comes from the side or from behind.

To add a bit of competition you can introduce 'runs', by revolving the bat around the body after a hit until the ball is retrieved.

Badminton

Badminton is a racket sport played by two or four people, depending on whether you're playing singles or doubles. Players volley a shuttlecock over a net until one player misses.

As in tennis, service is from the right-hand service area to the diagonally opposing area. Points can only be won by the server; the non-serving player can only win service. Badminton is a good sport to teach children as it's not too fast – a shuttlecock is very light so it's easy to hit back, which makes for long rallies. Hit the shuttlecock nice and high so that children have ample time to position themselves for the return.

The game is played on specially marked courts and every leisure centre in the land has at least one, so it's easy to find somewhere to play. However, a washing line in a back garden can serve just as well if you're playing for fun. For further details on rules and scoring see www.badmintonengland.co.uk

Rounders

Rounders is a similar game to cricket and is very much like the American sport of baseball. All you need to play is a tennis ball and a bat. Rounders bats are widely available but a cricket bat or even a tennis racket would be an adequate substitute.

Rounders is a great family game and is often played after picnics or on trips to the park. To play the game, set out four bases in a roughly diamond shape. Then divide your group into two teams and decide which team is going to bat first. One person from this team wields the bat whilst the others wait their turn. The fielding team nominates a bowler and then divides up so that a person stands at each of the four bases and the rest wherever they like.

The objective is for the batter to hit the ball far enough to enable them to run around all the bases and so score a 'rounder'. Batters are safe if they reach a base. The next player then steps up to bat, and earlier batsmen still standing at the bases can start running again after the ball is hit. Members of the batting team are out if their hit is caught, or if the base they're running to is touched before they reach it by a fielder holding the ball.

About six players on each side is best, but if you have more or less don't worry. Rounders is just a bit of fun, so adapt the rules to whatever suits you.

Table tennis

Table tennis or 'ping-pong' is, as its name suggests, a miniature version of tennis. It's played on a rectangular table with a low net across the centre. The ball is very light and the wooden bats are small and have a dimpled rubber surface.

This is a fun game for children and very easy to get the hang of. A crucial thing to remember is that, unlike proper tennis, the service ball has to bounce on each side of the table before it can be returned. Rallies then continue in the same manner as tennis, with each ball having to bounce once before being returned, so encourage your child to hit the ball at a downward angle so that it can bounce over the net.

Table tennis tables are quite expensive but there are plenty around in youth clubs, leisure centres and holiday camps. If you can't find one try playing on a dining room table, which is how the game originated. For further details on rules and scoring see www.englishtabletennis.org.uk

Games

Card games 72

Chess 74

Dice games 77

Pen and paper games 78

Battleships and Dead Ducks 80

Games for a car journey 82

Treasure hunt 84

Marbles 88

Card games

With a few good card games, you're well equipped to keep children busy and happy. A pack of cards is cheap and can be taken anywhere.

SOME DETAILS TO EXPLAIN TO CHILDREN

Jacks, Kings and Queens are called the court cards. An **Ace** is in some games considered higher or more valuable than a King, while in others it's considered the lowest card of all, below a Two.

The **rank** of a card is its number or title.

There are four **suits**: hearts, diamonds, clubs and spades.

The **pip value** of a set of cards is all the numbers added together, sometimes also including amounts for each of the court cards.

A **discard pile** is a stack of cards on the table that grows as players discard cards from their hands.

A **stock pile** is a stack of cards which gradually diminishes as people take from it during their turns.

Games vary, but for all the ones listed below you can agree that either the youngest player starts, or the player to the left of the dealer. Play continues clockwise.

Eights

Good for all ages from about 8+

2–8 players. One pack of cards for up to four players; two packs for more.

A traditional game, Eights bears some similarities to the excellent, popular game *Uno*. The aim of Eights is to get rid of your cards onto a discard pile by matching the rank or suit of the previous discard.

Use a standard 52-card pack, or two packs shuffled together if there are more than four players. The dealer deals five cards to each player, or seven if there are only two players. The remaining cards go face down on the table as the stock pile. The top card of the pile is turned face up and placed next to the stock pile to start the discard pile.

Each player must either play a legal card face up on top of the discard pile, or draw a card from the stock pile. The following plays are legal:

1. You can play any card that matches the rank or suit of the previous card. For example, you can follow the Ace of diamonds with any Ace or any diamond.
2. Eight is an exception. You can play an eight on any card, and then nominate the suit that must be played next.

The first player to get rid of all their cards wins. If you're scoring, the other players get penalty points according to the cards left in their hands – 50 for an eight, 10 for a court card, and other cards at pip value.

Last Card – If a player has just one card left he has to alert the others: choose your own codeword, such as 'Otto' (Italian for eight) or 'Last Card', or thump the table. If you don't alert them, you have to take two cards from the stock pile as a penalty.

Optional: cards with special actions – These extras make the game a little more complicated, but still simple enough for children aged 9 or so.

Queen – Miss a turn – When a queen is played, the next player misses a turn and play passes to the player after them.

Ace – change direction – If someone plays an Ace it reverses the direction of play.

Two – add two – When a Two is played the next player must either play another two or pick up two cards.

Beggar My Neighbour

Good for all ages from about 6+

2 players, using a standard 52-card pack.

This game requires no skill, just a sense of fun. The aim is to collect as many cards as possible and see your opponent run out of cards. Children love its simplicity. Dads need to remember to appear to get upset about losing all their precious cards, as that adds to the fun!

Divide the pack of cards roughly in half. Each player holds their cards, face down. Players take turns to turn over their top card and play it face up in the centre of the table, building up a pile.

There are two kinds of card – 'pay' cards and 'ordinary' cards. Aces, Kings, Queens and Jacks are pay cards. All the rest are ordinary cards.

Play continues until someone turns over a pay card. The other player has to pay for this card by adding cards to the pile as follows:

    4 ordinary cards for an Ace
    3 ordinary cards for a King
    2 ordinary cards for a Queen
    1 ordinary card for a Jack

When that player has paid up, the first player takes the whole pile and puts it face down underneath his own cards.

If, while paying for a card, a player turns over another pay card the previous pay card is cancelled, and his opponent has to pay for the new pay card instead.

The winner is the player who ends up with all the cards – or with the most cards if the game, which can go on for ages, has a time limit.

Cheat

Good for all ages from about 8+

2–4 players: one pack of cards; 5–8 players: two packs.
Shuffle and deal all the cards. Some players may end up with one or two more cards than others: that's fine. The aim of Cheat is to get rid of all the cards in your hand.

The first player starts the discard pile placing one or more cards, puts them face down declaring what they are – but he may be lying.

The next player must play further cards of the same value or upwards or downwards from what the previous player claims to have discarded.

As you discard cards face down, you don't necessarily have the cards you say you're putting down. For example, if you need to discard a Ten, Jack or Queen and don't have one, you can actually discard any card or mixture of cards.

But beware of being rumbled. Anyone who suspects that what's being discarded isn't what it's claimed to be, can challenge the player by saying 'Cheat!'. The challenged player then has to reveal the card(s) they've just discarded. If they *are* what they were claimed to be, the challenge is wrong, and the challenger has to pick up the whole discard pile; but if any of the played cards are different from what was called, then the player whose cheat has been exposed has to pick up the whole discard pile.

After a challenge, play continues with the next player putting down any rank or cards he chooses.

The first player to get rid of all his cards and survive any challenges wins. Consequently the last cards can be your downfall. If someone challenges you when you play them and you turn out to be a Cheat, then you have to pick up the whole pile and play continues.

Learning to lose

Card games are a great way of teaching children to lose with good grace. The best way of doing this is by making sure that a child wins enough times – either by a bit of subtle cheating to make sure you lose, or by showing them how to make good choices if the card game involves skill. The ideal win:lose ratio varies with each child, but you may find that a child under 8 will thrive on winning three games out of four, while one aged 8–11 is happy winning just two games out of four. Gradually they'll become happy to win less and lose more. Children over 12 are generally less bothered about winning and losing (in card games – it's rather different in other activities!). They're happy simply to take part, especially in larger group card games.

Rummy

Good for adults and children from about 10+

2–6 players, using a standard 52-card pack.
This game involves some skill and judgement. It can be played either as a one-off game, or as a series of games in which the eventual winner is the player who has either scored the most points or has reached a pre-agreed target within a set time limit.

The dealer deals ten cards to each player if there are two, seven cards if there are three or four players, and six cards if there are five or six. The remaining cards are placed in a pile in the middle of the table, face down, but with the top card turned face up next to it to start the discard pile.

The aim is to collect sets or 'melds', consisting of either three or more cards of the same rank, or sequences of three or more cards of the same suit – *eg* Ace, Two and Three of Hearts, or three Jacks.

On your go, you take the top card from either the discard pile (where you can see what the card is) or the stock pile (where you pick blind). If, after taking the card, your hand includes a set of three, you 'declare' them and place them face up on the table. Then discard one of your cards to complete your turn.

During your turn you can also add to other players' sets of exposed cards: for example, if someone has put down three Aces, you can add a fourth. If someone has put down the Two, Three and Four of Clubs, you could add the Ace and/or the Five.

If the stock pile runs out, turn the discard pile face down so that it becomes the stock pile.

The winner of the game is the first player to use up all their cards. If scoring over a series of games, the winner of each game gains points from the other players according to the cards still in their hands when play ends: ten points for every court card, one point for every Ace, and the pip value of every other card. It's a 'rummy' if the winning player declares and lays out all their cards in one turn, for which they receive double points. It can therefore be worth hanging on to complete melds in your hand if you think there's any chance of picking up the right one or two cards that will enable you to declare them all at one time. However, you run the risk of being caught with all these cards still in your hand at the end of a game!

Chess

Chess is a great game because it helps children learn about thinking ahead. Above all, it's good fun, whether you're a beginner or an experienced player.

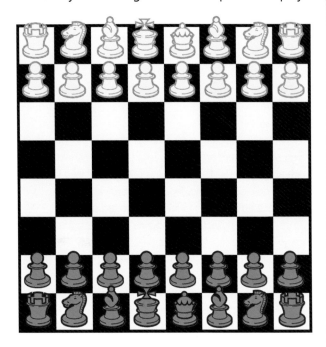

SETTING UP THE BOARD

A chessboard is made up of eight rows of eight squares. As you look at the board, the rows making lines ahead of you are called the files; the sideways rows are called ranks. The diagonal lines of squares of the same colour, are, unsurprisingly, just called diagonals. The half side of the board where the kings sit is called the kingside; and the half where the queens sit is called the queenside. Even when the pieces are other colours, the playing side that's darker is always called black, and the side that's lighter is always called white.

Turn the board so that both players have a white square in their right-hand corner. Place a line of pawns in the second rank.

Place the rooks (or castles) in the corner squares at far right and far left of the first rank, knights in the second square in, and then bishops. Your queen sits on her own colour – ie the black queen sits on a black square, the white queen on a white square. The king goes on his opposing colour – the black king therefore on a white square and vice versa – next to the queen.

Each piece should be directly facing its counterpart – therefore white rooks facing black rooks, white queen facing black queen, etc.

AIM OF THE GAME

The aim of chess is to trap your opponent's king, not to take as many pieces as you can. Sometimes it's a good move to sacrifice a piece in order to gain a tactical advantage. Knowing the value of the pieces or 'men' will help you decide when it's worth taking an opposing piece if it means sacrificing one of your own. Their relative values are: pawns 1; knights 3; bishops 3; castles 5; queen 9; king whole game.

LEARNING THE GAME

It's important to get to know all the pieces and their moves. Queen's attack (see page 76) is an excellent introduction to the pawns and the queen.

For children under 12, it may be better to leave more difficult manoeuvres like *en passant* and castling until later.

SOME GENERAL RULES

1 White has first move. Then each side takes turns in moving.
2 You can't miss a go, even if it means you have to put one of your pieces in danger.
3 Only one piece can be moved on a turn, except when 'castling' (see opposite).
4 A move is completed when one piece has been moved from one square to another. In serious games, if you so much as touch a piece you have to move it: you can't change your mind, even if the move will take it into danger. Also, if you put the piece down, let go of it and want to change your mind, you can't. However, it's less hassle and more fun to allow younger players second thoughts!
5 Only one piece can occupy a square at one time.
6 Except when castling, only the knight can leap over a square occupied by another piece.
7 Each piece can move in only one direction in a turn – except the knight (and pawns when moving *en passant* – see page 76).
8 Only one capture can be made in one go. You don't *have* to capture a piece just because you can – unless it's the only move that will save a king from capture.
9 You don't have to make any particular move, unless it's the only move that saves the king from capture.
10 You can't make a move or capture a piece that will allow your own king to be captured.
11 A pawn that gets past all your opponent's pieces and reaches the eighth rank can be promoted to become a second queen, a rook, a bishop or a knight: the choice is yours.

From check to checkmate

If a piece threatens the king, it's called 'check': the player who makes that move says 'check' and the other player has to either move the king out of check, by moving it to a different square or blocking the attack with another piece, or else take the attacking piece with one of their own. When the king can't move out of danger or can't be shielded or rescued by another piece it's called 'checkmate', and the game is over. If the king isn't in check, but the only moves he can make would put him in check, then it's a called a 'stalemate', and neither player wins.

Castling

This is the only time that two pieces are moved at the same time. After the knight and bishop have both moved from their original positions in the first rank, the king can swap round with the rook by moving two squares left or right. The rook therefore moves to the fourth or third square in.

You can castle on the kingside with the king and the king's rook; you can castle on the queenside with the king and the queen's rook.

What's the point of castling? Well, not only does it get the king away from the exposed centre of the board and over to the side, where he's easier to protect, but it also gets the rook away from a corner file into a centre file, where it's much better placed to attack. When castling, however, several special rules apply:

Before castling
BLACK
WHITE

BLACK
WHITE

After castling King-side
BLACK
WHITE
King-side

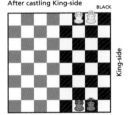

After castling Queen-side
BLACK
WHITE
Queen-side

1. There must be no pieces between king and rook.
2. It must be the first move of the game for both pieces.
3. The king must not be in check before or after the move.
4. The king mustn't pass over a square where he would (if he stayed on it) be in check – though if the rook passes over a square that's under attack you can still castle.
5. Each side can only castle once in game.

How do the pieces move?

All pieces except the pawns can move backwards as well as forwards:

King one square in any direction.

Queen any number of squares in a straight line, forwards, backwards, sideways or diagonally.

Castle any number of squares in a straight line, forwards, sideways or backwards.

Knight moves 3 squares in an L shape. Always lands on a square of a different colour from where it started.

Bishop any number of squares in a straight diagonal line.

Pawn one square forwards, except that on its first move only, if you so desire, it can advance two squares. However, pawns capture diagonally, and only diagonally.

! *The term 'rook', often used in place of 'castle', has nothing to do with birds. It comes from rukh, a Persian word meaning 'warrior'. 'Checkmate' comes from old Persian sháh, meaning 'king', and mát, meaning 'helpless'.*

Pawns

Top: A pawn can only move in one direction – forwards – on its own file, one square at a time. On each pawn's first move only, you can choose to move forward *two* squares if you want to, but a pawn can't capture on a two-square more.

Centre: A pawn can't capture a piece in front of it: it can only capture a piece that's on one of the squares *diagonally* ahead of it.

Bottom: A pawn can't move if there's another piece occupying the square in front of it. However, even if it can't move straight ahead it can still capture an opponent's piece diagonally.

EN PASSANT

An *en passant* ('in passing') capture is a special move where one pawn takes another. As already said, in a pawn's first move it can go either one or two squares forward. If it goes two, then on your opponent's next move one of his pawns can capture it, just as if it had moved only one square. To do this the enemy pawn must be on the square immediately alongside that on which your pawn has stopped. The enemy pawn then moves diagonally to occupy the first square over which your pawn passed. See the accompanying diagram.

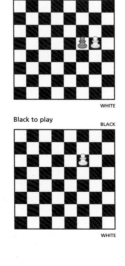

! *The word 'pawn' comes from Spanish peón, meaning 'worker'.*

Winning and losing

None of us much likes losing, and it's particularly difficult for children. A game like chess provides a great opportunity to show them how to enjoy losing as well as winning. If you can show surprise and even pleasure at losing a piece on the chessboard, then your child will learn to do the same. At first, try not to win by using your own skills, but rather allow your child's unwise moves to lead to a loss. Then you can help them see where they went wrong. This is much better than getting them confused by trying to explain your superior play.

You'll find that a useful phrase is 'Are you sure about that?' When your child is about to make a move that seems a bad idea, stop him so that he can work out the implications of what he's doing. He may well take back the move (which at the learning stage you can allow). It's also useful to query a perfectly good move, so that he checks it out and doesn't just rely on your hints.

Queen's attack

This is a great game for young and old players. It's got some of the excitement of full chess, you learn about tactics, and it's very quick.

Who's stronger, one queen or eight pawns? Your play will decide...

What you do: set up a row of white pawns in their normal starting position, *ie* in the second rank. Place the black queen on her square on the opposite side.

The aim of the game: if you're playing the queen, you've got to annihilate the pawns before any reach your first rank (their eighth) and so qualify to be promoted to a queen. Wipe them out and you've won. If you're playing the pawns' side, you've got to move them up the board in such a way that they can protect each other as much as possible, and try to get just one of them to the far side of the board. If you succeed, then you've won.

Pawns always play first. Take it in turns playing queen or pawns. It's very quick, so keep swapping. Play for the best of five or seven games. After you get to know the game you'll find you can play it really fast!

Dice games

Dice games can vary from simple and innocent to seriously dangerous if there's any gambling involved. Sometimes they involve no more than pure luck, while sometimes strategy is involved – a combination that makes dice games exciting for any age group.

Pig

2–6 players, about age 7 to adult.

This game requires just one dice, a pencil and paper to keep score, plus a lot of luck and a little strategy. Your aim is to achieve a high score, but with every extra throw you risk losing whatever you've scored in that go, so it's up to you to decide when to stop.

To start throw the single dice – lowest score starts, and the sequence of play goes clockwise. When it comes to their turn, each player can throw several times and accumulate an ever-growing running total. They can go on for as long as they like, but if at any point they throw a 1 then they lose all the points they scored in that go, and the dice passes to the next player. The first player to reach or exceed 101 points is the winner.

Chicago

2–6 players, about age 6 (or maybe younger) to adult.

For this game you need 2 dice, paper and a pen. It's a very simple and quick game, based only on luck. There are 11 rounds, and the youngest player starts; play then continues clockwise.

In round one, each player tries to throw 2, ie a double 1. Players who are successful get two points; everyone else none. In round two, everyone tries to throw a total of 3, ie a 2 and a 1. Players who are successful get three points; everyone else none. In round three each player tries to throw 4, ie a 1 and a 3, or two 2s, and those who succeed get four points – and so on, as in the following rounds the players try to throw 5, 6, 7, 8, 9, 10, 11 and finally 12. The winner is the person with the highest score at the end of the game.

After a few rounds the odds of getting the total you want are better than at the start. Then the odds go down again. Very young players may be put off if they don't throw winning combinations early on, so a junior version, to encourage them, works by introducing a rule that anyone aged under nine has two or three throws in each round.

Yacht

2–6 players, age 11+.

If teenagers reckon dice is only for kids, this game may persuade them otherwise. Yacht has some parallels to games such as poker, rummy and mah-jong – like them it combines strategy and luck, and once you've got your head around the rules it's just as absorbing.

You need five dice, a pen and paper (to draw up a score sheet). The aim of the game is both to achieve particular sequences from the five dice, and to work out how to make the most out of every go.

The players each throw two dice to decide who starts – lowest score wins. In each round a player then has up to three throws. On the first throw they roll five dice, and set aside any of them whose score they want to keep. Then they throw the remaining dice, and again set aside any more they want to keep. Finally, after the third throw all the dice are viewed side by side in order to decide how they should be grouped to achieve the best total:

- Yacht (5 of one kind – five 1s, five 2s, and so on) = 50 points
- Big Straight (2, 3, 4, 5, 6) = 30
- Little Straight (1, 2, 3, 4, 5) = 30
- Four of a kind (eg 3, 3, 3, 3) = total of all dots on the dice
- Full House (3 of one kind, 2 of another – eg 2, 2, 2 and 6, 6) = total of all dots on the dice
- Choice (any five dice – eg 1, 1, 3, 4, 6) = pip value of all the dice
- Sixes = 6 for every 6 thrown
- Fives = 5 for every 5 thrown
- Fours = 4 for every 4 thrown
- Three = 3 for every 3 thrown
- Twos = 2 for every 2 thrown
- Aces = 1 for every 1 thrown

There are 12 rounds. Each player must enter a score in every category of his score-sheet, even if their score for a category is nil. You can't enter a new throw in a category that you've already filled in on your sheet. For example, if you throw 4, 4, 4, 4, 6 that would be four of a kind, but if you've already entered a four of a kind result on your sheet from a previous go you must enter the score elsewhere, for example as Choice (scoring 22 points) or Sixes (scoring just 6 points).

	Mel	Tom	Han	Jon
Yacht				
Big Straight				
Little Straight	30			
Four of a kind				
Full House				
Choice				
Sixes			12	18
Fives				15
Fours				
Threes				
Twos				
Aces				
TOTAL				

Pen and paper games

Martian Consequences

3+ players, aged about 6+

This is a version of the well-known traditional game of Consequences, except that each player draws bits of an animal or monster, carrying a little bit of the picture, maybe just two lines, over onto the next panel so that the next player knows where to start from.

Leave the top panel blank. On panel two the first player draws hair or a hat, then folds the paper and passes it on.

On panel three the next player draws a head, then folds the paper and passes it on.

On panel four the next player draws the top half of a body, then folds the paper and passes it on.

On panel five the next player draws the bottom half of a body, then folds the paper and passes it on.

On panel six the next player draws the legs, then folds the paper and passes it on.

On panel seven the next player draws the feet, then folds the paper and passes it on.

The next player opens up the sheet.

Mega Noughts and Crosses

2 players

This is like normal Noughts and Crosses but with four horizontal and four vertical lines, making 25 squares to play in. The aim is to get as many sets of three in a row as possible, counted vertically, horizontally or diagonally. You can agree to use the same nought or cross twice where two sets of three intersect, or else agree to count them only once.

Million Pound Budget

1 child and 1 adult

How would you spend the money if you won a million pounds? Depending on who's playing, you can make the figures fanciful or use it as a way to help your child understand what things cost. A pony? A helicopter? A castle? If their tastes are especially extravagant you might allow a bigger budget of £10 million. Or more…

The target for spendthrifts is to use all the money down to the last pound. This can make for some fun maths, with or without a calculator.

A sample list might look like this:

HOW I WOULD SPEND £1,000,000

Sweets	£100
Ferrari	£120,000
Helicopter	£400,000
Present for my brother	£10
Nice camera	£50
Pet crocodile	£1,000
Food for crocodile	£400
Crossbow	£135
New bike	£250
Bike helmet	£25
Good book	£20
etc….	

Boxes
2 players

A simple but interesting game. Draw a grid of dots, 6 to 12 dots wide and 6 to 12 deep. Lined or graph paper is helpful for this. The aim is to complete as many boxes as possible, while preventing your opponent from doing so.

Each player draws one vertical or horizontal line, anywhere on the grid. When there are three lines waiting for a fourth to close a box, the next player can complete it. He then writes his initials in the box and has another go. The winner is the person with the most boxes when all the dots have been joined.

Dotty Drawings
2 players aged about 5+

Each player puts 20 dots at random on a sheet of paper and passes it to the other player. They then have to decide on ways to join the dots together to make as many pictures as possible.

Word games

MY GRANDMOTHER WENT TO MARKET
2 or more players

A classic game. Player One says 'My grandmother went to market and bought a…' and then adds something sensible or silly – eg a kangaroo. Player Two then says 'My grandmother went to market and bought a kangaroo and…' and adds an extra word, perhaps 'sausages' – and so on, with each player having to recite the entire growing list and add an extra item at the end of it. If a player can't remember the list (a little prompting is acceptable to help younger players) they're out. The winner is the last person to recite the list correctly.

FIRST AND LAST
2 or more players

Choose a subject – eg animals, first names, foods. Say you choose food: Player One then names a food, and Player Two has to think of another food beginning with the last letter of the food named by the first player – eg Player One says 'ice cream', so Player Two says 'mustard'. The next player must therefore think of a food beginning with 'd'.

A word can only be used once, and a player who can't think of a new word is out. If you're good at thinking of words beginning with 'e' you'll probably be the winner!

NEVER SAY THE START
2–5 players

A simple, quick game suitable for young and very young children. Each player starts with ten points. Player One chooses a word but doesn't pronounce the first letter. The other players then take it in turns to guess the missing letter that completes the word, and lose a point if they guess wrong. For example, Player One says 'ear'. Player Two suggests 'fear' but is wrong, Player Three tries 'beer' but is also wrong, and Player Four tries 'near', and is right. The player who gets the correct answer wins a point and starts off the next round with a new word. You can also play the game without bothering about scoring points at all.

FAST CONNECTIONS
2 or more players

This game has to be played fast. Player One chooses a noun. Player Two has to think of a noun connected with it, Player Three has to think of a noun connected with that, and so on. If someone calls out a noun that doesn't have an obvious connection, or takes more than an agreed time (eg ten seconds), they lose a point. Each player starts with four points and is out when they've all been lost. You can change the rules to allow adjectives as well, and you can agree that opposites count as connections.

Battleships and Dead Ducks

Battleship is a very well known game that has whiled away many hours for many generations. However, it can be a bit too long for younger children, so here we give two versions of it, plus an extra one for very young children.

Battleships – The big boys' version
2 players
You'll need a pencil and two sheets of paper (preferably lined or graph paper). Each player must sit so that their opponent can't see their paper. Both players then draw themselves two identical grids on their sheets, ten squares by ten squares. You could save time by running off photocopies, but it's a useful activity for children to learn to draw a grid with a bit of accuracy, and it will keep them occupied for a while. The players then number both sets of grid squares identically – A to J along the top, and 1 to 10 down the side. One grid is labelled 'Home', the other one 'Enemy'.

Each player then draws their fleet on their 'Home' grid. The fleet consists of:

- 1 battleship, occupying 4 adjacent boxes
- 2 frigates, each occupying 3 adjacent boxes
- 3 destroyers, each occupying 2 adjacent boxes
- 4 submarines, each occupying 1 box

These must be drawn in a straight line, horizontally or vertically, not diagonally. L-shaped ships are not allowed! If you want, other rules can be imposed governing the deployment of the ships:

- they must be placed so that there's at least one space between them; or
- they can be adjacent on diagonal squares; or
- they can be deployed alongside one another without gaps

The aim of the game is to locate and destroy the other player's fleet. Players take turns to 'fire', giving a grid reference – *eg* D4 – in which to drop a shell. The other player checks D4 on their 'Home' grid and must say if it's a hit, in which case you mark an 'X' in that square on your 'Enemy' grid. If it's not a hit, you mark the square with an 'O'. The other player also has to say if the hit has sunk the vessel. Only a submarine is sunk by a single hit: other vessels count only as damaged until every square they occupy has been hit. When a player scores a hit they have another go, but if they miss play passes to their opponent, who in turn chooses a place to drop a shell. The winner is the first person to annihilate the enemy's fleet entirely.

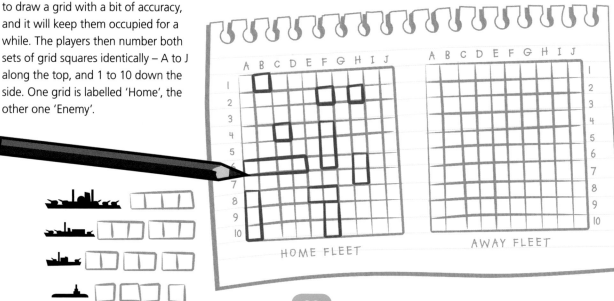

80

Battleships – The junior version
2 players

This is identical to the big boys' version except in using a smaller grid and fleet, which increases the odds of scoring a hit early on from 20 per cent to 50 per cent and makes the game quicker and more rewarding for younger players.

The grids measure six squares by six squares, numbered A to F along the top and 1 to 6 down the side, and the fleet comprises:

- ■ 1 battleship, occupying 4 adjacent boxes
- ■ 2 frigates, each occupying 3 adjacent boxes
- ■ 2 destroyers, each occupying 2 adjacent boxes
- ■ 3 submarines, each occupying 1 box

The rest of the game is played as described for the big boys' version, except that ships in the fleet can be placed next to one another.

Dead Ducks – The simple version

Younger children who can't get their heads round Battleships will enjoy this, though they may need a lot of help in the first few games. It requires little or no strategy, just a bit of imagination.

Though 'Dead Ducks' is a good name, younger children might be happier if you called it just 'Ducks', and pretended that you're a mother duck trying to find her ducklings rather than a hunter trying to shoot them!

Both players draw two identical grids on their sheets, measuring five squares by five squares, and number these A to E along the top and 1 to 5 down the side. One grid is labelled 'My Pond', the second one 'Other Pond'. Each player then places ten ducks on their own pond, each duck occupying one square – mark them in with a number '2' drawn to look like a duck. If you want to you can place them on adjacent squares.

The rest of the game is played as for Battleships, except that you don't say 'hit' or 'miss': you say 'quack' for a hit and 'splosh' for a miss.

My Pond   Other Pond

More word games

A LETTER IN MY HEAD
2–4 players

This is ideal for very young children just learning their alphabet, and older ones too. It's very simple, and parents can keep it going for as long as they like, not letting on that they may have guessed the answer. When you've chosen a letter, and your child is trying to guess it, remember that very young children may simply take a wild guess. Gently help them to work out the answer. They may get the hang of it one day, but completely forget on the next!

Player One says 'I've got a letter in my head' and thinks of a letter. The other players then suggest words that the letter may be in. For example:

Player One has S in his head.

Player Two says 'Have you got "bat" in your head?' to which the answer is 'No.'

Player Three says 'Have you got "sword" in your head?' 'Yes.'

Player Four says 'Have you got "island" in your head?' 'Yes.'

Then Player Two asks again, and so on.

Some players may find this much easier if they write the letters of the alphabet on a sheet of paper and tick them off as they're eliminated.

As you may have very young players in the game, remember to allow for the possibility of their answers being wrong!

THE OOO GAME
2–4 players or more

A rather silly game, related to Fast Connections, suitable for children aged four or more.

It's surprising how many words have an 'oo' sound in them. To win this game, a player has to come up with an associated word that has 'oo' sound in it. You play it like Fast Connections – each player has ten seconds to come up with a word (nouns and adjectives both count) – but instead of always picking connected words you can also choose complete opposites. The winner is the first person who can slip in an 'oo' word – so, for example, Player One may says 'tractor', Player Two says 'plough', Player Three says 'earth', and Player Four wins with 'moon'.

The 'oo' sound doesn't require a word to have a double 'o' – eg words like clue, wound, you, etc are also acceptable. You may even want to stretch the rules to include 'near-oos', such as 'dual'.

> **❗ Can you rearrange the letters at the top of this page to make a nine-letter word?**

Games for a car journey

'I'm bored...are we there yet?' Adults sitting in the front of a car tend to forget how boring it is in the back. You can't see as much, you don't know where the car's going, and if you're a child, sitting still for a long time is really hard. So games and activities designed to keep people's spirits up and stop the driver stressing out are valuable all round. Here are some great games to make a car journey pass quicker.

Let's Get Personal

Personalised number plates are very common these days, and as people choose them in order to get attention, they're fair game for fun for children from about age 7 upwards.

When you spot a personalised number plate, each player has a minute to make up an interesting and appropriate phrase in which the words begin with each of the number plate letters – depending on who's in the car, you can permit it to be as rude or as silly as you like. Teenage boys and girls relish the freedom. For example, a number plate such as AAA 321 could result in 'Alive And Active', while CD1 could be 'Cool Driver 1'. Teenagers in particular will probably come up with many far more interesting, imaginative and scurrilous suggestions!

My Auntie drove to Newmarket

This is a variation on the classic game 'My Grandmother went to Market' (see Word Games on page 79). Players add the place names – either real but silly, or sensible. For example:

'My auntie drove to Newmarket. On the way she went to **Cambridge**...'
'My auntie drove to Newmarket. On the way she went to Cambridge and **Buenos Aires**...'
'My auntie drove to Newmarket. On the way she went to Cambridge and Buenos Aires and **Pluto**...'
And so on.

Yes-No Game

This requires just two players. Player One starts as the questioner. His aim is to get the other player to answer a question by saying 'yes' or 'no', while Player Two has to find answers to all the questions without saying either of these words. For example:

Q: Is your name John?
A: It is.
Q: Do you like that name?
A: I do not.

The trick with this game is for the questioner not just to ask closed questions (ones normally answered with a 'yes' or 'no'), but also to ask open questions (ones that require all sorts of answers) and then slip in a closed question when their opponent's guard is down!

Legs Game/Pubs Game

Another classic, useful when driving through towns and villages but not when on trunk roads. One player or team look on one side of the road, the other on the other side. The task is to look at pub and inn names and signs and count the number of legs in the name. Legless signs such as 'The Ship' or 'The Globe' count zero. Animals such as 'The Bull' or 'The Red Lion' count as four. 'The Coach and Horses' can be counted as four horses, making 16. 'The Cricketers' could be 11 pairs of legs, making 22 in total – but don't cheat by including reserves or the opposing team! First one to reach an agreed total (a target of 20 may up people's interest) wins.

The trouble with the Legs Game is that you can sometimes find yourself driving through real deserts as far pubs are concerned. If you're desperate, an alternative spotting game is to choose two different door colours and then see how many red doors or blue doors there are on either side of the road. Younger children can do this.

Scissors, Stone and Paper

This two-player game has been around for centuries, and it's still fun for any age. Each player holds out one hand in a fist, and on a count of three they simultaneously change their fist to one of three positions: scissors (cutting action), stone (a fist) or paper (flat hand). Scissors wins against paper (it can cut it); stone wins against scissors (it can blunt them); and paper wins against stone (it can wrap it up). If both players opt for the same position, there's no score.

Number Plate Bingo

Traditional number plate bingo doesn't work so well with many of the newer-style UK (and foreign!) number plates appearing on our roads, so here's an alternative version.

This is a simple game in which young children who know their alphabet can take part. It requires two or more players plus a caller.

Each player draws a three by three grid and writes in nine letters (don't use I or Q). For a longer game, make it a four by four grid.

The caller (it can be the driver, but should preferably be the front-seat passenger) calls out the last letter on a number plate they can see. When a player has a full row of letters crossed off, he shouts 'Bingo'. The players then make new cards for themselves and start again.

Car-Spotting

Boys in particular like to show off special knowledge, and here are several car-spotting activities for a car journey. You can turn them into a competition – the first person to spot ten cars from, for example, Yorkshire or Wales; or the first person to spot two Porsches, and so on.

WHERE'S THAT CAR FROM?

In the UK, the vehicle registration mark system was changed in 2001. Here's what it means: the first two letters tell you where the car was first registered (the DVLA – Driver and Vehicle Licensing Agency – call them 'the local memory tag' and 'local identifier' respectively); the next two letters tell you the date the car was registered and are called the 'age identifiers' (eg 07 means March to August 2007; 57 means September 2007 to February 2008; 08 means March to August 2008); and the three last letters are generated at random from the alphabet, excluding I and Q.

Your children can impress people if they start to recognise the regional codes, which are revealed by the very first letter – the 'local memory tag' – of the number plate. They're not hard to learn:

A	East Anglia	**M**	Manchester and Merseyside
B	Birmingham	**N**	Newcastle and North
C	Wales (Cymru)	**O**	Oxfordshire
D	Deeside to Shrewsbury (Cheshire and Shropshire)	**P**	Preston and Pennines (Lake District etc)
E	Essex and Hertfordshire	**R**	Reading and area (Berkshire)
F	Forest and Fens (Nottinghamshire and Lincolnshire)	**S**	Scotland
G	Garden of England (Kent and Sussex)	**V**	Severn Valley (Worcestershire)
H	Hampshire and Dorset	**W**	West Country (Avon, Somerset, Devon and Cornwall)
K	Kettering and Luton (Northamptonshire)	**Y**	Yorkshire
L	London		

SPOTTING FOREIGN CARS

When you're car-spotting, it's interesting to know what the country codes mean. Here are some you might see around the UK and Europe:

A	Austria	**GBZ**	Gibraltar
AUS	Australia	**GR**	Greece
B	Belgium	**H**	Hungary
CDN	Canada	**I**	Italy
CH	Switzerland (actually *Confédération Helvétique*)	**IRL**	Eire/Ireland
		IS	Iceland
		L	Luxembourg
CY	Cyprus	**LT**	Lithuania
CZ	Czech Republic	**LV**	Latvia
D	Germany (actually *Deutschland*)	**M**	Malta
		MC	Monaco
DK	Denmark	**N**	Norway
E	Spain (actually *España*)	**NL**	Netherlands
		NZ	New Zealand
EST	Estonia	**P**	Portugal
F	France	**PL**	Poland
FIN	Finland	**S**	Sweden
FL	Liechtenstein	**SK**	Slovakia
GBG	Guernsey	**SLO**	Slovenia
GBJ	Jersey	**ZA**	South Africa (actually *Zuid Afrika*)
GBM	Isle of Man		

WHAT MAKE IS THAT CAR?

Boys in particular – and some girls too – enjoy learning to recognise car marques…you can help them pick out key features, such as logos and special design details.

Treasure hunt

Treasure hunts provide a great opportunity for thinking hard, dashing about, being silly, laughing a lot, getting frustrated and finally being delighted. You can use them as a team activity or as a one-to-one game with someone who's bored. They're perfect for a birthday party or family gathering, and an indoor hunt can turn a wet weekend into a great one.

You will need:

- Clipboard and paper
- Pencils and pens
- Containers for the clues
- Treasure

Planning the treasure hunt

You can have great fun thinking up the clues and places to hide them. You can do it by yourself, but it's more fun to have two people setting up a treasure hunt. A second pair of eyes can spot more locations as well as double-check that the clues work well.

Older children can help you work out excellent hiding places and clues. Get them involved in the hunt by thinking up clues for the younger children. If you leave them to actually put the clues in place, make sure you're with them, as otherwise you're likely to lose some.

LAST THINGS FIRST!

Work backwards. It's easier to describe a location if you work back from it. It's also a good idea to have the best clues at the end, and since you may find that it's harder to devise good clues after writing the first six or seven then it makes sense to do the last ones first. That way the first clue you write is actually the last clue of the whole treasure hunt. Try to make it a really unusual one.

PLANNING YOUR ROUTE

Decide how many stages/clues you want the hunt to be and how long you want the children to take. Tailor it to your specific group. A total of 10–12 stages usually works well, but 5–6 may be better for very young children.

The route is up to you. It's great fun to double back, maybe going backwards and forwards several times: it adds to the silliness, and no one will mind. However, watch out that children aren't likely to accidentally spot clues meant for one of the return trips.

All clues should be numbered: otherwise someone may find one in the wrong order, and then things can get very muddled indeed.

Make a note of the location of each clue: you can use your own secret marker to help you find the clue – for example, an unobtrusive large green leaf or a tin can always placed a couple of metres to the left of the clue.

Keep notes: a copy of the full list of clues, locations and instructions is invaluable, because you may need to check things from time to time. Don't rely on remembering where you put something.

Always have a plan B: it may happen that one of your clues goes missing, or you simply can't find it, in which case it's worth having a backup plan. This can mean simply having a copy of several of the clues in envelopes in your pocket ready to kick-start the hunt again if it staggers to a halt.

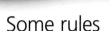

Hiding the clues

Generally, you should hide the clues at child's eye-level or lower: if you set them any higher they won't get spotted.

Once you start thinking about it you'll soon find many good hiding places. For example:

OUTDOORS

Trees, branches and bushes in gardens, woods and parks (if you stick a little coloured ribbon on the clues it'll make them easier for younger children to spot); under stones, perhaps choosing light coloured ones as a contrast, or marking them with a dot of chalk; under garden furniture or park benches; in a crack in a wall; under an outside mat, under a rock in a garden, hung on a clothesline and so on.

INDOORS

Under a table or bed; in the fridge, oven or washing machine; inside an ornament; behind or on a picture or in a picture frame; in clothing (*eg* a jacket pocket, a sock or a shoe); in a book or magazine; behind a radiator; in a saucepan, pot or cup; in a picture frame; tied to a key; in an envelope with the morning post and so on.

PROTECTING YOUR CLUES

It's worth considering using containers for your clues. Use food pots (they may need to be weighted down with stones); small fizzy drinks bottles (roll up your clue, put an elastic band around it, and pop it in); walnut shells (carefully break open some walnuts, then match unbroken shells together, put in your clue, and glue the two halves together with wood glue); sweet containers; or under large limpet shells for a beach treasure hunt.

Make sure the containers are waterproof. If you're using paper clues that may get wet (for example if you're laying a trail 24 hours in advance) you should use waterproof markers and put vegetable oil on the paper.

THE TREASURE

If your hunt involves teams, ensure that the treasure can be easily divided. If you have a large enough treasure chest, the spoils can replace the need for any other party bags: get the hunters to divide the spoils, and have bags at the ready. Sweets are an easy option, but it may be possible to find something as economical but more exciting, such as polished stones, sharks' teeth, marbles etc which also look more like treasure.

Some rules

It's important to establish some basic rules if the treasure hunt is for a team.

1. FINDING AND READING THE CLUES

Either one person is the leader and does all the reading (which is a good idea if there are any young children who can't read); or each child takes it in turns; or particular clues are marked for particular people or age groups. That way the clues can be designed for specific people – *eg* a wordy one for an 11-year-old, a mysterious picture for a 9-year-old, and a simple direction for a 6-year-old.

2. GROUPS OR PAIRS

Younger children may get discouraged on their own so it's a good idea to pair them with older ones, particularly if the latter can spot where the next clue is but don't mind letting the younger children find it.

3. LISTENING AND WAITING

Everyone has to wait together to hear or see the whole clue. They mustn't go off early. This is important, as otherwise some will dash off too soon, leaving the slow ones behind and possibly not having all the information they need. Either the group should talk the clue over and decide all together where to head; or pairs should go off unsupervised and work out the answer; or the individual treasure hunters should rush off individually *after* gathering quietly to hear the clue.

4. RUN OR WALK?

Depending on the setting and the company, it's always possible for things to get out of hand, and you don't want the younger participants trampled in a stampede. It may therefore be sensible to insist on 'Walking only, *no running*'.

5. FINDING THE NEXT CLUE

Either finders call out and wait for others to catch up; or finders take the clue to the leader.

6. PRIZES – WIN OR SHARE?

Either the first one there gets the prize if there's one with a clue, and everyone shares the final treasure; or everyone shares any prizes from start to finish.

Fun with clues

There are many options for interesting clues that'll entertain and challenge children of all ages, and even adults. Some people like riddles and rhymes. Younger children will like very simple clues such as 'This sounds like "head",' to get them rushing off to bedrooms. or 'You wear them on your feet,' to get them turning every pair of shoes in the house upside down.

Don't get hung up about being clever or original, though. Make sure you enjoy setting up the treasure hunt, and you'll find writing and hiding clues gets easier the more you do!

Depending on your treasure hunters, you may want to make some clues hard and some dead easy.

You could use codes (see page 146), use invisible writing (see page 147), or write on a sheet with white wax crayon so that only if the hunters write on top of it with markers or pour tea over it will they see the clue.

You could also use cunning co-ordinates. If you want to challenge children's ability to work out positions, try different ways of identifying locations other than by co-ordinates. For example:

- 'Face the door: your clue is at two o clock.'
- 'Look at the table: turn 45° left.'
- 'Walk 20 steps north-east.' (Provide a compass.)
- 'Full ahead 20 steps, turn to port (left) 10 steps, to starboard (right) 20 steps, and face the stern (*ie* look behind you).'

Alternatively you could use different measurements – yards, feet and inches, metres and centimetres (provide tape measures); strides, spans, arm-lengths, star-stretches (*ie* both hands out wide), and so on – young assistants are really valuable for helping to measure these.

USE CLUES OF DIFFERENT SIZES

Use tiny writing on a postage stamp, but make sure it doesn't get lost – perhaps put it in a jam jar in the fridge. The next clue could be an enormous arrow made of socks on a bedroom floor. In the woods or on a beach, you could make a really huge clue that's only readable from a distance.

USE PICTURES

Consider using photos and drawings: you can take photos from unusual angles, or of some detail which children can work out. Or a clue could be a captioned: 'This is your view from the next clue,' with a funny photo or drawing.

USE A MAP

Think about providing a treasure map. It could be a real map, or a pirates' treasure map (see page 87) on which you've marked things to find.

Off to an exciting start

If you want to add some drama, think of a special way of finding clue number one. For example:

- Put a mobile phone on the table: it rings, the birthday child answers, and the caller gives the starting clue.
- Special messages via email or videotape or audio tape.
- A letter comes through the letterbox addressed to the birthday child.
- There's a mystery box of bits of paper: get the group to scrabble through and find the clue.
- There's something in the food: everyone eats a fairy cake, and there's a bit of paper in one of them: a clue's been baked into the cake! Or everyone has to eat a sandwich – one of them contains the clue.

The end of the trail

It's good to end with a touch of drama too. For example, you could hide the treasure under a pile of leaves or a pile of dirty washing, or bury it in an old biscuit tin under a layer of soil and provide a couple of spades; or have it hanging up in a tree by means of a lot of knots that have to be undone. For an indoors hunt, the treasure could be wrapped for a game of pass the parcel.

Making a pirate treasure map

Whether as part of a treasure hunt, or to put in a treasure chest or just as fun to make for its own sake, drawing up a treasure map can provide hours of pleasure. All you need is a large sheet of paper and some pens, pencils and markers. To make it look authentic, try the following.

TORN EDGES
Hold a ruler about 10mm from the edge of the paper and carefully tear the paper against it. This produces a satisfying rough edge.

STAINS AND MARKS
Try dipping the paper in vinegar, carefully singeing the edges with a candle, or splattering it with wine or beer. A drop or two red food colouring will show there was a fight over it; dripping wax on it will make it look like people pored over it in a murky tavern. A word of warning, however: you might want to test these techniques before applying them to your finished map, because it's a bit of a disaster if they go wrong after hours of work!

FINISHING OFF
You can fold the map up and out again several times to make it look creased and worn; add a few grubby fingerprints; bake it in an oven at a low heat to get it looking brown (test this on a piece of plain paper first); jump on it and rub it in the ground to make it look like it was buried, or roll it up and tie it with a ribbon and maybe seal it with some wax.

GET DRAWING
Your child may say 'I can't draw,' but nor could most pirates. You don't need to be able to draw well to make little icons or pictograms that look fine on a map. Have a go for yourself and get your child to work at images like the ones on this page.

A simple tip: any illustration on a map looks better if you imagine the light is coming from the top left, so make lines thicker on the right and bottom, and work out where the shadows would be. Shadows can be black. To make things look three-dimensional, use very simple shading too – either short lines in one direction about 1mm apart, or cross hatching (lines cutting across at right angles).

Treasure Map

Marbles

Playing marbles can be simple and fun, and also challenging. It can help improve your child's concentration and hand/eye co-ordination, and it's sometimes useful as a gentle (or sometimes not so gentle!) outlet for aggression – there's a real thrill in the smash of one marble striking another.

HOW TO SHOOT MARBLES

We often say we need to 'knuckle down' to something. It's a very old phrase, and comes from marbles: to shoot your marble, you 'knuckle down'.

There are two basic methods, one easier and less accurate, the other trickier but reckoned to be better. In the simpler version, your forefinger knuckle goes on the ground, with the marble balanced on your bent finger and your thumb held lightly behind it, and you release your thumb with a flick to propel the marble.

'Proper' knuckling down, which experts prefer, involves holding your thumb back with the middle finger; keeping your hand quite still with the top of your forefinger on the ground; and then releasing your thumb to hit and shoot the marble.

For most children, however, any way that works is fine!

MARBLES AND THEIR NAMES

Marbles have many names around the country, some hundreds of years old. You usually shoot with the best, larger marbles, often called 'taws', 'alleys' or 'allis' (originally probably meaning real alabaster marbles, though the term is now sometimes applied to opaque marbles). Other names include 'bombsies' (great for dropping from a height), 'cats'-eyes' (clear glass marbles containing a colour twist), 'keepsies' (ones you really don't want to lose) and 'commonsies' (ones you don't mind losing).

FORFEITS

In most games you capture some marbles and forfeit others. To enjoy this, make sure each player has a good stock, as it's not much fun losing from a very small and fast-dwindling supply.

Precious marbles can usually be ransomed for commonsies, by swapping perhaps two commonsies for a regular taw, or maybe three commonsies for a special taw.

MARKING UP

Traditionally, markings for most marble games are scratched in the dirt with a stick. You scratch a line where everyone starts, and this will show how good they are – hence the phrase 'see if someone comes up to scratch'. Alternatively you can make a chalk or charcoal line. If you're playing indoors, improvise with string or something like a wooden spoon placed on the floor.

Hundreds

2 players

Mark a circle about 30cm in diameter and then mark a line about 60cm away from it (you can change dimensions in later games). You choose any size and distance. Shoot a marble from the line, trying to reach and stay within the circle. If both players get in, no one scores. If only one player gets in, they score 10. The first player to reach 100 wins.

Picking Plums

1–6 players

Use a taw for shooting. Each player then contributes an equal number of regular marbles to make a wide line of 'plums' about 30mm apart, ready to be picked off.

You shoot from a line 1–2m away, taking it in turns, and win any plum you hit, removing it from the playing area immediately.

Dobblers

1–4 players

A step on from 'Picking Plums'. Two to four marbles are collected from each player and arranged in a line, with a gap of about two marbles between each. You then agree a line from which to start, and shoot in turn. Any marble you hit you win. Your taw or shooting marble stays where it lies, and you shoot from there when your turn comes round again. If your taw is hit during play, you don't lose it but must add a regular marble to the line.

'Off-Wall Dobblers' is played the same way but close to a wall, enabling skilled players to use rebounds to win a marble.

Marble Arches

1–4 players

This game is also known as 'Archboard' or 'Bridgeboard'. To play it you'll need a piece of wood or card with arches cut in it and a good supply of marbles. You can have five, seven or nine arches, and can make them larger for younger players. Unusually, the middle arch scores lowest, as in this game it's the easiest one to hit, but your team might prefer a different numbering scheme. Each arch is slightly wider than two marbles, and the columns between the arches are about a marble wide. Set the arches up about 50cm–2m away.

There are two versions:

1. Simple scoring: Each player shoots from the same middle starting point, in line with the middle arch, and has three goes. The scores of these three goes are added together at the end of each round. The winner is the player with the highest score after a pre-agreed number of rounds.

2. Marbles money: This is played the same way as with simple scoring, but all the players contribute four commonsies to a 'bank'. One player acts as banker. When a player scores they're 'paid' the equivalent number of marbles from the bank. If they miss, they pay a marble and have to become banker until another player misses.

Bounce Eye

1–6 players

Mark a 30cm circle on the ground (the 'pond'), into which each player puts two marbles (the 'shoal'). Then the players take it in turns to stand over the pond and drop a marble into it from eye level. A player who knocks a marble out of the circle wins it and is allowed to retrieve their dropped marble. Fail to knock a marble out, however, and you lose your marble into the pond. The game is over when all the marbles have been knocked out.

Spanners and Screwdrivers

1–2 players

This is a simple game for any age. Player One rolls or shoots a marble across the ground. The other player then tries to roll or shoot a marble as close as possible to their opponent's. It's a 'spanner' if it stops within a span of the target marble (*ie* the distance between thumb and little finger of the bigger player's outstretched hand), and this wins one point or one marble. It's a 'screwdriver' if it touches and/or moves the target marble. This wins two points or marbles.

Ring Taw

1–6 players

This game can be a bit depressing for younger players but exciting and tough for older ones, as you can win or lose lots of marbles with aggressive tactics. It's quite an old game, in which you have to 'step up to the bar' and see who you can get out of the 'pound' (an old name for a prison).

Mark out two circles, the inner one about 30cm in diameter, the outer one about 2m. Each player puts the same number of marbles into the middle ring (the pound). Player One then shoots a taw from any position around the outer ring (the 'bar'). If any marbles are knocked out of the ring the player takes them and has another go, shooting from wherever the taw landed. If no marbles are knocked out of the pound then the taw stays where it is and it's the next player's turn. If any player hits an opponent's taw, the taw's owner has to pay a forfeit of one marble, but each player can only claim the forfeit once. The game continues until the pound is cleared.

Tricks

Conjuring tricks 92

Card tricks 94

Coin tricks 98

Secret codes 100

Conjuring tricks

Learning to do magic tricks is fun for all the family. Doing them wrong is very funny – almost as enjoyable as watching the kids' amazement when you get it right. Don't give away how it's done too soon, but if it's a trick they can learn, show them and help them practise. It'll help their dexterity and confidence, and learn that perseverance pays off.

Secrets for success

To succeed as a conjuror you need to concentrate on three essential elements:

Practice: even the simplest tricks call for initial and ongoing practice, until your movements become positive and confident.

Patter: chatting to the audience, whether one child or a crowd, is vital for the trick to be fun, so think up jokes and stories to accompany your 'act'.

Misdirection: getting the audience to look away from where the trickery is happening is fundamentally important. For example, if you're trying to conceal something in your right hand, try pointing at something with your left or looking somewhere else.

'Vanishing' things with a hankie

You can make coins and other small things disappear quite effectively with the help of a large handkerchief or dishcloth and a little practice. Children can spend ages practising it. For best results they need to develop some manual dexterity and learn how to put on a bit of a performance, in particular regarding the misdirection of their audience. The trick itself is simple and quick, but you can make it a little longer and funny.

1 Spread the handkerchief over your left hand, palm upwards, with one corner lying up towards your forearm. Hold the coin in your right hand, show it to everyone dramatically, then place it between the thumb and the first and second fingers of your left hand. Hold it upright through the handkerchief.

2 Pick up the corner of the handkerchief closest to you between your right thumb and forefinger and start to cover the coin. As you do this, turn your left hand slightly downwards and to the right so that the handkerchief hangs over the coin. Say that you're going to make it disappear, then dramatically lift the handkerchief and pretend to be shocked that the coin is still there. Your left hand has changed position and turned a little more to the right, but your audience should be sufficiently distracted not to notice.

3 Keep talking about being surprised that the trick didn't work. Pull the handkerchief back over the coin with your right hand and continue moving your left hand down and right. For added misdirection you can look upwards in the opposite direction as though the coin is flying through the air. At the same time turn your left hand downwards even more, and drop the coin so that it falls unseen into your right hand – the handkerchief hides what's happening. At this point you can either surreptitiously slip the coin into your right-hand pocket or keep it in your right hand under your finger: both moves require a little practice.

4 Ask your audience for some magic words, while pretending that you're still holding the coin in your left hand. Bring your right hand up, keeping the coin concealed (if you haven't dropped it into your pocket): point with your forefinger and have the second, third and fourth fingers curled over the coin. Point somewhere or wiggle your forefinger to distract attention and add a sense of magic!

5 Grasp one corner of the handkerchief with your right hand and let go with the your left. As the handkerchief floats down, grab it with your right hand. Show your left hand is empty, then take a corner of the handkerchief with your left hand and open it out to show that the coin has completely disappeared.

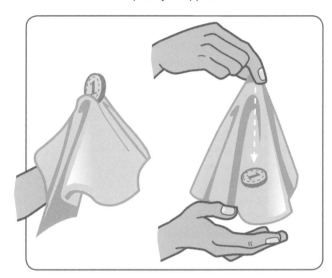

Levitating pens and pencils

In this trick a pencil or pen (or a magic wand if you have one) mysteriously rises out of a bottle. To perform it you'll need a pencil, a bottle and some thin fishing line or black thread – and you'll also need to wear a buttoned shirt.

Tie, glue or tape about 60cm of thread to the bottom of the pencil, and loop the thread around a button on the cuff or front of your shirt. Move the bottle so that the thread is taut. Then, by simply moving your arm or body slowly away from the pen, you'll be able to make it rise out of the bottle seemingly unaided.

What can make this trick particularly funny is that it's by moving away in mock fear that you make the pencil move. The same trick can be used to make other objects pop up out of a bottle.

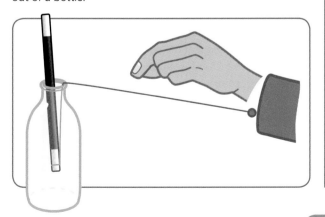

Sticky pencil

In this trick a pencil seems to be magically stuck to your fingers. It's simple, effective, and amusing for everyone.

1 Hold up a pencil, horizontally, in your left hand. Tell your audience that to do this trick you have to squeeze special sticky energy into your fingers with your right hand. Then grip your left wrist tightly with your right hand; your right thumb needs to be on the back of your left hand.

2 Turn your left hand so that its back is to the audience and the pencil can be seen sticking out on either side. The audience doesn't see your move here: quickly raise the index finger of your right hand to hold the pencil in place as in the picture.

3 Slowly straighten out the fingers of your left hand, and move your thumb so that it no longer holds the pencil.

4 Have a way ready to end the trick before your amazed audience can work out what's happening. A good one is to say that the sticky energy is beginning to hurt – let out a yelp, throw your hands wide and chuck the pencil in the air.

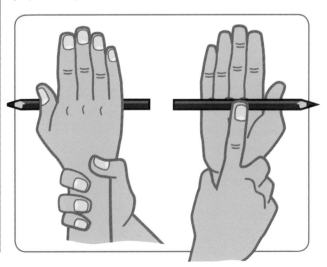

Card tricks

The 21-card trick

This isn't so much magic as maths, but the effect is excellent. You can do it after minimal practice, and it can be taught to children quickly. It can also help children learn how to deal cards.

The trick involves getting someone to pick a card, which you put back in the pack, and then in a couple of minutes you find it again. No sleight of hand is needed. You just have to be able to deal cards on a table.

You start by taking a pile of any 21 cards. Get someone to pick a card from this pack, show it to everyone else, and then return it anywhere in the pack. Tell them you're going to deal out the cards face up, and ask them to look out for their card as you do so but not to say anything if they see it.

1 Deal the cards face up in three piles, dealing from right to left. When you've finished, ask which pile the card was in. Take that pile, and put it between the other two as you pick up all three piles.

2 Repeat stage 1.

3 Repeat stage 1.

4 Pick up the three piles and again put in the middle the pile that you're told the card is in. Turn the whole pack face down and count (in your head) ten cards. Then say something that sounds appropriately magicky, like 'I feel some tingling here,' and with a flourish show the 11th card, which should be the one that was originally picked out.

How does it work? It's quite simple really: all the shuffling just puts that particular card into the middle of the whole pack of 21 – ie it becomes the 11th card.

Turnover Surprise

This is a classic trick that's easy to learn. Despite its great simplicity, an audience can be taken in completely and totally impressed.

Someone picks a card from a pack and puts it back in the same way up, but when you fan out the cards it's magically turned itself the opposite way up from all the other cards.

You need a full deck of cards (though an incomplete one will do). The only preparation required is to ensure that all the cards are the same way up except the bottom one, which you turn the other way. The whole deck can then wait in its box or on a table.

1 Slightly fan out the cards, face down, and allow someone to pick out a card that you can't see. Ask your helper to show the card to everyone else, or, if there isn't anyone else, tell them to help the magic by showing the card to two walls or pictures on the wall. This is a simple piece of misdirection that adds fun and gives you the chance to execute stage 2 unnoticed.

2 Hold the pack together, and lower your hand to your side in a relaxed way, turning the pack over in your fingers so that when you raise your hand the pack is the other way up. All the cards will now be face up except for the top card, which because its back is showing makes the rest of the pack still appear to be face down.

3 Ask your helper to slide his card back into the pack wherever he wants.

4 Remind your helper and audience that you have no way of knowing which card it was. Then say something like 'Look directly into my eyes and I'll try to see your card.' This is another piece of misdirection, to keep people's eyes away from your hand as you lower it and again turn the pack over in your fingers.

5 Raise your hand and the pack, which will now be face down except for your helper's card and the card at the bottom.

6 Slowly fan out the deck, but keep the bottom card hidden. Your helper's card will appear the wrong way up. Either ask them to pull it out and show the audience, or whip it out yourself and say something like 'Voila!'

Double X card trick

This is a clever yet simple and very surprising trick that requires a deck of cards and two identical marker pens. One helper picks a card from a pack and marks it with an 'X'. A second helper then does the same. Unbelievably, it turns out they've marked the same card.

To prepare for this trick one of the marker pens needs to be left to dry out for several days with its cap off – it should look fine, but will no longer work. Then take the other marker and put an 'X' on the front and back of any card. Put this card somewhere in the middle of the deck. Keep the good marker in your right-hand pocket.

1 Ask for two volunteers. Ask them if they'd like you to make them mind readers.

2 Give volunteer number 1 the deck of cards, face up, and ask him to shuffle it behind his back. Then, giving him the marker pen that's dried out, ask him to put a cross on any card while they're still behind his back, and then shuffle them again.

3 Take the pack back and pass it to volunteer number 2, face down. Ask her to hold the cards behind her back, shuffle them, pick a card and mark it with an X, and then shuffle them again.

4 Take the pack back, and also the dried out marker pen, which you need to slip into your left-hand pocket. Then turn the pack face up and ask volunteer 1 to find his card and pull it out. He will take out the card marked with an 'X'. While he's doing that, take the other marker out of your right-hand pocket.

5 Turn the pack over and ask volunteer 2 to find her card. Where is it? It's not there...so you ask her to turn over volunteer 1's card, and – amazingly – it's the same card! Place the working marker pen by the cards (in case they want to examine it) and thank the volunteers.

Shuffling cards

Children often find it difficult to manipulate cards, and need help learning how to shuffle.

FLICKED SHUFFLE

This is fun for everyone, and some younger players can master it more easily than shuffling by holding the deck in their hands. However, this method does risk ruining your cards.

1. Split the deck in two, and lay the two half-decks on the table close to one another at an angle, corner to corner.
2. While holding them down firmly with your other fingers, lift up a corner of each half-deck with your thumbs, then let the cards flick down past your thumbs so that come down overlapping, with most of the cards alternately mixed.
3. Push all the cards together. Repeat two or three times if you like.

OVERHAND SHUFFLE

This is simple enough, providing the child's hands are large enough to hold cards comfortably.

1. Hold the pack lightly in your left hand. Take about half of it in your right hand, lift the cards up and over to the left and drop them back into the rest of the pack.
2. With your left thumb, push some cards up.
3. Pick them up with your right hand and place them to the right of the pack.
4. Keep repeating as long as you like.

The Lost Hearts

This is a very simple 'con' which works wonders with younger children, some older ones, and even adults. Under-6s are liable to find stories like this a bit scary and probably won't understand the trick anyway. It needs no conjuring skills, just a convincing performance. Children will love it if you carry it off with panache.

The trick involves a group of cards getting lost and magically reappearing. It works best with a small audience, and calls for a bit of inventive storytelling. A sample story is given here, but you can adapt yours to suit a birthday party or make it special for a particular child. You can also elaborate the story by adding more cards and characters.

All you need is two *identical* packs of cards and eight identical envelopes (to hold eight cards). It's also useful to have an assistant lurking in another room ready to take away any incriminating evidence.

You need to take the Ace, King, Queen and Jack of Hearts from one pack and put the rest of that pack away. Place each of these four cards in individual envelopes and hide them in different places around the room where you'll be performing the trick. You need to remember which card is hidden where. When your audience arrives you take the full pack of cards and lay them out in front of them, either on a table or on the floor.

The following is a sample of the kind of story you need to tell: you can adapt this one or make up one of your own:

'Once upon a time, there were some happy cards. They were kings and queens and princes, and these little ones [the aces] were babies. Can you help me find them here?' (You then get some of your audience to help you sort out all the aces and court cards.)

'So here we've got the Spades and Diamonds, the Clubs and Hearts. Let's imagine they were having a picnic by a river.

'But suddenly something awful happened. Guess what? Baby Heart was flying a kit and got blown away by a big gust of wind.' (Get a child to put the Ace of Hearts in an envelope, take it out of the room and blow it away – in fact you give it to your assistant.)

' "Oh dear," said all the other cards. Then, guess what? Jack Heart went canoeing and got washed out to sea.' (Get a child to put the Jack in an envelope, then take it out of the room and whoosh it away to your assistant.)

' "Oh dear," said all the other cards. Then, oh no, guess what? Mummy Heart [the Queen of Hearts] was mending the car when the brakes went wrong and she went flying down the hillside.' (Get a child to put the Queen in an envelope, take it out of the room and pass it to your assistant.)

' "Oh dear," said all the other cards. Then, oh no, guess what? Daddy Heart [the King of Hearts] was making the sandwiches and a great big bear came out of the woods and chased him out of sight.' (Get a child to put the card in an envelope, take it out of the room with growling noises and give it to your assistant, who puts all of the envelopes away well out of view.)

' "Oh dear," said all the other cards. And oh dear, what was to be done? They searched and searched but couldn't find the Hearts. All the other cards packed up their picnic things [start picking up the other cards] and went home very sad, except for one girl who was having a tenth birthday. She was called Lucy [pick out the Ten of Diamonds and lay it on the carpet or table] and she didn't want to give up. She lay listening very quietly.' (Tell your audience to be dead quiet if they aren't already.)

'Suddenly she heard a noise. [Make a muffled "Help" noise.] It was coming from over there [point, and get a child to go and discover the envelope with the King of Hearts]. Hooray, it's Daddy Heart. However did he get there? But where were the others? Wait, there's another noise… "Help!" …Can you hear it? It's coming from over there [send a child in the direction of the next hidden envelope.] Hooray, it's Mummy Heart. However did she get there? But where are the children? What's that noise? [Muffled "Mummy I'm here."] Can you find it? [Send a child to discover the next hidden card.] Hooray, here's Jack Heart, however did you get there? But where's the baby? [Muffled cries.] Where's the baby? [Send a child to find the last envelope.] Hooray, its baby Heart! However did he get there?

'And so Lucy Diamond found all the hearts and they all went home very happy after a magic time.'

Magician's Jacks

This is also an easy trick, in which four Jacks are put in different places in a deck of cards and magically appear at the top of the pack. It's very simple but is very effective if you can tell a story well.

Take the four Jacks and four other cards from the pack, and hold the Jacks up in a fan with the other four cards hidden behind them as shown in the picture. Then tell your story:

'A magician had four servants – these four Jacks. He sent them all over the world to find magic secrets. [Show your audience the fan of what appears to be four cards; then place what is really eight cards on top of the pack.]

'He sent Jack number 1 down into the deepest caves. [Dramatically take the top card – which people will think is a Jack – and insert it near the bottom of the pack.]

'Jack number 2 he sent up to the highest heavens. [Take the next card – which people think is another Jack – wave it in the air and insert it near the top of the pack.]

'Jack number 3 he sent over the hills. [With an undulating motion of your hand, take the next card – which the audience will think is the third Jack – and insert it into the pack about a quarter of the way down.]

'Finally he sent Jack number 4 to sail over the seven seas. [With a wavy motion of your hand, take the fourth card – which people will think is the last Jack – and insert it near the middle of the pack. Your audience will think that the four Jacks are now scattered right through the pack.]

'So the four Jacks were scattered around the world. The days went by and the Jacks didn't come back with any magic secrets, and eventually the magician got fed up. He clapped his hands and shouted, "To me, all Jacks" – and hey presto, here they are.'

And then, with a flourish, you turn over the next four cards in the pack – and all four Jacks appear.

Magic paper rings

You can teach children aged about 6 to do tricks with paper rings. Anyone will find them intriguing, as they don't do what you'd expect.

Start by cutting some strips of paper about 120cm long and 5cm wide (or thinner if adults are doing the cutting). You can make the strips by simply cutting an A4 sheet in four lengthways and taping the pieces together.

Draw a line all along the middle on one side of each strip. Then tape the two ends of each strip together. You need to make two each of three different types of ring: one with a single twist, one with a double twist, and one with no twist. Make a small mark on each to distinguish which is which.

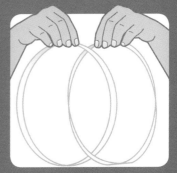

RING NUMBER 1

This is the ring with one twist. Explain to the audience that you plan to cut the ring in two, and ask them to guess what the result will be. Cut slowly – see if you can invent a story to tell as you do so. The result? You get one larger ring.

RING NUMBER 2

This is the ring with no twist, and this time you can ask a member of the audience to help. Although it looks like the same sort of strip as you cut the first time, the result this time is two separate rings.

RING NUMBER 3

This is the ring with two twists. Cut it as before, but this time you'll end up with two interlinked rings. What a surprise!

Finally, you can throw in a mathematical puzzle which older children will find interesting. How many sides does a strip of paper have? We all know the answer is two, but if you make a ring of paper with one twist in it and then draw a line on one side as far as you can it will end up traversing both sides without a break! It's a puzzle known as the Mobius Strip – a piece of paper with only one side.

Coin tricks

It's often handy to have a few tricks up your sleeve, especially ones which will keep your children puzzled for a while and then, once they've rumbled you or you've explained it, will keep them busy practising for hours.

Keep up the patter

Effective tricks require multitasking. Concentrating on hand movements and talking too is not so easy, so practise your words separately from the trick. You can collect funny phrases ready for you to use without breaking your concentration. Get a bit of audience interaction that distracts them but not you. For example. ... "That's nice hair .... Did you buy it from Sainsburys?" "You in the back do you always pick your nose at parties?"; "See this envelope, I'm going to burn £20 in it (dig around in pocket) oh I haven't got one can someone lend me £20? Don't you trust me? OK I'll use this pound coin"

Coin catching

This isn't so much a trick as a skill that anyone can learn. The challenge is to bend your arm back close to your ear, rest a coin on your elbow, and then pick it up without using your other hand. To anyone who's never seen it, it seems impossible. The solution, of course, is to move your hand very quickly in a circular downwards motion: the coin slips off your elbow, but is suspended in the air momentarily by inertia so that your hand manages to catch it before it drops. You can even do it with several coins at once, so you can turn it into a competition. However, since coins can go flying everywhere and break favourite ornaments it's best to practise in an open space!

Coin move challenge

This is another trick that's a puzzle children enjoy. You start by putting three coins (A, B and C) in a row so that they're touching, and then put down a fourth coin (D) about 10cm away. The challenge is to move coin A away from coin B without touching it with your fingers, without moving coins B or C, and by moving coin D just once.

The solution? Hold down coins B and C with two fingers of your left hand. With the forefinger of your right hand, shoot coin D across the table to hit coin C hard. Coin A will shoot away. How does it work? You're creating a pulse that travels through the coins. It's interesting to vary this with more coins and experiment with different arrangements.

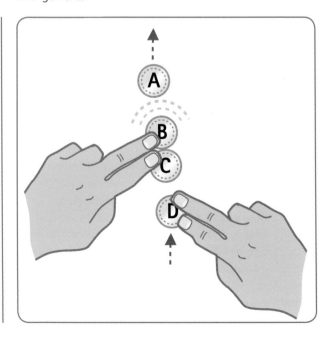

Money-burn trick

This requires only a little practice and minimal preparation, and makes good entertainment. You drop a coin into an envelope – it's clearly there – and seal the envelope. You then set fire to the envelope, and the coin has disappeared! All you need is a coin, a cardboard disc, an envelope and a cigarette lighter.

1 Take an envelope that's reasonably opaque. With a pair of scissors or a knife, cut a very thin sliver off a bottom corner, slightly wider than the coin. Cut a circle of cardboard the same size as the coin and the same colour as the envelope, and glue it inside, in the middle at the bottom.

2 Show the audience the empty envelope, making sure they can't see the card disc. Slowly place the coin inside so that it slips to the cut corner. Stick down the envelope, holding it at both corners. Then raise the uncut corner slightly so that the coin slides down to the slit in the opposite corner.

3 Keep up your patter while you let the coin drop unseen into your right hand. Then hold the envelope in your left hand while you put your right hand in your pocket, drop the coin, and pick up the cigarette lighter, which you light, holding it behind the envelope so that people can see the coin shape in silhouette. After a dramatic pause set fire to the envelope and amaze everyone. The coin has disappeared!

Hand-to-hand trick

In this trick you have a coin on the palm of each hand. You turn your hands over on a table, and when you raise them there are two coins under one and none under the other.

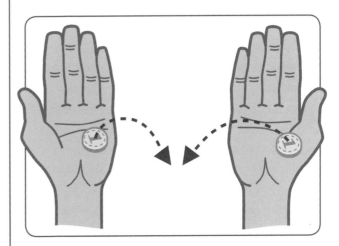

1 Show the audience you have a coin on each palm. They need to be placed quite carefully: the coin on the left hand should be directly below the third and fourth fingers; the coin on the right hand should be close to the base of the thumb. Hold your hands, palm up, 25–30cm apart, over a table.

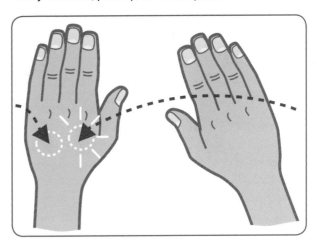

2 Turn both hands over at the same moment and slap them down on the table so that your thumbs touch or almost touch, then draw your hands apart immediately. It looks like there should still be a coin under each hand, but if you've done it right you'll have flicked the coin from your right hand underneath your left hand as you slapped them down – the noise and speed with which you do this should have concealed it from your audience. Then you lift your right hand to show that the coin has gone. Where is it? Two coins will be under your left hand. Amazing!

Secret codes

People have been disguising messages for thousands of years. Strictly speaking, a code is where letters or words are substituted for others, to make up another message that may seem entirely innocent. So, for example, you can change meanings – white could mean black; Sunday could mean Saturday; morning could mean evening; and shopping centre could mean pub. A coded message 'see you at the Black Lion Shopping Centre on Sunday morning' might thus mean you end up having a good evening out – or, if you've forgotten the code, sitting at home confused.

Technically, it's a cipher when you change a message by using a series of letters or numbers hidden within it. You're encrypting the message. But most of us would say we're putting it into secret code. Here are several easy codes or ciphers to try.

Shifty Code

Here's a quick and easy method for a substitution code.

Mark out two rows of 26 boxes about 10mm wide. Write the full alphabet across each row and separate the strips.

Shift the lower strip across by a number of spaces and tape it in position. Cut the right end off and place it at the left of that row.

Then either do the same again with another pair of strips, putting them in the same position for your partner in spying, or tell them the number of boxes to shift by, or write it at the end of your message – *eg* write 'AADD', meaning set D to line up with A.

Speedy Code

In English, if you remove the vowels (a, e, i, o, and u) from words, you can usually still work out what a sentence says. It's this principle that provides the starting point for some systems of speedwriting, and for the Speedy Code. While it may be too difficult for many children, especially those under 9 or so, some older ones will find this quite challenging and very enjoyable.

Write your secret message with the vowels removed, leaving spaces where the vowels should be as well between words. Leave the letter 'i' in only when it means 'me'.

Now fill the gaps between the letters and words with random vowels selected from a, e, o and u – but don't add any 'i's. As you get better at it, you'll be able to choose vowels that make confusing word patterns.

To decipher this, you and your fellow conspirators simply need to know that you have to remove all the vowels except i. Once you've done that, look carefully at what's left and you'll probably be able to work out what the message is.

Encoding
1. MEET IN PARK THIS AFTERNOON
2. M T N P RK TH S FT RN   N
3. MOATOANUPURKETHESOEFTURNEEN

Decoding
4. MØ̸ATØ̸ANU̸PURKƏTHƏSØ̸ƏFTURNƏƏN
5. M__T _N P_RK TH_S _FT_RN__N

Foldy Code

This is easy for most children aged over 8, and is very quick to set up.

Take an A4 sheet of paper, fold it in half and in half again along its width and open it up. Then fold it in half along its length, in half again and then in half again. Open it up, and you'll have 32 panels (see diagram). Number them from 01 to 32 with small numbers in one corner. Then write all the letters of the alphabet and the numbers 3, 4, 6, 7, 8 and 9 (but not 1, 2 or 5) in the boxes at random. Put 1 in the same box as I, 2 in the same box as Z, and 5 in the same box as S.

Now you have a code for converting anything, using two digits per letter or number. Make other copies for your fellow spies and deciphering is easy – in fact easier than encoding!

Foldy code: 07, 17, 21, 09, 17, 27 = SECRET
07 = S, 17 = E, 21 = C, 09 = R, 17 = E, 27 = T

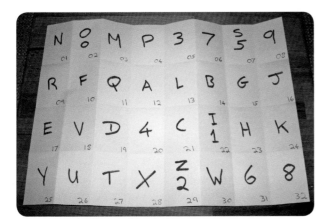

Code Red

This is great fun and intriguing for anyone over 6
– and adults too.

You will need:

A piece of white paper; a piece of red-coloured
transparent plastic, cellophane or similar, any size
(a sweet wrapper will do; larger is better); felt tip pens –
light red, pink, orange and/or yellow, light blues and greens

Write your secret message
in letters of light green and
blue, leaving spaces between
all the letters.

Now write other letters
in between in orange, pink,
yellow and light red. You can
also add lots of squiggles to
confuse the enemy. They'll
now just see a confusing mess.

Your friends can find the secret message easily by
putting the red plastic over the paper. It's a bit like magic.

Invisible ink

You can make invisible ink from many things.
There are three basic types: inks revealed by
light (eg the ink of ultra-violet security pens
is invisible to us but visible under ultra-violet
light); by chemical reaction; and by heat. The
last are those that are easiest to try at home.

Many liquids make invisible ink that can be revealed
by a bit of heat. Try lemon juice, orange juice, onion
juice, vinegar, milk or sugar solution. Some of these
are noticeable on white paper when they've dried,
so it may be better to use cream-coloured paper to
avoid detection.

Using a brush, a dip pen or a very tightly rolled
bit of paper as a sort of stick pen, write your secret
message with your chosen ink and allow it to
dry completely.

You can reveal the secret message in several ways:
put it in a medium to hot oven for a few minutes
(but watch it carefully); use an iron on high setting;
or pass the paper near a hot light bulb. The most
exciting way, as in pirate stories, is to pass the paper
over a candle flame. It's excellent, but it obviously
requires adult supervision to make sure the results
aren't too exciting! Move the paper across the flame
quickly several times, without pausing, then pause
to allow it to cool a bit before continuing.

Out and about

On the beach   **104**

**Woodlands, parks
and countryside**   **108**

Birdwatching   **112**

Sky at night   **114**

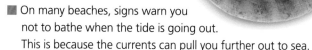

On the beach

A beach provides parents and children with a mixture of activities, some of which they can do together, and some which give the adults a bit of well-earned peace and quiet!

Useful hints for a good day

■ When you get sunshine on a beach, it's extra-powerful because of reflected light from the sea and sand. Don't forget that when the sun is out between June and September it's particularly fierce, and its strength is greatest from about 11:00am to 3:00pm. As children's skin is sensitive, be sure to use high factor sun cream and cover up.

■ It's important to get a good idea of what the tides are doing, by picking up local tide tables or looking at websites such as www.bbc.co.uk/weather. On many beaches, the best time to bathe is when the tide is coming in over sand that's been warmed by the sun during the afternoon. Many visitors start to leave busy beaches in the afternoon and miss the best time!

■ On many beaches, signs warn you not to bathe when the tide is going out. This is because the currents can pull you further out to sea.

■ There are two high tides and two low tides every lunar day – which is about 24 hours 50 minutes, so every day the tides are about 50 minutes later than the day before. Spring tides, when the high tides are particularly high and the low tides particularly low, occur around the new moon and full moon. Neap tides, when there's less difference between high and low tides, occur midway.

■ Very low tides are particularly good for looking at sea-life, because if you go down to the low tide margins you often see far more sea creatures than at other times. Search round rocks and seaweed at very low tides and there are typically more shrimps, crabs and small fish to be found.

■ It's often possible to see clearly how high the tide will go. Keep an eye out for the tide line, a line often composed of seaweed that's been left behind by the last high tide. As well as helping you plan where to be on the beach, it's also a good place to hunt for interesting treasures.

■ If you have a choice of beaches, it's really valuable to check local weather information to see which way and how strong the wind is blowing.

■ On many beaches you can work out where the weather's coming from. Often the winds are predominantly in one direction, so keep an eye out what's happening and you'll be able to spot rain clouds and be ready for a dash to the car faster than anyone else; or pick out good patches of blue that spell better weather so you don't need to pack up and go.

Beachcombing Treasure Hunt

For a few minutes of peace and quiet, you can set the kids a challenge. Give them a long or short shopping list (depending on their age and independence) itemising things you want them to pick up.

You can write the list or just tell them: 'Find me...'

- 1 flat stone
- 2 stones with stripes in them
- 3 feathers
- 4 leaves
- 5 pieces of driftwood
- 6 different shells
- 7 pieces of seaweed
...and so on.

When your treasure hunters have finished, get them to lay out the spoils in neat patterns on the sand. You might have prizes ready, or you may find they simply want to do another treasure hunt. The best collection can win first prize, everyone else gets second prize. Don't necessarily be the judge yourself – it's better to encourage the youngsters to use their own critical faculties, so get each of them to say which they think is best and why.

Finding fossils

Fossils can be found in many places in Britain. You can obtain details from local tourist offices, by using the keyword 'fossils' to search www.channel4.com/history, or by looking at www.discoveringfossils.co.uk.

You can get your child interested by explaining that fossils are millions of years old and that some come from the time of the dinosaurs. While you probably won't find any dinosaur fossils, you may find evidence of fossilised shells and plants. This is especially true of beaches where there's substantial cliff erosion. If you're hunting for fossils it's worth taking an old chisel, some newspaper to wrap any finds, and plastic bags to put the newspaper in. If you plan more serious fossil hunting, you need a hammer and chisel, and must ensure that everyone wears safety goggles and gloves.

Skimming stones: Ducks and Drakes

We all know how to skim stones, right? Wrong. We all have to learn, and children in particular need some help.

Get them to find good small flat stones, show them where the water is calm and show them how you have to throw very flat – children tend to throw stones up in the air. Get them to bend at the knees and be as close to water level as possible. Show them how to send something off spinning. Some children can't get the hang of a spin, with the hand starting from the chest and moving outwards; but you can also achieve good bounces by sending a stone spinning backhanded with a flick of the wrist, so that's something else they can try.

IMPORTANT – SAFETY RULES

When children throw, things tend to fly off in all directions. It's important to introduce safety rules suitable to where you are and who's around. A vital basic rule is that you should never throw a stone if you can't see clearly where it's going to land. For young children you have to work out particular rules, such as taking it in turns and making sure people stand back.

Beachcombing

You can find a wide variety of shells and live molluscs on the beach and seashore. Here are some you're likely to see on many British beaches.

TOPSHELLS – PRETTY AND NUMEROUS

You may find various topshells around and under rocks, sometimes in great numbers. They get their name from being quite like a spinning top. They're usually a grey or mauve chequered pattern, often with some pearly inner layer showing. The shells are usually easy to find and well worth looking at closely with a magnifying glass.

PERIWINKLES – SEA SNAILS HAPPY OUT OF WATER

The largest type of periwinkle in the UK is the edible periwinkle, as wide as 30mm. Smaller ones, from 20mm down to 10mm, tend to take the colour of their surroundings as camouflage and are often orange or yellow. They can survive out of seawater for weeks.

WHELKS – VAMPIRES ON THE ROCKS

Periwinkles and topshells graze on seaweeds. Not so whelks – they're hunters, vampires even. They prey on barnacles and mussels. They bore into the shell, stick in an appendage that's like an elephant's trunk and a rasp, and squirt in liquid that dissolves the flesh, suck out the juices and scrape out the rest of their victim. They have a distinctly different shape from periwinkles. They're usually found on the lower shores, especially under rocks.

RAZOR SHELLS – SHARP BUT SHY

The razor shell is a 'bivalve', – two long thin shells covering its body. You won't normally see a live one because usually it will have buried itself about 45cm deep in the sand while the tide is out. If you tread on a live one, or just a shell, it can be quite painful, since razor shells are very sharp.

STAR BARNACLES – LUNAR LANDSCAPE ON ROCKS

There are millions and millions of these on seashore rocks, but we hardly notice them. Get a magnifying glass and take a look. Close up, they look like something out of a sci-fi story. The middle section opens up underwater like a trapdoor, and the barnacle flicks out special feathery legs to bring tiny particles of food to its mouth.

COCKLES – TASTY LITTLE NUMBER

Common cockles have very distinctive shells, which may often be found on sandy beaches. Dig down and you may find live ones. Birds and people alike find them tasty.

WRACK – BUBBLY SEAWEED

There are various types of wrack. They usually have little lumps like small eggs or peanuts. These are gas bladders that enable the plant to stand upright when the tide is in so that they can get more light. Its other name is popweed, and it's fun for children to pop the bladders.

MERMAID'S PURSE – COOLEST EGG BOXES EVER

Mermaid's purses are egg cases of the dogfish, a small shark common around the UK. At each corner there's a tendril that works its way around seaweed, anchoring the purse. Each egg case holds one egg, from which the baby shark emerges, leaving an empty case. If you're lucky, you may find a purse washed up on the high water mark, and they're a real treasure for taking home.

ANEMONES – LOADS OF TENTACLES BUT ARMLESS

There are various anemones, the beadlet and snakelock varieties both being very common. The beadlet anemone is most recognisable, as a reddish jelly-like blob stuck to rocks. Children often enjoy making them squirt water by putting their fingers in them, which is a safe, harmless activity for the children, but not for the anemones. Snakelock anemones have a cool name and a friendly disposition. Put a finger near their tentacles (which they cannot retract) and they may stroke and touch it to investigate the taste.

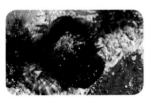

SHRIMPS AND PRAWNS – MANY AND VARIED

The brown or edible shrimp is mottled grey or brown, giving it excellent camouflage on sandy surfaces. There are various types of prawn. The most common are semi-transparent. Always on the search for little bits of food, they're great fun to watch in rock pools and buckets. Prawns are remarkable, and are very complex compared to the little piece of them that we get to eat! They have 20 pairs of appendages, consisting of a pair of antennules, which are for balance; a pair of antennae, which are sensory organs; six pairs of limbs around the mouth, including biting jaws and limbs to hold food; maxillae which pump water over the gills; four pairs of walking legs; and five pairs of limbs for swimming.

Fancy being nibbled by an anemone? Sampled by a shrimp? If you can find a sea anemone with tentacles in a pool, be sure to get your children to hold a finger close to it so that they can feel it nibbling them. If you're still and patient, shrimps may also emerge from seaweed and delicately nibble at fingertips, taking off microscopic bits of dead skin.

Hunting for sea life

Any beach or shore has masses of life – if you know where to look. Apart from rock pools, don't forget to look carefully under rocks at the water's edge at mid to low tide. There's a good chance of finding crabs, small fish and sometimes a starfish. Replace stones carefully after a peep.

USEFUL THINGS TO TAKE

☐ Crablines – very cheap, and well worth buying for hours of fun. Warn your children to watch out for the hooks (usually two or three on a line) then wait for them to learn the lesson the painful way when, like everyone else, they forget and get a hook stuck in a finger. The bright orange lines don't seem to warn off sea creatures if you hold the crabline still for a while, and hanging crablines over rocks and in rock pools can produce great results – crabs, fish, even starfish. The line doesn't harm the creatures, which generally just cling onto it.

☐ A good-sized household plastic bucket – seaside buckets tend to be too small if you catch anything large.

☐ A clear plastic jug – this will enable your child to get a better look at little sea creatures.

☐ A magnifying glass.

☐ A jam jar, for small shells that can easily get lost.

☐ A penknife.

LOOKING AFTER CAPTIVES

Ensure that whatever your children catch is kept safe from harm in a bucket of water while they examine it. The bucket should contain seaweed and rocks for the captured fish and other creatures to hide under.

Keep an eye on what's put into the bucket – it's upsetting for a child to discover that some of their prize catch has been eaten by another of their captives! Keep the bucket in a shaded spot. If the water becomes too warm it loses much of its oxygen, and your captives may suffocate. Be sure to release everything back into a rock pool before you leave.

Woodland, parks and countryside

You don't need to be an expert to open your children's eyes to the wonders of nature. What's more, kids have a natural excitement and inquisitiveness, and walking with them can be just as much an eye opener for adults!

If you're planning a trip outside it's common sense to choose a day when the weather's good. However, rainy days can be good fun too. Avoid very windy days, as falling branches can be a serious danger.

You don't need any special equipment for a great day out, but the following will come in handy:

- A groundsheet or old blanket to sit or lie on
- A plastic container (an old ice-cream or margarine box)
- A paintbrush to pick up insects
- Magnifying glass
- Sheet of white plastic
- A toilet roll or Smarties tube
- Something for insects to hide in (eg an old envelope)
- Bottle of water (to drink, to wash hands, to clean wounds and specimens)
- A jam jar
- First Aid kit

Sensational observations

The great outdoors provides excellent opportunities for interesting observations. If you focus on a specific sense it will help catch a child's interest and imagination.

WHAT CAN YOU SEE?

Lie on your back and stare up at the trees. Then get on all fours like an animal and look around. Finally, look through a Smarties tube or toilet roll. These three ways of looking around can help you focus on different things. When you're on your back, you appreciate something of the tree canopy. When you're on your knees, you start to see (and smell) the woods from an animal's perspective. Using the cardboard tube helps you focus on particular things.

WHAT CAN YOU HEAR?

Choose a good time to make your group be really quiet. Either stand still or lie on the ground. First you can play a quick game of 'Who can stay quiet the longest'. When the game is over, take some time to enjoy the peace and quiet. Then, get everyone to *whisper* things they can hear. Listen to the natural sounds: creaking trees, rustling grass, buzzing insects, the wind in leaves and branches.

WHAT CAN YOU SMELL?

Lie on the ground or sniff around a small area and you can pick up interesting woodland scents – woody smells, decaying smells, flowery smells, moist smells, earthy smells, leafy smells. Most children won't notice them unless you point them out. For example, in autumn a sycamore leaf smells like brown sugar (quite different from its spring smell). All plants have their own specific smells. Look out for wild herbs such as mint and garlic. In open chalky areas there may be marjoram and thyme.

WHAT CAN YOU FEEL?

You can set children off on a hunt to find things that feel soft, hard, shiny, cold, and so on. Get them to put their hands behind their backs and let someone else put something in them – what is it? Can they describe it? Feeling something 'blind' in this way sharpens our sense of touch. Another interesting way of doing this is touch and feel things not with our hands but with our noses: just try feeling different trees and their bark with your nose. It's a very different sensation!

Woodland dangers?

Though woodlands may seem to be dangerous, they can be safer than your local High Street. Life is full of risks. The best way to prepare children for life is to help them understand risk by assessing it for themselves. For example, the best way to learn about stinging nettles is to get stung by them! Look out for wide dock leaves which often grow near nettles. These are traditionally good for nettle stings and they do seem to work, if only as a distraction!

The fact is, we're very lucky in the UK in not having many dangers in our countryside – as long as you don't eat anything. There are few poisonous fungi, and no insects with dangerous stings (unless someone has specific allergies). You're unlikely to come near a dangerous animal, and very unlikely to see an adder, our only poisonous snake, not only because they're relatively rare but also because they're shy.

Dead wood and lively minds

In any woodland you can find dead wood in different states of decay. Show children how weak it is by taking a branch and breaking it either over your knee or by stamping on it – but watch out for bits flying everywhere! Show them how light and crumbly it is. Bend a living branch, then see the difference when you bend a dead branch.

Dead wood is full of life. Many woodland creatures rely on it for food. Some eat the organic matter. Some eat the creatures grazing there. Look out for a wide variety of insects, especially beetles.

Encourage your child to be sensitive to wildlife. Breaking up one or two pieces of dead wood is a good experience, but you're also breaking up the homes of many small creatures, so don't allow the experiment to go on long!

Look under logs and branches, lift stones carefully and slowly; look for rotten wood and leaf litter – lift it carefully with a twig. Examine any insects, then put them back where you found them. Remember to return logs and stones to their original positions, and be sure to put the insects back *afterwards* rather than before (which can have disastrous consequences!).

Climbing trees

Climbing trees is great for all ages, and is usually safe if you establish a few simple rules, explain them, and keep reminding children of them. Here are some useful guidelines to emphasise as occasion demands.

- Only stand on mature, strong branches.
- Avoid dead branches (show children how to spot these: they have no leaves or only dead leaves; bark may be coming off; there may be fungus; the branch may feel rigid, not flexible).
- Look for leafy branches: it's more likely they won't be dead.
- Aim to have three points of contact – standing on two feet and holding on with one hand, or standing on one foot and holding with two hands. Always hold on with at least one hand.
- Don't climb a branch with someone immediately above or below you.
- Only share a branch with someone if you're sure it's strong enough.
- Don't step too far out from the trunk (how far depends on the tree and the child).
- Never jump between branches.
- Stay close to the trunk unless a branch is very thick. (If you can put your hand round a branch, it's probably too thin to carry your weight. If a branch is as thick as your leg at the knee, it's probably OK to stand on. But you have to use judgement.)
- Don't wear gloves (your hands are more likely to slip if you do).

Limit the number of children on a branch and in a tree. What's safe will depend partly on their age and size and partly on how sensible they are!

Minibeast hunt

You need no expertise to find and observe minibeasts, and no special equipment. The best times to look for minibeasts are spring, summer and early autumn. Look under logs and stones. In the UK there are no minibeasts that will hurt you (other than a little nip if you're rough with them), so there's no need to be afraid.

Keep your eyes open for a variety of spiders, ants, millipedes, centipedes, beetles, woodlice and pill bugs (like woodlice, but they can roll up into a ball). You can tell children going through a dinosaur phase that their favourite dinosaurs would have probably recognised woodlice, as their ancestors have been scuttling around the earth for millions of years.

Don't worry about knowing exactly what the creatures are. Chat over what they look like, what they're doing, and the way they move. You can always pick up a reference book at the local library or bookshop if anyone wants to follow the subject up. Look at the colouring too; many woodland insects and minibeasts are brown, whereas on grassland they're often green. If they're red, it's often nature's way of saying 'Don't eat me, I'm poisonous!'

Handle them all carefully, and when you've looked at them put them back. Let them crawl onto a piece of paper if you want to look at them closely. Let them crawl onto you if you're brave. If you have a camera you could try to take a photo, both of the creature and where it was living.

Is it OK to take some creatures home? No – they shouldn't be removed from their natural environment, and most would quickly die. There's a nice saying: take nothing but photos, leave nothing but footprints.

It's also worth remembering that some minibeasts and insects, such as the stag beetle, are protected by law, and it's an offence to disturb them.

WHAT'S THE DIFFERENCE BETWEEN MILLIPEDES AND CENTIPEDES?

'Millipede' means a thousand legs, 'centipede' mean a hundred legs, but they don't actually have that many. Look at one segment of the creature's body: if you can see two pairs of legs per segment it's a millipede; one pair per segment means it's a centipede. But the real giveaway is the way they move. Millipedes are slow-moving, as they eat plants and organic debris, but centipedes are fast-moving predators.

INTERESTED IN SPIDERS?

If you wait long enough in the woods you'll see hunting spiders on the ground. You may spot a wolf spider (there are various types) carrying a big white egg sac. Don't disturb her or she'll dump the eggs. A scary detail that will delight children: wolf spider mums eat the dads. They carry the eggs, then carry the babies on their backs, sometimes for weeks. And then the babies sometimes eat the mother.

To see a great selection of different shapes of web, one of the best places to look is in a garden shed. If you see a funnel-shaped web, you've probably found a funnel spider – tickle the edge with a feather and see if it'll come out thinking you're dinner.

HOMES IN HOLES

- Rabbit holes: smaller than a dinner plate, usually more like a side plate. Look for rabbit droppings around the entrance.
- Rodent holes: golf-ball size holes could be for a mouse, weasel, vole or stoat; near a riverbank and a little larger it could be for a water vole.
- Fox holes: dinner plate size and very smelly.
- Badger holes: larger than a dinner plate. An active sett usually has clear paths and a mound of earth outside, Badgers use the same paths under hedgerows and fences. If there's barbed wire you may see some badger hair on it. Badgers clean their holes each spring and you may see their old chucked-out bedding. They also have their own special toilet, usually a little hole near the sett.

Who's been here then?

Look out for evidence of animals. Nuts broken in half probably means squirrels, but if they've been nibbled it's probably a mouse or a vole. If you find pine cones eaten away down to the core it's probably a squirrel; look out for his special eating spot too – squirrels like to sit on a favourite log for their meals. Like children, they make quite a mess and don't tidy up afterwards.

Kids find animal poo funny and interesting. There's the 'ugh, disgusting' factor, and the inquisitive side too. You can encourage both. For example, show them hedgehog poo, which looks like a black slug and smells like something else, and try to find some owl pellets at the foot of an old tree (don't make too much noise, as the owl may be dozing up above); then take them away and break them up to see what was on the menu.

If you can find droppings you may also be able to find animal tracks, and the paths they make through the undergrowth. Some routes are like major roads, worn away by loads of animal traffic.

HOW TO MAKE A NOISE WITH GRASS

- Pull out a piece of grass about 10cm long and at least 3mm wide.
- With your palms together, hold the bottom end of the grass between the heels of your thumbs. Hold the top taut between the tops of your thumbs (it may be easier to position it with your forefingers first).
- Now blow, gently and then more firmly, with your lips over your thumbs and your breath going over the blade of grass.
- You should get a nice whistling or screeching sound, which will carry a long way.

Woodland games

CAPTURE

Four or more players – the more the merrier! Great for outdoor rough and tumble at any age, this is best played in a woodland or park with lots of hiding places.

You have a base that's a prison. One team are the catchers, and the other team hides. The catchers have to find them and escort any prisoners to the prison. Catching can involve some rough and tumble, but it can be made less scary for younger children by just having two or more catchers make a ring around them.

Prisoners have to stay in prison until they're released by one of their team, who has to touch the captive without getting caught doing so. Catchers can stay on guard at the prison. The teams swap roles when everyone's been caught or when people want a change.

FORTY FORTY OR POM POM

Three or more players. Excellent for young children, teenagers and adults too.

This game can be quite quick, and you'll want to play it again and again. It works best in woodland, parks with open areas and occasional bushes and trees, and beaches with few people and lots of rocks to hide behind.

Choose a tree or rock as base. The person who's 'on' counts slowly to 40 while the others hide. His aim is to find them; their aim is to creep back unnoticed. As soon as the seeker has spotted someone hiding or running back, he shouts 'Forty Forty' (or 'Pom Pom') and 'I see…' plus the person's name, and then dashes back to base – and the person who's been spotted tries to get back first, shouting 'Forty Forty Home' if he succeeds. If he doesn't get there first, he has to stay there as a prisoner. If he is there first, he's home safe and stays until the end of the game.

The person who's 'on' mustn't stay at the base for very long. The best games are when he moves away from base to entice people to break cover.

The game is over when everyone has either reached home safe or been caught by the hunter getting there first. In some versions of the game, someone getting home without being caught can release all the prisoners (saying 'Forty Forty Release') and they can all go off again, but if they're named they have to rush back to base or be caught again.

Birdwatching

Birdwatching is as interesting as you make it. The problem is that for most children just *looking* at something isn't very exciting; but if it involves doing something, or if it comes with a story, then things start to become more interesting.

The birds on these pages are all relatively easy to identify. Most of them are resident in large areas of the UK all year round, and there's something memorable about each of them. However, identifying birds can be difficult, as you may only see them in silhouette or at a distance. It also helps to observe the way it moves and the sound it makes.

Recognising a bird is easier when you look at the way it behaves as well as the way it looks, but since children are generally fairly unobservant and can miss things it's often easier to get them to listen out for a birdcall first and then try to spot the bird.

THE MAGPIE – AN UNLUCKY BIRD?

The Magpie has a distinctive loopy flight, with its long tail acting as a rudder. The black feathers are vibrant – you can see other colours in it because of iridescence. Look out for deep black and bright white feathers on walks, since these will usually indicate a Magpie. And listen out for its 'chack chack' and chuckling sounds. You can also tell when a Magpie is around by smaller birds setting up a chorus of alarm calls.

Magpies are scavengers, and are often seen eating carrion on the road. They're also hunters, and will steal eggs and attack not only fledglings in nests but on occasion larger animals such as rabbits, lambs and even sheep.

THE GOLDCREST – THE UK'S SMALLEST BIRD

Listen out for a beautiful tingly sound in a wood, and this will be the tiny Goldcrest – only 9cm long, and similar to a wren but for the tell-tale golden stripe on its head. The high-pitched notes of its song go a little lower towards the end and finish with a flourish. It's a delightful bird to watch, as it busily searches for insects and other small invertebrates. Because it feeds in tall conifers it tends to be high up in the trees, but it isn't shy. During the mating season the male's gold crest brightens to reveal a streak of orange.

THE ROBIN – THE FRIENDLIEST OF BIRDS

'Robin Redbreast' is really a misnomer, since it actually has an orange breast and face. It makes a sharp 'tik' alarm call, and its song is a high-pitched warble. It's a very sociable bird that seems to appear from nowhere, especially when you dig in the garden. It may even feed from your hand. However, though it may be friendly to humans it isn't so keen on other robins coming into its territory, and will see them off quite aggressively. But its territory is quite small, and you'll find two pairs of Robins living happily next door to one another in a single garden.

THE GANNET – HUGE DIVE-BOMBER

85 per cent of the world population of Gannets live in the UK. Another detail children will like is that they're called Boobies in other parts of the world.

Gannets are huge white birds, nearly a metre long with a wingspan of about two metres. Watch out for what looks like a great flying cross, made up of the bird's cigar-shaped body and long, straight, narrow wings (black tipped in adults). It's worth finding some binoculars to see them better as they plunge spectacularly into the sea a few hundred metres off the coast, skewering fish on their beaks. Fisherman used to watch gannets to guide them to a shoal of fish.

THE KINGFISHER – THE FLASHIEST BIRD

Being very, very elusive, it's a real treat if you see a Kingfisher, which you'll recognise by its unmistakable flash of electric blue. It flies in a very straight line, making sharp turns, and hunts

from a perch, looking for small fish such as minnows and sticklebacks – but you're unlikely to see that except in books or on TV. Expect only to see a bright blue flash and hear a high piping call of 'chee tee' or 'tseet tseet'.

THE GREEN WOODPECKER – JOKER ON THE LAWN

The Green Woodpecker is a beautiful bird that's comic too. It laughs like a jester ('yah, yah, yah'), and looks a bit like one too, flashily dressed in green and golden yellow, with a red crown and black face. It has a funny undulating flight, and a very bouncy walk. It can be found in towns and villages and

around the coast. It climbs and walks up trees, head up, and feeds on the ground searching for ants. Mowing the lawn sometimes encourages one to visit soon afterwards. It isn't very shy: if you scare it, it will fly off laughing but probably be back again after a few minutes.

THE PEREGRINE FALCON – THE FASTEST BIRD

This is the largest European falcon, at 45cm. Watch out for them round church towers, steeples and quarries, their

favourite nesting spots. They circle high waiting for prey, then fold their wings and dive at up to 115mph (185kph). In flight, you can spot their scythe-shaped wings. Listen out for a distinctive 'yickering' noise or 'keck keck' sound.

THE KESTREL – EASILY SPOTTED ON A JOURNEY

This is the only commonly seen British bird that hovers. It heads into the wind, spreads its tail in a fan shape and, flapping its sharp pointed wings lightly, appears motionless as it hovers looking for small rodents. It also eats flies and insects. Usually solitary, it's quite small and is found in both town and country. Areas by roads and motorways provide good hunting ground. Its call sounds like 'kee, kee, kee'.

Swifts, Swallows or Martins?

It's afternoon or evening in spring or summer. Birds are zooming around fields catching insects – and people often wonder 'Are they Swallows, or Swifts, or Martins?' Here's some help in distinguishing which is which.

SWALLOWS (ABOVE)

Visiting from April to September, these are larger than Martins, measuring 20cm including their long, deeply forked tail. They have red faces and a more fluid flight with straighter wings. They nest in outbuildings such as barns, not under eaves. They're quite chatty in flight: listen out for their musical chattering, and sharp chirrups of alarm if they sense predators.

HOUSE MARTINS

House Martins are small – 12cm – and are in Britain from May. They look rather like a blackbird with a white rump and white underside plus some vibrant royal blue, and have a stubby forked tail. They nest under the gable ends and eaves of houses, and fly in groups, sometimes very high. Listen out for their unmusical calls – harsh chirruping and tuneless twittering.

SWIFTS

Visiting from May, Swifts are slightly smaller than Swallows (18cm) and have a dark underside, a short forked tail and sickle-shaped wings. They nest in high towers, steeples and suchlike, because they need height for launching. Look out for parties of six or so flying at very high speeds in circles as if in a giant air race, screeching and screaming.

One amazing thing about Swifts is that they never land to go to sleep. They're constantly in flight for 11 months of the year.

Sky at night

Though children find the night sky fascinating, their boredom threshold is usually quite low, so it's useful to have activities that will keep their interest while you're star gazing – and some simple signposts to find the right stars.

Getting started

First, it's important not to hurry. Spend some time out of doors before you start, as our eyes take a while to adjust to darkness. You can see much more if you wait in the dark for at least 10–20 minutes.

The trouble is, few children happily wait that long. So fill the time looking out for other things – for example, between spring and autumn you might see bats flitting past at dusk if you're out in the country. In gardens and woods you might see the way certain flowers seem to be slightly luminous, their colouring designed to attract moths, and on a spring or summer evening you may notice that some plants give off much stronger scents than in the day. Listen out for the sounds of nature too. You may be lucky enough to hear snuffling hedgehogs, croaking frogs, the twit-twoo of owls, barking foxes or even the cry of a deer; or, in a town, human noises like banging dustbins and windows being opened.

Get everyone to shut their eyes and count to one hundred. Get them to do deep breathing for a hundred breaths. Go through the alphabet. Chat about who's best friend at the moment, what's their favourite activity at school, and so on. It will pay off – each time you open your eyes you'll find that you can see more stars.

USEFUL EQUIPMENT

■ **Binoculars or telescope** – helpful for viewing the moon, though they're generally difficult for children to use. You'll need a serious, costly astronomical telescope to get detailed views of stars or planets.

■ **Torch** – needs to be dimmed, either by using old batteries or covering the lens with red cellophane (red light won't spoil your night vision).

■ **Compass** – useful for getting your bearings. Alternatively, simply remember to note where the sun goes down, which indicates due west: 90° to its right is north, and you may be able to find the North Star. Constellations can usually be seen clearest towards the south.

■ **Warm clothes and a warm blanket** – looking at the sky is more fun if you do it lying on a blanket.

■ **Toilet roll telescope** – a simple but very useful tool. Just take a cardboard toilet roll tube and look through it: it helps you to see more clearly, and restricts your field of vision to about 20°, which is quite handy in helping children pick out stars and constellations.

THINGS TO LOOK FOR

■ **Shooting stars** – a streak of light across or down the sky, appears and disappears suddenly, evidence of a meteor shower.

■ **Space stations, satellites etc** – small lights, sometimes flashing, moving slowly across the sky.

■ **Stars** – many different brightnesses. To our eyes some of them seem to form patterns, or constellations. Because of the rotation of the earth, stars seem to move in the sky each night, but they keep their positions in relation to one another, so the constellations change their position but not their shape. What looks like a very bright star may be a planet.

■ **The Milky Way** – very clear on some nights, a band of what seems like cloud but is in fact billions of stars.

■ **Planets** – sometimes very bright, visible at different times of year. It's best to check a newspaper for detailed information, and there's great information on the BBC's website, www.bbc.co.uk/science. When visible, Venus is the brightest star in the sky, appearing as the evening star at sunset and the morning star before sunrise. Jupiter appears as a bright yellowish white point of light. Saturn is a bright yellow star (its rings are only visible with a powerful telescope).

THE MOON

As it's so easily seen, the moon is both easy and interesting to watch in all its phases. From earth we always see the same side of the moon, and with the naked eye or binoculars you can easily point out some of its features to a child.

SEAS

Confusingly, parts of the moon are called 'Seas' but are actually more like deserts – there's no water on the surface. Back in 1609, groundbreaking astronomer Galileo thought there might be seas on the moon and gave 'sea' names to different areas.

1 Mare Nectaris (Sea of Nectar)
2 Mare Fecunditatis (Sea of Fertility)
3 Mare Crisium (Sea of Crises)
4 Mare Serenitatis (Sea of Serenity)
5 Mare Imbrium (Sea of Showers)
6 Mare Frigoris (Sea of Cold)
7 Mare Nubium (Sea of Clouds)
8 Mare Humorum (Sea of Moisture)
9 Mare Tranquillitatis (Sea of Tranquillity)

Unfortunately, these Latin names aren't designed for children, so you may prefer to use child-friendly, totally unofficial names such as Honey Sea, Rich Sea, Dangerous Sea, Smooth Sea, Wet Sea, Cold Sea, Cloudy Sea, Damp Sea and Peaceful Sea.

CRATERS

There are enormous craters on the moon, up to 250km wide, blasted out by asteroids falling millions of years ago. They're named after famous scientists.

A Tycho Crater (Tycho Brahe, Danish astronomer 1546–1601)
B Ptolemaeus Crater (Claudius Ptolemy, Egyptian astronomer and scientist, lived around 40AD)
C Copernicus Crater (Nicolaus Copernicus, Polish astronomer 1478–1543)
D Kepler Crater (Johannes Kepler, German astronomer 1571–1630)
E Aristarchus Crater (Aristarchus, Greek mathematician and astronomer c.310–230BC)
F Plato Crater (Plato, Greek philosopher and mathematician 427–347BC)

PHASES

The moon appears to change size as the weeks pass, but this is just the effect of sunlight and shadow as it orbits the earth. Unlike stars the moon has no light of its own, but merely reflects the sun. It waxes (grows) and wanes (diminishes). How do you tell what it's doing? One way to remember is that if you can imagine the crescent appears to face Left, the Moon is getting Larger, i.e. waxing; if Right, it's Reducing (waning).

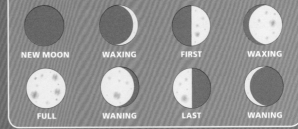

| NEW MOON | WAXING | FIRST | WAXING |
| FULL | WANING | LAST | WANING |

Constellations to look out for

Constellations move all over the sky, and some are only easily visible at certain times of year. Newspapers provide good information as to what's clearest in the sky. Here are ten of the less difficult ones to point out to children. They are all visible most times of year, and make quite distinctive patterns.

ORION
Named after Orion the Hunter in Greek mythology: it's often easiest to pick out his belt – three bright stars close together – and then work out the full pattern.

CYGNUS (THE SWAN)
Look for its distinctive cross – the reason it's also known as The Northern Cross.

PEGASUS
Named after the winged horse of Greek and Roman legends. First look for the four bright stars that make a sort of square, then work out the rest.

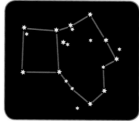

CASSIOPEIA
Named after a Greek lady. Look for a very distinctive W or M shape.

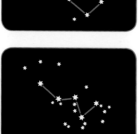

URSA MAJOR (THE GREAT BEAR)
One of the best-known constellations, visible in the UK on most clear nights. Seven of its brightest stars make up the Plough.

DRACO (THE DRAGON)
A long line of faint stars, with a tail that loops around Ursa Minor, so you may be able to locate it from Polaris. Rather difficult to pick out as it winds its way across other constellations.

GEMINI (THE TWINS)
Look for a kind of box with arms and legs. At one end are two very bright spots, named after the twins Castor and Pollux of Greek and Roman legend.

BOÖTES (GUARDIAN OF THE BEAR)
Pronounced bo-oh-tays. Look for a kind of kite shape of bright stars, sometimes easy to spot, plus some fainter ones.

AQUILA (THE EAGLE)
Makes a diamond or kind of bow and arrow shape.

HERCULES
You may be able distinguish the great hero of legend by starting with the box shape of his body, then his arms and legs – but he doesn't seem to have a head.

STAR MAP

This is an extremely simplified map to help young stargazers identify just a few constellations. First look North to pick out Polaris, or search the sky for the Plough (Ursa Major). Turn the chart round so that the Plough is roughly in the same place and same way up as in the sky, and you should be able to pick out some other constellations.

Polaris – the Pole Star or North Star – is often easy to see. It's the only star that seems to stay in the same place in the sky. You can find it relatively easily if you know where north is.

If Orion is clearly visible, or just his belt, follow it across and you may pick out the W or M pattern of Cassiopeia. In line with Orion's 'back' you can pick out Gemini with the two bright points Castor and Pollux.

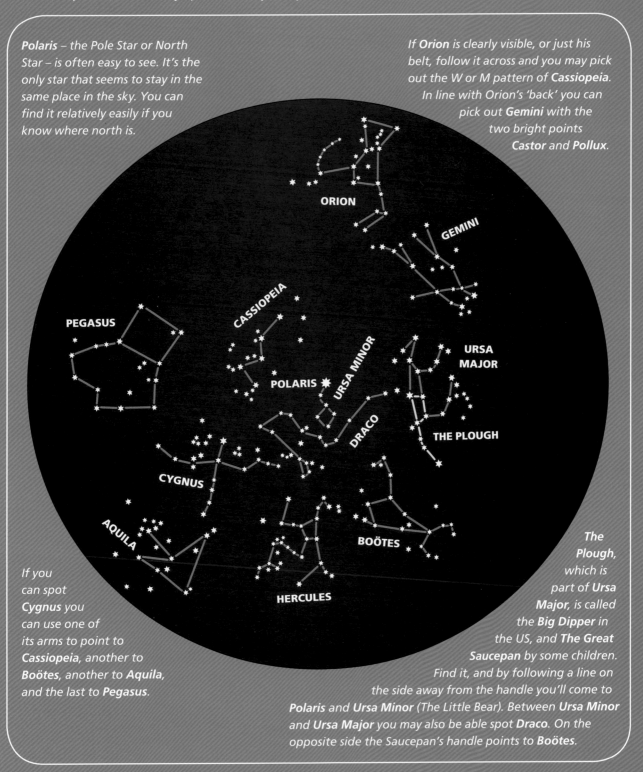

If you can spot Cygnus you can use one of its arms to point to Cassiopeia, another to Boötes, another to Aquila, and the last to Pegasus.

The Plough, which is part of Ursa Major, is called the Big Dipper in the US, and The Great Saucepan by some children. Find it, and by following a line on the side away from the handle you'll come to Polaris and Ursa Minor (The Little Bear). Between Ursa Minor and Ursa Major you may also be able spot Draco. On the opposite side the Saucepan's handle points to Boötes.

Kitchen fun

Let's get cooking   **120**

Yummy snacks   **121**

Fruit smoothies   121
Thousand island dip   121
Fruity French toast   122
Chocolate dip   122
No-bake chocolate biscuit cake   123
Quick & easy vegetable soup   124
Cheesy corn & bacon frittata   125

Pizza mania   **126**

The Italian favourite   126

Quick mid-week meals   **128**

Sweet & sour with noodles   128
Mozzarella pasta bake   129
Chicken tikka pouches   130
Salmon and bacon risotto   131

Wet afternoon baking   **132**

Coconut flapjacks   132
Banana cake   133

Easy roast dinner   **134**

The perfect roast dinner   134

Let's get cooking

Not only is cooking with your kids a fun activity, but by encouraging them to get involved in planning and preparing their meals they're also much more likely to develop good eating habits and an appreciation of the importance of a healthy diet. Children who cook at home learn essential skills that will stand them in good stead as they grow up and need to cater for themselves and their own families. And teaching them to cook is a great way to motivate fussy eaters!

Children enjoy cooking. It's practical, creative and satisfying as well as educational, and is an activity which parents and children of all ages can enjoy together. Whether you're simply rustling up a few snacks, preparing a weekend roast to wow your family and friends or looking for some entertainment for a wet weekend, cooking always comes up trumps. So get the aprons on and cook up some fun in the kitchen.

Tips for healthy kids

1 Only buy the foods you want your children to eat.

2 Encourage children to be adventurous, to try new foods and dishes, and to experiment with cooking by trying out different ingredients. Tasting in the kitchen provides a no-pressure opportunity to explore new flavours.

3 Prepare and cook a range of different recipes so as to learn about a variety of foods, flavours and cooking skills.

4 Children learn by example so if they see parents or older brothers and sisters eating something unfamiliar, they're more likely to try it themselves.

5 Make all mealtimes a social occasion, a time to sit down at the table and chat, avoiding distractions such as the TV and computers.

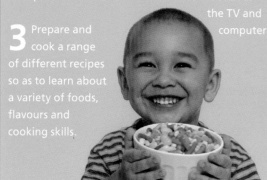

Safety know-how

- Wash and dry your hands before you start preparing food.
- Clean work surfaces with an antibacterial spray.
- Use separate chopping boards and knives for raw and cooked food, or wash them thoroughly between different uses.
- Check and ensure food is eaten by its 'use by' date.
- Keep perishable foods in the fridge.
- If you're not eating cooked dishes immediately, allow them to cool and then cover them before putting them in the fridge.
- Take care with knives, graters, peelers, processor blades and anything else with a sharp point or blade.
- Always wear oven gloves when putting anything in or taking anything out of the oven.
- Always put hot pans and dishes down on a heatproof work surface or pot stand.
- Always turn pan handles to the side when cooking so that you don't knock into them.
- Hot liquid is dangerous and so is steam, so never reach across a hot pan, and take care when draining food.
- Beware of the steam when you uncover food that's been cooked in a microwave.
- Make sure your hands are dry before touching plugs on electrical appliances.
- Always turn the hob, grill or oven off as soon as you've finished cooking.
- Always clear up and wash up when you've finished – keep your kitchen clean and tidy!

Fruit smoothies

Smoothies are the ultimate versatile drink. They can be made just with fruit but including milk or yoghurt makes them more nourishing.

SERVES 2

Ingredients

- 1 large ripe banana
- Handful of strawberries or raspberries
- 150ml (¼ pint) natural Greek yoghurt (or a fruit yoghurt)
- 200ml (⅓ pint) orange juice

Fruit smoothies provide a delicious drink at any time of day. Put all the ingredients into a blender, food processor or smoothie maker and mix. Add ice cubes if you'd like it chilled. Pour into two tall glasses.

You can actually use any soft fruit – fresh, frozen or canned. Try mango, peaches, passion fruit or mixed berries. You can use milk in place of the yoghurt or add a scoop of ice cream for a creamy consistency. Play around with any concoction you fancy.

Thousand island dip

You can of course buy dip from the supermarket, but it's so quick and easy to make your own. Quantities can be doubled for a party.

SERVES 4

Ingredients

- 100g tub soft cheese (Philly type)
- 2 tablespoons tomato ketchup
- 2 tablespoons mayonnaise
- 2 tablespoons hamburger relish

To serve

- Raw carrot, cucumber and celery sticks
- Pitta bread and/or Italian breadsticks

1 Peel the carrots and cut into sticks. Cut the cucumber and celery into sticks. Break the breadsticks in half.

2 Put the soft cheese in a bowl, add the ketchup, mayonnaise and relish and stir together.

3 Warm the pitta either under the grill or in a toaster. Then cut into strips.

4 Serve the dip with the vegetable sticks, pitta and/or breadsticks. If not serving immediately, cover the dip and keep it chilled in the fridge. Wrap the salad sticks in cling film.

Fruity French toast

A variation on eggy bread but made with a fruit loaf. You could also use a brioche loaf or just regular, thickly sliced white bread.

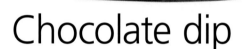

SERVES 2-4

Ingredients

- 4 slices of fruit loaf, halved diagonally
- 2 eggs
- 2 tablespoons milk
- 2 tablespoons caster sugar
- Pinch of ground cinnamon or mixed spice
- 25g (1oz) butter
- 1 tablespoon sunflower oil

1 Whisk the eggs and milk together in a shallow dish.

2 Sprinkle the spice over the sugar on a large plate.

3 Lay each slice of fruit loaf in the egg mixture then flip it over to coat the other side.

4 Heat the butter and oil gently in a large frying pan. Using a fork, lift each slice of fruit loaf into the pan and fry it gently on both sides until golden and crisp.

5 Sprinkle the slices with the spicy sugar then serve immediately.

TIP

This toast is extra delicious served with a fruit compote, such as apricot or peach, or mixed soft berries.

Chocolate dip

Guaranteed to be a real hit and a good way of encouraging kids to eat fruit.

SERVES 4

Ingredients

- 6 tablespoons chocolate and hazelnut spread
- 4-5 tablespoons milk
- 1 tablespoon golden syrup

To serve
- Apples, strawberries and marshmallows

1 Mix together the chocolate spread, milk and syrup.

2 Core the apples and cut into wedges. Remove the stalks from the strawberries.

3 Serve the dip with the fruit and marshmallows to dunk into it.

No-bake chocolate biscuit cake

This couldn't be simpler, yet it's fun to make and tastes yummy. Though the main recipe lists digestives you can actually use any plain biscuits you like for this cake. For variety try an oaty type, or Ginger Nuts.

1 Line a 30 x 20cm (12 x 8 inch) tin or shallow plastic container with cling film, leaving plenty of film at the edges to turn the cake out.

2 Put the biscuits in a plastic food bag and crush with a rolling pin, making sure that the pieces don't fall out of the top of the bag.

3 Break the chocolate up into squares and put in a large Pyrex bowl with the butter and syrup. Microwave on a medium setting for about 2 minutes until the chocolate has just melted. Alternatively, you can place the bowl over a pan of simmering water on the hob and heat it gently until the chocolate and butter melt.

4 Stir the mixture with a wooden spoon then stir in the crushed biscuits, and the nuts and cherries if you're using them. Stir thoroughly to make sure that everything is combined and coated with the chocolate.

5 Pour the mixture into the tin and level the surface. Put in the fridge for 2–3 hours until firm. Turn out, peel away the cling film and cut into chunky slices.

12 SLICES

Ingredients

- 200g (8oz) digestive biscuits
- 200g (8oz) dark or milk chocolate
- 140g (5oz) unsalted butter
- 1 tablespoon golden syrup
- 100g (4oz) walnut pieces (optional)
- 50g (2oz) glacé cherries, chopped (optional)

TIP

You can use any glass, heatproof bowl in a microwave, but no dishes or pans made of metal. And remember that cooking times vary in microwaves depending on the wattage. It's always best to slightly undercook, then take the dish out and give it a stir.

Quick & easy vegetable soup

Soup is one of the quickest and easiest recipes to make, and homemade soup tastes so much better than anything bought ready-made. It's also incredibly versatile, so you can add whatever you have available to suit anyone's particular likes or dislikes.

1 Tip the can of tomatoes into a large saucepan and add the stock. Bring to the boil then add the macaroni. Cook for 5 minutes until the pasta is almost tender.

2 Add the vegetables and bring back to the boil, then cook for 3–4 minutes until the macaroni and vegetables are tender. Stir in the beans and pesto sauce and heat through.

3 Sprinkle with Parmesan cheese and serve with garlic bread or crusty rolls.

The recipe suggests frozen mixed vegetables for convenience and because they're frozen when they're really fresh. However, you could add any leftover vegetables, diced into small pieces.

Buy a wedge of Parmesan rather than using the ready-grated that's sold in tubs – freshly-grated tastes so much better. If you have no Parmesan, serve with a grated mature Cheddar cheese.

The pesto sauce adds an instant Italian basil flavour to the soup, but if you don't have any add a sprinkling of fresh or dried herbs, such as parsley or oregano.

SERVES 4

Ingredients

- 400g can chopped tomatoes
- 500ml (18fl oz) chicken stock (made from a stock cube and boiling water)
- 50g (2oz) short-cut macaroni or other small pasta shapes
- 140g (5oz) frozen mixed vegetables
- 400g can cannellini (or other) beans, drained and rinsed
- 2–3 tablespoons pesto sauce

To serve
- Freshly grated Parmesan cheese
- Garlic bread

Cheesy corn & bacon frittata

A flat Italian-style omelette made using ingredients that you're likely to have in the fridge and store-cupboard. It's also very versatile, so you can ring the changes.

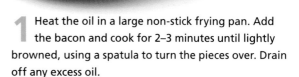

1 Heat the oil in a large non-stick frying pan. Add the bacon and cook for 2–3 minutes until lightly browned, using a spatula to turn the pieces over. Drain off any excess oil.

2 Crack the eggs into a jug and lightly whisk with the milk and a little salt and pepper to season.

3 Drain the brine from the can of corn, then add the corn and grated cheese (and the spring onions if you're using them) to the egg mixture. Pour the mixture into the frying pan over the bacon.

4 Cook the omelette over a low heat for about 8 minutes until the egg starts to set.

5 Place the pan under a medium grill (make sure the handle isn't under the heat) and cook for a couple of minutes until set and lightly golden on top. Cut into wedges and serve.

If you like you can add thawed, frozen peas or diced red pepper in place of sweetcorn. If you have any leftover boiled potatoes you can also add them: sauté them first with the bacon. Chopped ham or pieces of cooked chicken can be used in place of the bacon.

SERVES 4

Ingredients

- 2 tablespoons oil
- 4 rashers lean smoked rindless bacon, cut into pieces
- 5 large eggs
- 1 tablespoon milk
- 198g can sweetcorn (plain or with peppers)
- 50g (2oz) mature Cheddar, grated
- 2 spring onions, chopped (optional)

TIP

The easiest way to chop bacon is using a pair of sharp kitchen scissors. Cut away the fat so that the bacon is lean.

The Italian favourite

Everyone loves a pizza and they're fun to make. Just remember that you need to start preparing it some time ahead, to allow time for the dough to rise before rolling it out. You can go off and get on with doing something else in the meantime. The following recipe makes a thick-crust pizza large enough to serve four. If you prefer thin crust, divide the dough in half and roll out two pizza bases. Alternatively, you could make four individual pizzas, each about 18cm (7 inch) across.

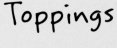

Toppings

- 200g jar pizza sauce or passata topping
- Pinch of oregano, basil or mixed herbs (optional)
- 140g (5oz) mozzarella or Cheddar cheese, grated or thinly sliced

Plus your choice of:
- diced courgettes or peppers
- sliced mushrooms or tomatoes
- sweetcorn
- pineapple pieces (fresh or canned)
- thinly sliced salami, pepperoni, ham, spicy chicken or cooked bacon, cut into strips
- chunks of tuna or anchovy fillets
- 2 tablespoons pesto sauce or humous
- a few pitted black olives

SERVES 2-4

Ingredients

- 375g (13oz) strong white bread flour, plus extra for kneading
- 1 teaspoon salt
- 1 sachet (about 7g) of easy-blend dried yeast
- 1 teaspoon caster sugar
- 1 tablespoon oil
- 250ml (9fl oz) warm (hand-hot) water

1 Put the flour, salt, yeast and sugar in a large mixing bowl. Add the oil to the warm water and gradually mix in with a round-bladed knife, to make a soft but not sticky dough. Add a little more water if the dough feels too dry. The water needs to be warm (hand-hot) to activate the yeast. If it is too hot it will kill the yeast.

2 Sprinkle the work surface with a little flour then knead the dough for 5 minutes using the heel of your hand, until smooth and stretchy.

3 Place the dough in a large, lightly oiled bowl, cover with cling film or a clean tea towel and leave to rise in a warm place (somewhere in the kitchen, near a radiator, or in the airing cupboard) for about an hour or until doubled in size.

4 Turn the risen dough out onto the lightly floured work surface and knock it back, then knead very lightly.

5 Roll out or press into a round, about 30cm (12 inch) in diameter, and transfer to a non-stick baking sheet.

6 Spread the sauce or passata onto the pizza, leaving a border around the edge. Sprinkle with herbs if you want to, scatter over your choice of toppings, and then sprinkle with grated cheese. If using pesto or humous, simply dot it on randomly.

7 Leave the pizza to rise in a warm place for about 20 minutes or until the bread is puffy around the edges. Meanwhile set the oven to 220°C (fan oven 200°C), gas 7.

8 Bake the pizza for 12–15 minutes until the crust is golden and the cheese has melted. Cut into wedges and serve warm.

Other ideas

■ To make a Four Seasons pizza, cover each quarter with different toppings.

■ For a cheese crust pizza, roll out the dough into a 40cm (15 inch) round. Scatter 140g (5oz) of grated mozzarella around the edge, leaving a 5cm (2 inch) border. Dampen the inner edge of the cheese ring then bring the outer edge over to cover the cheese. Press down firmly to seal the cheese inside the dough. Carefully turn the pizza over on to a baking sheet so that the joins are underneath. Top as you like, then continue as above.

■ To make calzone, make four individual pizzas, each about 18cm (7 inch) in diameter, then simply fold the topped pizzas in half and seal the edges with water to make pizza-style parcels, like Cornish pasties. Leave to rise then bake as in the main recipe.

■ To make your own tomato sauce topping, simmer a 400g can of chopped tomatoes, with 3 tablespoons of tomato purée and herbs to season for about 10 minutes until thick.

■ To make a monster or teddy bear face, cut the toppings into face features. You can also make a teddy bear template to cut out the shape of the pizza dough.

■ For really fast pizzas, add toppings to ready-made pizza bases or ready-rolled puff pastry then bake in a hot oven for 10–15 minutes (for pizza bases) or 20–25 minutes (for puff pastry). Or you can use muffins, crumpets, French bread or ciabatta – just split in half lengthways for the base, top as you like, and heat under a hot grill until the cheese has melted.

Sweet & sour with noodles

This recipe is made using Quorn pieces, so it's suitable for vegetarians, but you could easily substitute pieces of chicken breast or pork fillet. To make the dish fun to eat, lay the table with chopsticks rather than cutlery.

SERVES 4

Ingredients

- 2 carrots, peeled and cut into strips
- 1 red pepper and/or 8 baby corns
- 2 tablespoons sunflower oil
- 300g pack frozen Quorn pieces
- 227g can pineapple pieces in juice, drained and reserved for sauce
- 375g medium noodles (13oz)

Sauce
- Pineapple juice, from can
- 1 tablespoon cider or wine vinegar
- 1 tablespoon tomato purée or ketchup
- 2 tablespoons soy sauce
- 1 teaspoon caster sugar
- 1 teaspoon cornflour

1 First drain the juice from the pineapple and mix it with the rest of the sauce ingredients in a jug.

2 Cut the stalk from the pepper, cut the pepper in half, then remove the seeds. Cut the pepper into strips the same size as the carrots. Cut the baby corns in half lengthways, if you're using any.

3 Bring a full kettle of water to the boil for the noodles and pour it into a saucepan.

4 Heat 1 tablespoon of the oil with 2 tablespoons of water in a wok or large frying pan. Add the carrots, peppers and/or corn and cook on a medium heat for 4–5 minutes, stirring occasionally, until the vegetables are almost tender. (If you're using strips of chicken or pork rather than Quorn, stir-fry the meat with the oil for 8–10 minutes until it's cooked, and then add the vegetables to the pan.)

5 Add the remaining oil to the pan, then add the Quorn pieces and stir-fry for 3–4 minutes. Pour in the sauce and cook over a high heat for a couple of minutes until the sauce has thickened. Stir in the pineapple and heat through. Meanwhile cook the noodles for 3 minutes until softened in the boiling water.

6 Drain the noodles and serve immediately with the Quorn and vegetables on top.

To add extra flavour to your noodles, toss them in a tablespoon of toasted sesame oil before serving.

For a crunchy finish, serve the dish sprinkled with some toasted (unsalted) cashew nuts. Toast them in the dry frying pan before you start cooking the vegetables then remove and set aside for garnishing at the end.

TIP

Quorn can be cooked from frozen, making it really handy to keep in the freezer for quick meals after school.

Mozzarella pasta bake

Pasta dishes are always popular and this recipe adding spicy sausage is really packed with flavour. Mozzarella is the cheese used on pizza and gives a great stringy texture, but you could use grated Cheddar instead.

Ingredients

- 250g (9oz) penne (pasta quills)
- 115g (4oz) chorizo sausage
- 700g jar herb and garlic pasta sauce or passata
- 140g (5oz) mozzarella cheese, grated
- 2 tablespoons freshly grated Parmesan cheese

1 Preheat the oven to 200°C (fan oven 180°C), gas 6. Cook the pasta in a large saucepan of lightly salted boiling water for 10 minutes, until just tender.

2 Meanwhile, fry the chorizo in a frying pan without adding any oil. Cook for 4–5 minutes then drain on kitchen paper. (Discard the oil that's released from the sausage.)

3 Drain the pasta and return to the pan. Stir in the pasta sauce or passata, the chorizo and the grated mozzarella, then tip into an ovenproof dish and sprinkle the Parmesan cheese over the top.

4 Bake for 10 minutes then serve with a crisp green salad and some garlic bread. Bake the garlic bread at the same time as the pasta dish is in the oven.

You could also add a drained can of tuna to the dish, or pieces of cooked chicken. Stir the tuna or chicken into the pasta in step 3. As an alternative to chorizo, you could use salami, cut into strips. It doesn't need frying first, so omit step 2. For a lovely herb flavour, tear some fresh basil leaves into the pasta in step 3.

TIP

Cook pasta in a large volume of boiling water, using a large saucepan, to prevent it sticking together. Cook until al dente – just tender – or firm to the bite. You could also use quills or spirals.

Chicken tikka pouches

Fun to serve and eat. When it's ready, put the spicy chicken, pitta pouches, salad and minty yoghurt dip on the table and let everyone assemble their own!

SERVES 4

Ingredients

- 4 skinless chicken breast fillets
- 4 tablespoons Greek yoghurt
- 2 tablespoons tikka (or korma) curry paste
- juice of half a lemon

Sauce
- 4 tablespoons Greek yoghurt
- 2 teaspoons mint sauce
- 4 pitta breads
- 4 tablespoons mango chutney (optional)
- ¼ cucumber, sliced
- Rocket or herb salad

1 Cut the chicken widthways into bite-sized pieces. Stir the curry paste and lemon juice into the yoghurt, then add the chicken and stir to coat. Cover with cling film and keep chilled in the fridge for 15–30 minutes or until ready to cook. Meanwhile, stir the mint sauce into the remaining yoghurt.

2 Line a grill pan with foil and spread the chicken over it in an even layer. Heat the grill to medium then cook the chicken for about 15 minutes, turning it from time to time to make sure it is cooked through.

3 Remove the grill pan and put the pitta under the grill to warm on both sides. (Alternatively, pop it in the toaster for a few minutes.)

4 To serve, cut the pittas in half widthways then split open to form two pouches. Spread a little mango chutney inside, if liked, then half fill with salad leaves and cucumber. Pop the chicken on top then drizzle over a little of the minty yoghurt. Eat immediately.

Salmon and bacon risotto

We should all aim to eat oily fish at least once a week. Salmon has a mild flavour and the fillets have no bones. Try it in this delicious rice recipe, flavoured with a pesto stock, and serve with crusty French bread.

SERVES 4

Ingredients

- 3 salmon fillets, skinless and boneless
- 2 tablespoons sunflower oil
- 2 rashers lean smoked bacon, chopped
- 300g (10oz) risotto rice
- 150ml (¼ pint) dry white wine
- 2 tablespoons pesto sauce
- 850ml (1½ pints) hot fish, chicken or vegetable stock
- 140g (5oz) frozen peas
- 50g (2oz) Parmesan cheese, freshly grated

Traditional Italian risotto rice is recommended for a creamy texture, but long-grain rice could be used instead.

1 First cook the salmon. Either cover and cook in a microwave for 4–5 minutes or under the grill for 8–10 minutes, lightly brushed with oil. Set aside, covered to keep it warm.

2 Heat the oil in a large deep frying pan, add the bacon and cook for 4–5 minutes until lightly browned. Stir in the rice.

3 Pour the wine into the pan and cook, stirring on a moderate heat for a few minutes until the wine has been soaked up by the rice.

4 Stir the pesto sauce into the stock. Gradually start adding the stock to the rice, about 150ml (1/4 pint) at a time, adding more stock as it gets absorbed.

5 Just before adding the final amount of stock, add the peas to the pan. By the time all the stock has been used up the rice should be tender. Add a little more stock if necessary. Season to taste.

6 Flake the salmon into large pieces then gently stir it into the risotto. Sprinkle the Parmesan over the top and serve immediately.

TIP

The wine boosts the flavour but isn't essential – you could just use extra stock. Stock can be made up using stock cubes dissolved in boiling water. You'll need two stock cubes for 850ml (11/2 pints) of boiling water.

Coconut flapjacks

A popular favourite but with a coconut twist. These are quick and easy to prepare and are great for a teatime treat, for packing into lunch boxes, or for taking on a picnic.

1 Preheat the oven to 180°C (fan oven 160°C), gas 4. Line the base of a greased, shallow 23cm (9 inch) square tin with baking parchment (lay the tin on the paper, draw round the base with a pencil, then cut it out). If your tin is non-stick, there's no need to line it.

2 Put the butter, syrup and sugar in a large saucepan then place it on the hob and heat gently until the butter melts and the sugar dissolves. Alternatively, put the ingredients in a large Pyrex bowl and place it in the microwave for about 2 minutes on a medium heat.

3 Remove the pan from the heat and carefully stir in the oats and coconut, making sure that all the oats are coated with the buttery syrup.

4 Turn the mixture into the tin and, using the back of a spoon, press it down firmly so that it reaches right into the corners and is level on top. This makes sure that the mixture holds together and that the bars are an even thickness.

5 Put the tin in the oven and bake for 20–25 minutes until the flapjack looks golden on top.

6 Using oven gloves, carefully remove the tin from the oven. Allow the flapjack to cool for 5 minutes then mark it into 12 even-sized bars, using the back of a knife. Leave to cool completely before cutting into bars and removing from the tin using a palette knife. The flapjacks will keep for up to a week in an airtight tin.

MAKES 12

Ingredients

- 175g (6oz) butter
- 3 tablespoons golden syrup or honey
- 3 tablespoons light muscovado sugar
- 250g (9oz) porridge oats
- 25g (1oz) desiccated coconut

You can make fruity flapjacks by replacing the coconut with 50g (2oz) of chopped ready-to-eat dried apricots, sultanas or dried cranberries. Muesli could also be used in place of porridge oats.

Banana cake

This cake is a good way of using up ripe bananas when the skins are beginning to turn black. They need to be ripe so that they're soft and mash easily.

Ingredients

- 250g (9oz) self-raising flour
- 1 teaspoon baking powder
- 140g (5oz) light muscovado sugar
- 7 tablespoons sunflower oil
- 7 tablespoons semi-skimmed milk
- 2 large eggs
- 2 large ripe bananas
- 75g (3oz) ready-to-eat dried apricots
- 75g (3oz) sultanas

10 SLICES

This cake can be baked either in an 18cm (7 inch) round cake tin or a large loaf tin measuring about 13 x 23cm (5 x 9 inch) and 7cm (3 inch) deep. Lightly grease the base and sides then line the base with baking parchment.

1 Preheat the oven to 170°C (fan oven 150°C), gas 3. Sift the flour and baking power into a large bowl then stir in the sugar. (If the sugar is hard and lumpy, crumble it in your fingers before adding it to the flour.)

2 Whisk the oil, milk and eggs together in a jug and mash the bananas in a bowl using a fork. Snip the apricots into small pieces using a pair of scissors.

3 Using a wooden spoon, stir the egg mixture, the mashed bananas and the dried fruit into the flour mixture until all the ingredients are well combined.

4 Pour the mixture into the prepared cake tin and place in the oven.

5 Bake for 50–55 minutes until the cake has risen. To test it's cooked, insert a skewer into the centre – it should come out clean, with no raw mixture on it. If the cake isn't quite cooked, give it another 5 minutes cooking time then test again.

6 Using oven gloves, remove the cake from the oven. Run a knife around the edge then turn it out onto a cooling rack and leave to cool completely. The cake will keep for 4–5 days in an airtight tin or wrapped in foil.

If preferred you can use just apricots or sultanas and leave out the banana, or you can add chopped dates, glacé cherries or walnuts instead. Some chocolate chips would also be good – just use whatever you have in the cupboard that you know everyone will like.

The perfect roast dinner

This is everyone's favourite meal of the week and a time to enjoy sitting around the table to eat together. Follow the time plan to get it all ready together without hassle.

SERVES 4

Roast chicken with sausages

Ingredients
- 1 fresh chicken, about 1.3kg (3lb) without giblets
- 25g (1oz) butter, softened
- ½ lemon, cut in two
- 8 chipolata sausages

1 Preheat the oven to 190°C (fan oven 170°C), gas 5. Rinse the chicken, allowing cold water to run through the inside, then pat it dry with kitchen paper. Put the chicken in a roasting tin, breast side up.

2 Smear the breast with the butter and sprinkle with freshly ground black pepper. Gently squeeze some lemon juice inside the chicken then put the lemon shells in the cavity and tie the legs together with a piece of string. Tuck the flap of skin at the neck end under the bird and secure it in place with the wing tips tucked underneath. Cover the tin loosely with foil.

3 Put in the oven and cook for about 1¾ hours. Remove the foil for the last 30 minutes to allow the skin to brown, basting the bird with the juices in the tin. At the same time, put the sausages around the chicken to cook.

4 To check the chicken is cooked through, pierce the flesh with a skewer between a leg and the body – the juices should run clear. If they still a little bloody, return the chicken to the oven for a little longer. (It's important that chicken is cooked thoroughly.)

5 Aim to have the chicken cooked about 15 minutes before the potatoes and vegetables are ready. Then cover it with foil to keep it warm and leave it to rest. Once the juices have settled it will be easier to carve.

> **TIP**
>
> Chickens come in different sizes. A medium bird should be about the right size for an average sized family meal, but if you want to have some meat left over then cook a larger one. Free-range chicken has the best flavour but does cost more. If you buy a frozen bird, make sure it's thoroughly defrosted before cooking it.

Beans with carrot sticks

Ingredients
- 2–4 carrots, peeled
- 200g (8oz) French beans

1 Cut the carrots into thin sticks using a sharp knife. Top and tail the beans.

2 Cook together in a pan of lightly salted boiling water for 8–10 minutes, until just tender.

3 Drain, and reserve the cooking water to make the gravy.

Really crisp roast potatoes

Ingredients
- 700g (1 lb 9oz) potatoes, peeled
- Sunflower oil

1 Cut the potatoes into large chunks then put in a saucepan and pour boiling water over them. Put on the heat, add a pinch of salt and bring the water back to the boil.

2 Turn the heat down so that the water is simmering, put the lid on the pan and cook the potatoes gently for just 5 minutes to par-boil. Drain, return them to the pan and shake it vigorously to rough up the edges. (This will help them to crisp up in the oven.)

3 Pour enough oil (about 4–5 tablespoons) into a roasting tin to just cover the base, then put it in the oven to heat for a few minutes. Remove using oven gloves, and spoon the potatoes into the hot oil. Turn the potatoes so that they are coated in oil then put them in the oven.

4 Roast the potatoes for about 45 minutes until golden and crispy, turning them from time to time. Remove using a draining spoon.

For extra flavour you might like to add some sprigs of fresh rosemary or a few cloves of garlic to the roasting tin.

> **TIP**
>
> King Edward, Maris Piper and Desirée are good varieties for making roasties that are crisp on the outside and fluffy on the inside.

Getting it all ready on time

11:00am – Prepare crumble.

11:15am – Preheat the oven to 190°C (fan oven 170°C), gas 5. Prepare the chicken.

11:30am – Put chicken in oven. Prepare potatoes and the rest of the vegetables and set aside, covered until ready to cook.

12 noon – Lay the table. Put potatoes on to par-boil.

12:40pm – Heat oil in tin for roasting potatoes.

12:45pm – Put the sausages in the tin with the chicken, and also put the potatoes in the oven to roast. If making the Mediterranean medley, put this in the oven too.

1:00pm – Put crumble in oven. Make custard, if serving with the crumble. It can be reheated just before serving.

1:15pm – Remove roast chicken and sausages from oven and cover with foil to keep warm. Put vegetables on to cook.

1:25pm – Make gravy and carve chicken.

1:30pm – Serve main course.

Broccoli trees

Take a head of broccoli and cut off the thick stalk. Then cut or break the broccoli into florets (small heads). Broccoli is best steamed or microwaved. To steam, place the florets in a steamer over a pan of boiling water and cook for 5–8 minutes. To microwave, arrange the florets in a shallow glass dish with the stalks pointing outwards, cover with cling film, pierce the film, then cook for about 5 minutes.

Mediterranean medley

Ingredients
- 2 courgettes
- 1 red pepper and 1 yellow pepper
- 3 tablespoons olive oil
- 2 garlic cloves
- 1 tablespoon runny honey

1 Trim the stalks then thickly slice the courgettes. Cut the peppers in half and remove the core and seeds.

2 Put the vegetables in an ovenproof dish, drizzle with the olive oil then tuck the garlic cloves in between (leave the papery skin on). Roast for 30 minutes at 190°C (fan oven 170°C), gas 5.

3 Drizzle the honey over, turn the vegetables in the oil, then return to the oven for a further 10 minutes.

Peas with corn and cherry toms

Ingredients
- 200g (8oz) petits pois frozen peas
- 198g can sweetcorn, drained
- 8–12 cherry tomatoes

1 Put the tomatoes in an ovenproof dish then pop them in the oven for 5 minutes.

2 Cook the peas in a small amount of boiling water for 3–4 minutes, then drain and toss with the sweetcorn and baked tomatoes.

Perfect gravy

Ingredients
- Chicken cooking juices
- 1½ tablespoons flour or cornflour
- 1 wineglass white wine (optional)
- 300ml (½ pint) vegetable cooking water or stock

1 Remove the chicken and sausages from the roasting tin and pour off excess fat, leaving 3–4 tablespoons of the cooking juices in the tin. Stir in the flour, scraping up any meaty pieces in the tin. Cook on a gentle heat for a few minutes until the flour has browned.

2 Gradually add the stock, and the wine if you're using it, stirring all the time using a wooden spoon. Bring to the boil, still stirring until thickened, then reduce the heat and simmer for about five minutes. Season to taste with salt and pepper.

TIP
If you have some redcurrant jelly, add **1** tablespoon to the gravy for a delicious flavour and to add a shine. If you want the gravy to look a little darker in colour, add a splash of gravy browning, Marmite or Worcestershire sauce.

Apple crumble

You can't beat this old-fashioned favourite – luscious fruit of the season with a crunchy oat topping. The apples are cooked in orange juice for a fruity twist. Ideally use Demerara sugar for the best crunch, flavour and colour.

Ingredients

- 175g (6oz) plain flour
- 100g (4oz) porridge oats
- 140g (5oz) butter
- 140g (5oz) Demerara sugar
- 3 Bramley cooking apples
- 2 tablespoons caster sugar
- 3 tablespoons orange juice

Serve with custard, cream or vanilla ice cream.

TIP

If it's more convenient the crumble can be cooked in advance, then just warmed through in a moderate oven for about 15 minutes before serving. It's also equally good served cold.

1 Preheat the oven to 190°C (fan oven 170°C), gas 5. First make the crumble. Put the flour and oats into a large bowl. Cut the butter into small pieces then add it to the flour mixture. Using your fingertips, rub the butter into the flour until it resembles rough breadcrumbs. (For speed, this can be done in a food processor.) Stir in the Demerara sugar.

2 Peel the apples. Cut the apples into slices (removing the cores) and put in a large, deep ovenproof dish. Sprinkle the caster sugar and orange juice over them.

3 Evenly sprinkle the crumble mixture over the fruit. Bake for 50–60 minutes until the crumble is crisp and golden and the juices are starting to bubble up around the edges.

You can make a crumble with many different fruits depending on what's in season:

- Use 2 apples with 225g (8oz) of blackberries.
- Use 800g (1lb 12oz) of rhubarb, chopped into pieces, or 600g (1lb 5oz) of rhubarb with 200g (8oz) of strawberries. Sprinkle with a little extra sugar, but use just 1 tablespoon of orange juice.
- Use 900g (2lbs) of plums, quartered and stoned. Add 150ml (1/4 pint) juice or water and sprinkle with sugar.

Growing
fun things

Gardening basics   **140**

Making a vegetable plot   **142**

Delicious pots   **144**

Cress heads   144
Cherry tomatoes in wall pots   146
Sweet & simple strawberries   147
Flowers and salad in a window box   148

Water for wildlife   **150**

Beautiful barrel pool   150

Flower power   **152**

Sowing sun-worshippers   152
Flowers in welly boots   153

Gardening basics

Gardening with children is fun and can be educational too. Their excitement as a tiny seed turns into a flower or something to eat is infectious, and by caring for their plants your children will instinctively learn how they grow. All the projects outlined on the next few pages are easy for children to tackle with a little help from you, but without the right preparation things can go wrong, so here are a few gardening tips to ensure that you get great results every time.

Basic tool kit:

- Hand trowel
- Hand fork
- Border spade
- Border fork
- Gardening gloves for you and children
- Secateurs
- Watering can with a rose head

BASIC EQUIPMENT

Unless you're completely new to gardening you may already have a few tools at home, but if not, here's a basic kit to get you started. Choose spades and forks with stainless steel heads, which will last a long time and require little maintenance – simply clean off excess soil and dirt after use. Avoid plastic tools made for children, as they break easily. Invest instead in a good quality trowel and hand fork, which are generally small enough for young children to handle. You'll need a full-sized spade and fork to dig over large areas: border spades and forks have slightly smaller heads which older children will find easier to use.

Always wear gardening gloves when cutting with secateurs or pruning saws. Gloves will also protect children's hands from thorns and prevent dirt from getting into cuts.

A large watering can with a rose head is essential, but you may find a smaller one useful for seedlings and for little hands.

CHOOSING POTS

Children love pots because they're easy to plant up, and the plants are at eye – or mouth – level. There's a huge range of pots to choose from, but if you have very young children opt for plastic types. These may not look as attractive, but they won't split or break when they're knocked over or during frosty weather. Metal containers are also robust, but they can get very hot during the summer and become painful to handle. They're also unpleasant for plants, which will dry out very quickly. Place a layer of pebbles at the bottom of plastic and light metal pots to prevent them from blowing over.

Terracotta or clay pots can be inexpensive and look decorative, but they break easily, smashing into sharp shards, and if they're not frost-proof they'll also crack in sub-zero temperatures.

ASSESS YOUR SITE AND SOIL

When planting, it's a good idea to first assess the conditions in your garden. The direction in which it faces has a great impact on what plants will grow well there; for example, a south-facing plot will be warm and sunny for most of the day, and plants that thrive in heat will do well, while a north or east-facing garden will be cool and shady, so choose plants that enjoy these conditions. To find out which way your garden faces, simply stand with your back to the house wall and use a compass, or check where the sun rises and sets.

The soil type also affects plant growth. A light, sandy soil, for example, drains freely and, because plant foods dissolve in water, holds few nutrients. This may sound like terrible news, but many beautiful plants have evolved to thrive in sandy soil conditions. Heavy clay soil holds water and nutrients well but is prone to waterlogging, and in hot weather dries out to form a solid, concrete-like mass, yet despite these disadvantages many plants do very well on clay.

Testing your soil

To test your soil, dig out a sample and add a few drops of water if it's dry. Then try to roll it into a ball – sandy soil will feel gritty and just fall apart in your hand, while clay is smoother and will keep its ball-like shape. A loamy soil, which is a mix of sand and clay, will keep its shape but be a bit crumbly at the edges.

CLAY

SANDY SOIL

WATERING TIPS

When watering, aim your can or hose at the soil rather than spraying the leaves and flowers. This ensures that the moisture reaches the roots, where it's needed – a canopy of leaves can prevent the water from ever reaching the soil, especially in a pot – and is less wasteful. When planting up containers, always leave a gap of at least 2cm between the compost and the rim of the pot, to allow space for watering. If you fill pots up to the rim with compost, the water will simply run over the sides and your plants will die.

FEEDING TIPS

Whatever your soil type, dig in some well-rotted organic matter, such as homemade compost or well-rotted farmyard manure – apply it every year in the autumn if you have clay, or in the spring on sandy soils. Organic matter improves both types of soil, adding vital nutrients and helping sandy soils to retain water, and increasing the drainage in clay soils.

You may also need to add some slow-release fertiliser to poor soils, such as Growmore or blood, fish and bone – remember to wear gloves when applying it. And every couple of weeks in the summer give a dose of tomato fertiliser to fruiting vegetables and other fruit, and to flowers in baskets and pots. Alternatively, apply a slow-release plant food when planting up flowers in pots and baskets. This should last most of the summer.

Making a vegetable plot

You don't need a large allotment to grow vegetables – a sunny space in an ordinary garden can accommodate a few favourites. Alternatively, you can grow some in large pots on a patio. Children are more likely to eat what they've grown themselves, so try these easy veg and hopefully they'll enjoy the results.

For more inspiration on growing all types of fruit and veg see the Royal Horticultural Society's website: www.rhs.org.uk

Preparing your plot

Vegetables grow best in an open, sunny site, sheltered from strong winds and hard frosts. Don't plant them too close to trees and shrubs, as some prevent seeds from germinating, and they drain the soil of valuable moisture and nutrients that your vegetables need to thrive.

Before you start planting, weed the plot carefully. Skim off annual weeds with a hoe, severing the top growth from the roots, and dig out perennials, such as dandelions, bindweed, and couch grass, making sure that you remove all the root system – otherwise the roots left in the ground will simply grow into new plants. Also work in some organic matter, such as homemade compost or well-rotted farmyard manure, to improve and feed the soil. A dose of chicken manure is beneficial too. Remember to wear gloves when applying any plant fertiliser and wash your hands afterwards.

Growing broad beans

These delicious beans are easy to grow, and aren't readily available in shops. You can sow them either in pots indoors or directly into the ground outdoors from mid-spring. By sowing in pots in early spring you can get a slightly earlier crop.

1 Fill 7cm pots with good quality seed compost, and water to dampen it. Plant two broad bean seeds in each pot, pushing them down about 2cm below the surface, and then cover them with compost.

2 Leave the pots in an unheated greenhouse, or on a windowsill in a cool room. When germinated, acclimatise the young plants to outdoor temperatures by setting them outside during the day for a couple of weeks. When they've grown to about 10cm, plant them outside in rows.

3 Mark out a row with string, and dig a trench about 7–10cm deep. Plant the beans about 25cm apart and space the rows 30cm apart. Unless they start wilting you don't need to water them until they start to produce flowers. Once in flower, water them every few days, or more often if temperatures are very high.

The young shoots of broad beans are susceptible to aphids, which you can pinch off with your fingers as you see them. When the plants have produced plenty of flowers, and the beans have set, pinch out the growing tips to deter these sap-sucking pests.

Planting up potatoes

Potatoes are quite easy to grow, but they do suffer from a few diseases, such as blight and eelworm, which destroy the tubers. To prevent disappointment, choose varieties that are disease resistant, such as 'Premier', 'Nandine' and 'Cara'.

You can buy either 'earlies', which you plant in early spring and harvest from early summer to midsummer, or 'maincrop' potatoes, which are planted at the same time but are harvested from late summer onwards.

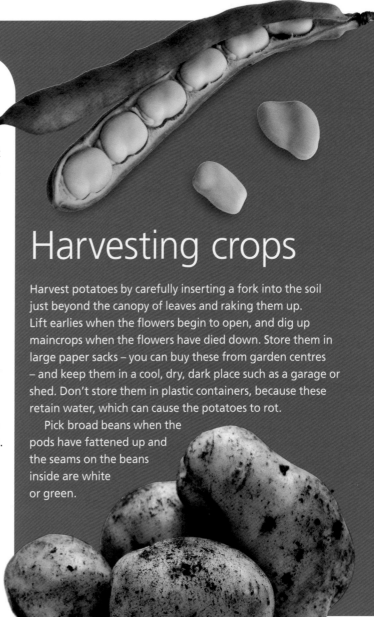

Harvesting crops

Harvest potatoes by carefully inserting a fork into the soil just beyond the canopy of leaves and raking them up. Lift earlies when the flowers begin to open, and dig up maincrops when the flowers have died down. Store them in large paper sacks – you can buy these from garden centres – and keep them in a cool, dry, dark place such as a garage or shed. Don't store them in plastic containers, because these retain water, which can cause the potatoes to rot.

Pick broad beans when the pods have fattened up and the seams on the beans inside are white or green.

1 In late winter, place your potato tubers in an egg box in a cool, light place indoors in order to 'chit' them (*ie* encourage them to sprout). Set the tubers with the knobbly buds or 'eyes' at the top. These will soon start to sprout and will be ready to plant after about six weeks.

2 In early spring, prepare a planting bed. Peg out a length of string to create a straight line and use this as a guide for sowing your row of potatoes. To prevent their leaves from being frosted, don't plant earlies until a month before the last frosts are forecast.

3 Dig out a trench along your string guide, 10cm deep for earlies and 15cm deep for maincrops. Place the tubers in the trench with the shoots at the top, at intervals of 30cm for earlies or 45cm for maincrops. Space the rows 45cm apart for earlies and 75cm apart for maincrops.

4 Cover the potatoes and water them in well. When the stems are about 30cm high, mound up soil around the shoots so that only 15cm of foliage is exposed. This prevents any potatoes that form close to the surface from going green, since green potatoes are poisonous. Water the plants once every two weeks, or more frequently if conditions are exceptionally dry and the plants start to wilt.

Cress heads

These funny-face pots will sprout edible hair within a week, and the cress itself is delicious on salads and in sandwiches. There are different varieties of cress to choose from, so select types you think your children will enjoy – some are quite spicy, while others have a milder taste. You can keep these nutritious snack pots going all year by sowing new seed every week or two – simply renew the kitchen towels and a little compost, and sow more seeds.

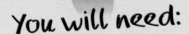

You will need:

- 7cm (3in) plastic pots
- Kitchen paper towels
- Marker pen
- Bug eyes (optional)
- All-purpose compost
- Cress seeds
- Sandwich bags

1 Draw funny faces on each pot – permanent markers are best, but remember to cover up before you start to keep clothes clean. You could also add some bug eyes, available from craft shops, using glue suitable for plastics.

2 Take one sheet of kitchen paper towel and fold it in four. Draw around the rim of the pot and cut out the circles with scissors. Repeat for all cress pots, so that you have four circles of paper per pot.

144

3 Fill each pot with compost to just below the rim and place the four paper circles on top. Water to dampen the paper towels.

4 Sprinkle some seeds evenly on top of the paper towel. You will have enough seeds in each packet for quite a few sowings, so reseal the seed packet with sticky tape and put it in a container in the fridge.

5 Place each pot in a sandwich bag and seal loosely at the top – these bags have sticky tags that are ideal for the job. Put the sealed pots in a cool dark place and check them daily. When the seedlings are 1cm (½in) tall, take the pots out of their bags.

6 Place cress heads on a window sill or in a light area out of direct sun, and keep moist until the cress is ready to cut. Snip off the cress with pair of scissors, and enjoy.

Super bugs

Some insects are gardeners' best friends, helping to pollinate plants and keeping pests at bay. Why not see if you and your children can spot these insects in your garden?

Ladybirds

Both the adults and larvae love nothing better than snacking on aphids, so encourage them to breed in your garden. To do this, cut up some bamboo canes into 20cm (8in) lengths, tie the canes together and hang the bundles from a tree. The flightless larvae look nothing like the adults, and are about 1cm long, bullet-shaped, and black with yellow markings.

Hoverflies

Sometimes mistaken for wasps, hoverflies are slimmer and hover in the air. The adults are great pollinators while their young love juicy plant pests.

Lacewings

The larvae of these pretty bugs with large lacy wings are great insect pest predators, munching on aphids and other small bugs. Lure the adults into your garden with open, daisy-like flowers.

Bees

As well as giving us delicious honey, bees are also wonderful pollinators, and will help to ensure you get a bumper crop of fruit on your apple or pear trees, as well a lots of runner beans. Encourage them with lavender, and open, daisy-like flowers.

Cherry tomatoes in wall pots

What could be more delicious than small, sweet cherry tomatoes picked fresh from just outside your back door? Try these in large wall pots or hanging baskets and hang them where they will get plenty of sun to ripen the fruits, and where you can water them easily because success depends on keeping them moist at all times. Garden centres and the large DIY stores sell young tomato plants from mid-spring, but do not put them outside until all danger of frost has passed, in late spring or early summer.

You will need:

- Large wall pot
- Good quality compost
- Water retaining gel
- One young Tomato 'Tumbler' plant
- Small bedding plants
- Gravel
- Tomato food

1 Make sure your pot has a drainage hole (if not, drill one or two), and then place a layer of crocks or bits of polystyrene on the bottom. Mix some compost with water-retaining granules and add a layer of this mixture over the crocks.

2 Plunge your tomato plant in its pot into a bucket of water and wait for the bubbles to dissipate. Remove the pot and allow it to drain. Plant the tomato in the centre of the pot, and if you have space, add one or two flowering plants, such as brachyscome, around the edge. Make sure that you have a gap of at least 3cm between the top of the plants' rootballs and the rim of the container, to allow for watering.

3 Fill in around the plants with more of the compost mixture, pressing the soil around the plant gently with your fingertips. Water and add more compost if the roots have become exposed.

4 Add a layer of gravel over the compost surface. This looks decorative and helps to prevent moisture from evaporating off the surface. Water the pot daily, making sure that the soil never dries out. The tomatoes will first produce little flowers and these will then turn into fruits. When the fruits start to swell, feed the pot every week with a liquid tomato fertiliser.

Sweet & simple strawberries

Sweet strawberries are a delicious summer treat for children, and are very easy to grow in pots. Raising the fruits off the ground also helps to prevent them from rotting, and they're less likely to be eaten by birds and mice (although they won't be completely immune). The special strawberry pots with holes up the sides look attractive but are more difficult to water, while inexpensive terracotta 25cm pots are ideal. Alternatively, you can mix strawberries with flowers for pretty pots all summer.

You will need:

- 25cm (10in) pot
- Multipurpose compost
- 3 strawberry plants

1 Make sure your pots have drainage holes in the bottom and cover them with a layer of crocks or bits of polystyrene. Water the plants about 30 minutes before planting.

2 Half-fill the pot with multipurpose compost and place the strawberry plants – still in their plastic containers – in it. Check that they'll sit at least 3cm below the rim of the pot when planted.

3 Carefully tip the plants out of their containers, slipping your fingers between the stems to avoid breaking them. Space the plants evenly in the pot. Add some slow-release fertiliser granules to the pot and then fill in around the plants with more compost. Press the compost down between the plants with your fingertips, and water the plants in well.

4 Take the flowers off as they emerge in the first year. This will encourage strong, healthy growth and result in a bumper fruit crop the second year. However, if you're impatient and want strawberries in the first year take off only about 70 per cent of the flowers after planting. Then you'll get a few strawberries during the first summer and still have a good crop the following year.

Flowers and salad in a window box

This pretty window box is literally good enough to eat. All the leaves and the nasturtium flowers are edible – the flowers are quite spicy but make a decorative garnish, even if your children find them a bit strong to eat. The best time to sow your salad box is in mid-spring when temperatures are 10–20°C (50–68°F) – lettuce seeds will not germinate in very hot weather.

1 Make sure you choose a window box with drainage holes in the bottom, or drill some if you have one without. Place a layer of crocks (pieces of broken clay pot) or bits of polystyrene (old plant packaging is ideal) in the bottom.

2 Fill the window box with roughly equal amounts of multipurpose compost and seed compost. Leave a gap of about 3cm between the rim of the box and the compost. Press the compost down gently to form a level surface.

3 Water the compost with a watering can fitted with a rose. Allow it to drain. Then take a short bamboo cane and gently press it into the surface of the compost three times to form three 'drills' or furrows about 5mm deep. Leave a gap at each end of the box for the nasturtium seeds.

4 Sprinkle the lettuce seed thinly and evenly along each of the drills, and cover lightly with some seed compost.

You will need:

- Window box
- Multipurpose compost
- Seed compost
- Loose-leaf lettuce or mixed leaf salad seeds
- Nasturtium (Tropaeolum minus) seeds
- Short bamboo cane or stick
- Tomato food

5 At each end of the window box press two or three nasturtium seeds into the compost to a depth of about 2cm and cover them. Then place your window box on a sunny or lightly shaded window sill and keep it well watered.

6 When your salad leaves are a few centimetres high you can either take a few out to allow the others more space or simply leave them all to grow. When the young leaves are about 15cm tall, snip them off, leaving stubs of about 25mm at the bottom – these will then sprout again to give you a second crop. The nasturtiums will take longer to mature, but they'll add colour and interest while the second crop of salad is growing.

Potatoes in pots

You can plant potatoes in large pots on your patio. Half-barrels are ideal containers and will hold two or three tubers. Drill drainage holes in the bottom of the barrel, and place a layer of crocks (pieces of broken clay pot) and grit on the bottom to cover them. Then add 17–20cm of loam-based compost, such as John Innes No 3. Plant chitted tubers evenly around the barrel and cover with a layer of compost. As the plants grow, simply add more compost to cover the stems and prevent the tubers from going green.

Keeping plant pests at bay

No garden is completely free of pests or diseases, but you can keep them at bay if you check vulnerable plants regularly and dispose of pests before they become a plague.

The most common pests are aphids – little green or black insects that feed on young shoots and buds – and slugs and snails. Aphids suck the sap from plants, so you'll notice them wilting or looking distorted. To dispose of aphids, either use an insecticide or, better still, pick them off and squeeze them between your fingertips. You can also encourage friendly predators into your garden, such as ladybirds, lacewings and hoverflies – the adults and offspring of these insects love nothing better than a feast of juicy aphids.

Slugs and snails can be lured into pots of beer sunk into the ground. They drown in the beer, but you then have to dispose of them. Copper tape set around pots helps to deter slugs and snails by giving them a mild electric shock when they try to cross it. Coffee grounds applied to the soil also seems to keep them at bay. If you use slug pellets, apply them sparingly and pick up and dispose of the dead pests to prevent birds and other animals from eating them. Nematode biological controls, which you water on to vulnerable plants, are safer for vegetable crops than chemical sprays, and there's a range of products available for controlling different pests, including slugs.

Beautiful barrel pool

You don't need acres of space for a large pond to enjoy frogs, toads, water skaters and water snails – this simple half-barrel is home to all of these creatures and will fit on the smallest of patios. Position the barrel in a sunny spot that's in shade for part of the day (you can use another plant in a pot to create some shade), and keep it away from deciduous trees that will drop leaves into the water and pollute it.

You will need:

- A wooden half-barrel
- Strong plastic or butyl pond liner
- Hammer and galvanised nails
- Small water plants
- Aquatic pond baskets
- Aquatic compost or garden soil
- Gravel
- A few bricks
- Hose
- Scissors or sharp knife

1 Place the half-barrel where you intend to keep your mini-pond, since it'll be very difficult to move once it's full of water. Place the pond liner over the top of the barrel, push it down around the edges and smooth it over the bottom. Make sure that you have enough liner to reach about 10cm above the rim at this stage.

2 Using a hose, add about 15–20cm of water – this presses the liner against the bottom and sides of the barrel. Then neatly fold the liner around the sides of the barrel and trim off the excess just above the rim.

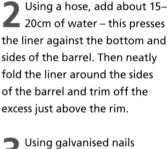

3 Using galvanised nails a little shorter than the width of the wooden edges of the barrel, tack the liner evenly to the sides. Then take a sharp knife or scissors and trim the liner just above the nails and below the rim of the barrel. Fill the barrel with water.

4 Plant up your aquatic plants in fine-meshed aquatic baskets, available from garden centres, pond specialists and DIY stores. Ideal plants include Japanese water iris (*Iris laevigata*), marsh marigold (*Caltha palustris*), arum lily (*Zantedeschia aethiopica*) and a small rush (*Juncus ensifolius*). Add a layer of aquatic compost or garden soil to the bottom of the basket – don't use ordinary compost, because it's too rich. Then take the plant out of its container, place it in the basket and fill in around it with more soil. Add a layer of gravel on top to prevent the soil from floating out.

5 All the plants listed in step 4 are 'marginals', which means that they like growing with their rootballs just below the surface of the water. To raise them up to this level, position the baskets on bricks or large flat stones so that the gravel on top of the soil is just below the surface. The plant baskets and bricks also allow frogs and toads to climb in and out of the barrel easily.

6 To keep the water clear you need to add one or two oxygenating plants. Good choices include hornwort (*Ceratophyllum demersum*) and water violet (*Hottonia palustris*), used here. Plant these in pots as in Step 4, and place them on the bottom of the barrel.

7 In the spring, ask friends or neighbours with a pond for some frog or toad spawn or tadpoles to add to your barrel. Your children can then watch them grow and develop. Place other potted plants around your barrel pool so that the frogs and toads have landing places to hop in and out of the water. Snails and water insects will soon find their way to your pool too. Scoop out duckweed (small round leaves that float on the surface) with a small net if it threatens to cover the whole pool.

Frogs and toads

These amphibians are great assets to the gardener, feasting on slugs and snails, as well as being fun for children to watch as they develop from spawn to tadpoles and then into adults.

Toads tend to be larger than frogs, and have drier, wartier skin – they also spend less time in the water. Adult frogs and toads like long grass or leafy flowerbeds in which to hibernate in winter, take shelter from strong summer sun, and hunt for insects and slugs, so make sure your garden offers this cover for them. Also, take care when gardening near your pool – a sharp spade or fork could be fatal.

IMPORTANT – SAFETY RULES

Young children can drown in just a few centimetres of water, so don't make a pool or have any open area of water in your garden if you have children aged under 5.

■ Don't allow young children who're visiting to go near your water features without constant adult supervision.

■ Empty and turn upside down paddling pools, buckets and other vessels that hold water, after every use.

■ Teach your children about the dangers of water from a young age, and encourage them to learn to swim.

Sowing sun-worshippers

Sunflowers are very easy for children to grow from seed. However, slugs may eat young seedlings, so it's best to start them off in pots and plant them out when the plants are more robust. It's also fun to watch the faces of these late summer flowers follow the sun round throughout the day, a characteristic that gave rise to their common name.

You will need:

- Packet of sunflower seeds (choose dwarf ones if you don't have much space)
- 7cm plastic pots
- Seed compost

1 Fill the pots with seed compost, firming it down gently with your fingertips. Water the compost and allow it to drain.

2 Take two sunflower seeds and plant them in each of the pots. Push the seeds down about a centimetre below the surface of the compost and cover them. Place the pots in a cool, bright place, and keep well watered.

3 When the seedlings are 10–15cm tall, plant them out in a sunny spot. Water the plants, then dig a hole for each one, spacing them about 45cm apart. Remove the plants from their pots and gently prise them apart, planting one seedling in each hole. Fill in around the plants with soil, firm down gently with your fingertips, and then water. Water them during dry spells.

Butterflies and bees

Gardens filled with flowers make a wonderful scene, but if you want an animated picture, plant those that'll bring in butterflies and bees. Children get really excited when they see flashes of colourful wings flitting through the flowerbeds! Try planting flowers such as lavender (*Lavandula angustifolia*), gayfeathers (*Liatris spicata*) and butterfly bush (*Buddleia davidii*) to encourage them.

Flowers in welly boots

This is a fun way to recycle old wellies your children have grown out of. You can use almost anything as a plant container if it has drainage holes in the bottom, and little boots will bloom all summer if kept well watered.

You will need:

- Old wellington boots or other unwanted footwear
- Cordless drill
- Pebbles or pea gravel
- All-purpose compost
- Bedding plants such as Busy Lizzies (Impatiens) and Flame nettle (Solenostemon)
- Slow-release fertiliser granules
- Water-retaining gel

1 Make some drainage holes along the bottom of the boots with an electric drill – take care that no children are close by, and wear gloves to protect your hands. Place a piece of wood inside each boot to help stabilise it while you're drilling.

2 Fill the bottoms of the boots with gravel or small pebbles. These help to prevent the compost from blocking the drainage holes and stabilise the boots when they're planted up. Add a layer of all-purpose compost over the gravel or pebbles.

3 Water your bedding plants well before planting. Remove them from their pots and position two or three in each of the wellies. Fill in around the plants with more compost mixed with some slow-release fertiliser granules and some water-retaining gel. Make sure that you leave a gap of at least 3cm between the top of the compost and the top of the boots, to allow space for watering.

4 Water the plants in well and place the wellies in a sheltered spot on a patio, doorstep, or at the front of a flowerbed. Water them every day throughout the summer. In autumn, when the summer bedding has died, you can replace it with small daffodil bulbs and little violas.

Building things

Go-kart   156

Playhouse   164

See-saw   170

Rope ladder   174

Doll's house   176

Ramps for bikes
and skateboards   182

Model railway layout   194

Go-kart

This go-kart design is very simple, and can easily be adapted for different sizes of driver. Although specific dimensions are given for all the components, in practice they can be varied to suit the materials to hand.

All the main components are made from wood, and the parts have been designed so that if you want to make the kart from new wood, everything can be cut from three basic lengths that can easily be obtained from most DIY stores.

The trickiest components to source are bound to be the wheels and axles. The wheels used on the kart shown here are 10in diameter sack-truck wheels, with pneumatic tyres and integral bearings to suit 5/8in diameter axles. These wheels are commonly available through hardware and tool shops, and from several internet-based component suppliers; 5/8in bright-steel round bar for the axles is easily available from steel stockists, and many fabrication and engineering workshops may have offcuts that they're willing to sell at a very reasonable price. Although we've specified a 2m length it will actually be cut into two, so you may find it easier to scrounge two 1m lengths.

You will need:

- Saw
- Hammer
- Sharp chisel
- Electric drill
- 4mm, 12mm, 5/8in diameter twist drills
- Countersink bit
- Pencil
- Tape measure or 1m steel rule
- Bradawl
- Square
- Marking knife
- Screwdriver
- 2 large adjustable clamps

- 1 x 2.4m length of 38 x 89mm finished, planed (50 x 100mm nominal) pine
- 1 x 2.4m length of 38 x 63mm finished, planed (50 x 75mm nominal) pine
- 1 x 1m x 1m sheet of 12mm marine ply
- 1 x 1m length of 12 x 33mm finished, planed spruce
- 1 x 2m length of 5/8in diameter bright steel round bar
- 4 x 10in pneumatic-tyred wheels with integral bearings to accept 5/8in axles
- 1 x M12 x 75mm bolt
- 2 x M12 x 100mm bolts
- 8 x 5/8in flat steel washers
- 9 x M12 flat washers
- 3 x M12 Nyloc nuts
- 4 x 6mm cotter-pins
- 4 x split-pins to suit cotter-pins
- 16 x No8 60mm long screws
- 2 x No8 35mm long screws
- 6 x No6 35mm long screws
- 2m nylon rope
- Paint/wood sealant/varnish, as required
- PVA glue

Main chassis

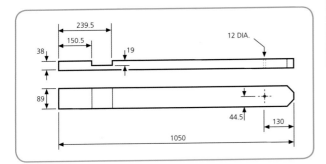

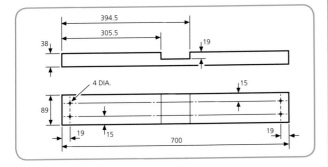

1 The main chassis is made from two lengths cut from the 38 x 89mm pine. Cut one of them 1,050mm long and the other 700mm long.

2 The two lengths are joined together using a half-lap joint, as follows:

■ Take the 1,050mm length and, using a rule and square, mark out the material to be removed from the half-lap joint (see the drawings).

■ Make two vertical saw-cuts across the 89mm faces, down to the horizontal lines on the 38mm faces, taking care not to cut too deep.

■ Working from each side of the wood in turn, use a sharp chisel and mallet to remove the waste material. Work slowly, and make sure that the chisel is sharp. The aim is to end up with a flat horizontal surface halfway down from the top face of the wood.

NOTE: It will help accuracy, and make your cuts neater, if all the marking out is done using a marking knife.

3 Repeat the procedure with the 700mm length, again marking out the wood as shown in the drawing.

4 Trial-fit the two pieces together, sanding or trimming as necessary until the joint is a tight fit. Then round off all the edges and remove any splinters.

5 Working on the bottom face of the 1,050mm chassis section (the face with the joint material removed), use a bradawl to mark the position of the hole for the steering pivot bolt, as shown in the drawing. Drill a 12mm hole centred on the bradawl mark.

6 Cut off the corners at the front of the 1,050mm section using a saw, then round off the edges.

7 Working on the top face of the 700mm length (the face with the joint material removed), use a bradawl to mark the locations of the four main chassis-to-rear axle carrier screw holes, as shown in the drawing.

8 Drill 4mm holes centred on the four bradawl marks, then use a countersink bit to countersink the holes in the top face so that the screw heads will be slightly recessed.

Axles

The front and rear axles are the same length, so cut the 5/8in diameter bar as necessary to give two 860mm lengths. Chamfer the ends and deburr them with a file to make them smooth.

Front axle carriers

■ Cut a 200mm length from the 38 x 63mm pine.

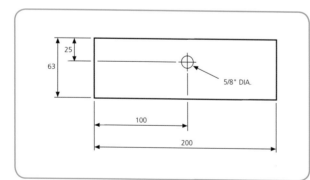

1 Using the bradawl, mark the position of the hole for the front axle as shown in the drawing. Drill a 5/8in diameter hole centred on the bradawl mark.

2 Repeat the procedure to make the second front axle carrier (both are identical), then round off the edges of both carriers and remove any splinters.

Rear axle carriers

■ Cut a 245mm length from the 38 x 89mm pine.

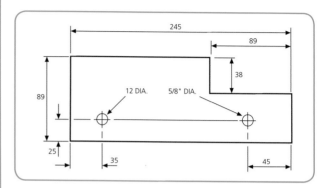

1 Mark out the rectangular section to be removed to accommodate the main chassis, as shown in the drawing.

2 Make a saw cut from the end of the wood down to the line across the 89mm face. Then turn the wood round, and make a second saw cut down from the 38mm face to remove the waste material.

3 The next stage is to drill the 5/8in diameter hole for the axle. Using a bradawl, mark the position of the hole as shown in the drawing. Using a pillar drill if possible, drill a 5/8in diameter hole centred on the bradawl mark.

4 Now mark out and drill a 12mm hole for the brake block pivot bolt, as shown in the drawing.

5 Repeat steps 1 to 5 to make the second rear axle carrier (both are identical), then round off the edges of both carriers and remove any splinters.

Seat

■ Cut a 400 x 700mm section from the 1m x 1m sheet of ply.

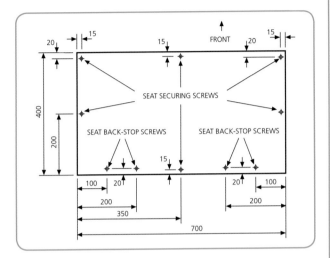

1 Using the bradawl, mark the positions of the six seat securing screw holes as shown in the drawing.

2 Drill 4mm diameter holes centred on the six bradawl marks, then use a countersink bit to countersink the holes in the top face of the seat sufficiently to ensure that the screw heads will be slightly recessed.

3 Turn the seat over and, working at its back edge, use the bradawl to mark out the positions of the four seat back-stop securing screw holes.

4 Drill 4mm diameter holes centred on the four bradawl marks, then use the countersink bit to countersink the holes in the bottom face of the seat so that the screw heads will be slightly recessed.

5 Round off the edges of the seat and remove any splinters.

Seat back-stop

■ Cut a 700mm length from the 38 x 63mm pine. Round off the edges and remove any splinters.

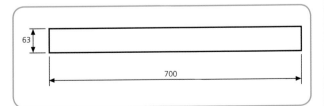

Footboard

■ Cut a 200 x 700mm section from the sheet of ply.

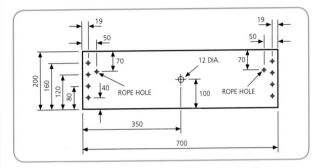

1 Using the bradawl, mark out the position of the steering pivot bolt hole, as shown in the drawing. Drill a 12mm hole centred on the bradawl mark.

2 Again using the bradawl, mark the positions of the four front axle carrier securing screw holes on each end of the footboard, as shown in the drawing.

3 Drill 4mm holes centred on the eight bradawl marks, then use the countersink bit to countersink the holes, as for the seat.

4 Mark the positions of the rope holes in the footboard, as shown in the drawing. Drill holes to suit the rope you intend to use.

5 Round off the edges of the footboard and remove any splinters.

Brake block bar

■ Cut a 780mm length from the 12 x 33mm spruce.

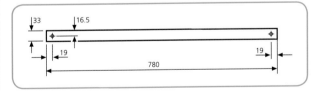

1 Referring to the drawing, mark out the locations of the two holes for the screws that secure the brake block bar to the brake blocks.

2 Drill 4mm holes centred on the two marks, then use the countersink bit to countersink the holes. Round off the edges and remove any splinters.

Brake blocks

■ Cut two lengths from the 38 x 63mm pine, one 280mm long and one 120mm long.

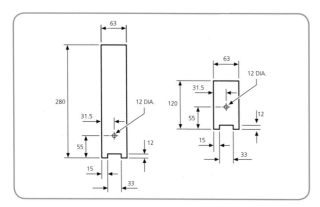

1 Working on each brake block in turn, mark the position of the pivot bolt hole and drill a 12mm hole.

2 Referring to the drawing, mark out the slot to be removed from the longer brake block to accommodate the brake block bar.

3 Make a saw cut from the end of the wood down one of the marked lines to the lines across the 63mm face. Then make a second saw cut down the remaining line.

4 Working from each side of the wood in turn, use a sharp chisel and mallet to remove the waste material. Work slowly and make sure that the chisel is sharp. The aim is to end up with a flat horizontal surface 12mm down from the top face of the wood.

5 Repeat steps 2 to 5 to make a slot in the bottom of the shorter brake block. Then round off the edges of both blocks and remove any splinters.

Assembling the parts

1 Begin by assembling the main chassis. Apply PVA glue to the two joint faces and push the two sections together firmly. To ensure that they bond, clamp the joint and allow the glue to dry overnight.

2 Once the main chassis is dry, lay one of the rear axle carriers in position on the chassis with the wider end of the carrier pointing forwards. Make sure that the outer edge of the carriers is flush with the outer edge of the chassis member, then clamp the carrier into position. Push the bradawl through each of the holes already drilled in the outer ends of the chassis member, and make corresponding marks in the top face of the axle carrier.

3 Remove the clamps and lift off the axle carrier, then drill small pilot holes at the four bradawl marks ready to accept the 60mm No 8 screws that secure the carrier to the chassis.

4 Slide the axle carrier into position on the main chassis again, then fit two 60mm screws and tighten them to secure the axle carrier in place.

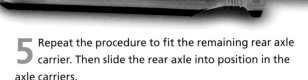
5 Repeat the procedure to fit the remaining rear axle carrier. Then slide the rear axle into position in the axle carriers.

6 Slide one of the two front axle carriers into position on the footboard, making sure that the outer end of the carrier is flush with the end of the footboard. Clamp the carrier into position.

7 As with the rear axle carriers, make bradawl marks in the top face of the axle carrier and drill pilot holes ready to accept the 60mm No 8 screws which will secure the carrier to the footboard.

8 Slide the axle carrier into position on the footboard again and fit four 60mm screws to the footboard. Tighten the screws to secure the axle carrier in position.

9 Repeat the procedure to secure the remaining front axle carrier to the footboard. Then slide the front axle into position in the carriers.

10 Working on the right-hand side of the main chassis, fit the longer brake block and its pivot bolt (you could fit the longer block on the left-hand side if you want to

– the longer block is used as the lever to operate the brakes). The bolt fits from the outside of the brake block: fit a washer under the bolt head, another to the bolt between the brake block and the axle carrier, and a third to the end of the bolt. Fit a Nyloc nut to the end of the bolt, but don't fully tighten the nut at this stage.

11 Repeat the procedure to fit the shorter brake block to the other side of the main chassis, then tighten the Nyloc nuts so that the brake blocks rotate freely on the pivot bolts without being loose.

12 Fit the brake block bar into position across the brake blocks, making sure that the ends of the bar are flush with the outer ends of the brake blocks. Then push the bradawl through the two holes in the bar to mark the bottom face of each block.

13 Drill small pilot holes at the two bradawl marks ready to accept the 35mm No 8 bolts used to secure the brake block bar to the brake blocks. Then slide the bar into position. Fit and tighten the two screws to secure the bar to the blocks. Depending on the shape of the wheels/tyres you've used, you may need to modify the rear edge shape of the brake blocks slightly by filing or sanding, so that they both contact the tyres at the same time when the brake lever is operated.

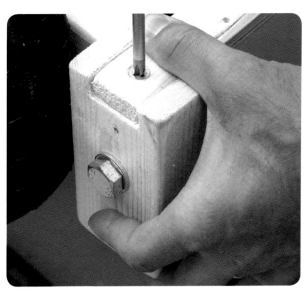

14 Working on the rear axle, make sure that the axle is central in its carriers – *ie* that the same length is protruding from the end of each carrier – then slide a washer on to one end of the axle before sliding on the wheel. Slide on another washer, then mark the position of the hole for the cotter-pin which secures the wheel on the end of the axle. Make sure that there's enough clearance between the hole and the washer to allow the wheel to rotate, and bear in mind that most cotter-pins have a flanged head. If you mark the hole accurately it's possible to leave just enough clearance so that if you file a flat (see photo) on the flanged end of the cotter-pin, the flat will stop the cotter-pin rotating when it's fitted to the end of the axle. Once the cotter-pin position has been marked, use a centre-punch to mark the exact drilling position on the axle.

15 Repeat the procedure for the other end of the rear axle.

16 Remove the rear axle from the axle carriers and, ideally using a pillar drill, drill the ends of the axle to accommodate the cotter-pins, centring the drill bit on the punch marks. File the holes in the axle to remove any burrs, then refit the axle to the carriers.

17 Repeat the procedure to drill the cotter-pin holes in the front axle.

18 Slide a washer onto the steering pivot bolt, then push the bolt through the hole in the front of the main chassis member. Note that it may be necessary to shorten the bolt so that its end doesn't foul the front axle. Slide another washer onto the bolt, then slide the bolt through the hole in the centre of the footboard. Slide another washer onto the bolt, followed by a Nyloc nut. Tighten the nut to secure the footboard/front wheel assembly to the main chassis, but not so tight that the assembly can't pivot.

19 Feed the rope through the holes in the footboard and tie the ends securely around the front axle.

20 Refit the washers to the ends of the axles and slide on the four wheels, followed by another washer for each wheel. Secure the wheels by fitting the cotter-pins to the holes in the axle. Lock the cotter-pins in position using suitable split-pins.

21 Slide the seat into position on the top of the chassis, making sure that it's square, that the sides of the seat are flush with the ends of the main chassis, and that the rear of the seat is flush with the rear of the main chassis.

22 Push the bradawl through the holes in the seat to make pilot holes in the top of the chassis and the rear axle carriers for the six 40mm No 6 seat-securing bolts. Fit and tighten the bolts.

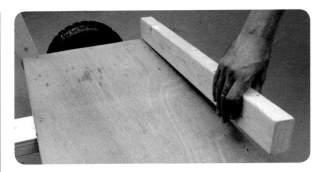

23 Clamp the seat back-stop into position at the rear edge of the top of the seat. Then, working under the seat, push the bradawl through the back-stop securing screw holes in the bottom of the seat to mark the screw positions on the bottom of the back-stop.

24 Remove the clamps and remove the seat back-stop. Then drill pilot holes in the bottom of the back-stop for the 60mm No 8 securing screws. Slide the back-stop into position on the seat again, then fit and tighten the securing screws.

25 Congratulations! The go-kart is now complete. Once you've made a final check that everything is correctly assembled and secure, it's time for a trial run.

26 Once you're happy that everything is correctly assembled, and that the go-kart works satisfactorily, then in order to help it last longer it's a good idea to dismantle it, varnish or paint all the wooden parts, and reassemble it using PVA glue in addition to the securing screws. Hopefully your go-kart should then provide many years of enjoyment to kids and dads alike!

Playhouse

This is a project that will provide children with hours of enjoyment. You may be daunted by its size, but don't be – it's really only sheets of plywood joined together with battens and pegged with dowel rods.

Cutting list

- Front and back walls – 2 @ 1,222 x 1,219 x 6mm (plywood)
- Side walls – 2 @ 1,219 x 914 x 6mm (plywood)
- Gable ends – 2 @ 1,160 x 304 x 6mm (plywood)
- Roof section – 2 @ 1,222 x 660 x 6mm (plywood)
- Vertical wall battens – 8 @ 1,219 x 43 x 22mm (timber)
- Horizontal wall battens – 4 @ 828 x 43 x 22mm and 4 @ 1,163 x 43 x 22mm (timber)
- Battens to secure roof – 2 @ 502 x 43 x 22mm (timber)
- Battens for curtain track – 4 @ 404 x 43 x 22mm (timber)
- Window valances – 4 @ 355 x 60 x 22mm (timber)
- Door battens – 2 @ 600 x 65 x 22mm (timber)
- Roof battens – 3 @ 1,222 x 43 x 25mm (timber)
- Battens for gable ends (to be cut to fit) – 4 @ 1,222 x 43 x 25mm (timber)
- Chimney stack sides – 2 @ 216 x 184 x 6mm (plywood)
- Chimney stack fronts – 2 @ 184 x 171 x 6mm (plywood)
- Chimney pot base – 1 @ 194 x 146 x 6mm (plywood)

Measurements are approximate and can be adapted to suit.

You will need:

- Stanley 'Jetcut Fine' panel saw
- Bradawl
- Jigsaw with fine cutting blades
- Orbital sander
- Screwdrivers
- Tenon-saw
- Stanley knife
- Mallet
- Chisel
- Hammer
- Selection of drill bits
- Countersink bit
- Battery screwdriver/drill
- Steel rule
- Expanding rule
- Timber and plywood (see cutting list)
- 122 x 70mm diameter plastic tube (chimney pot)
- Length of nylon cord for roof hinge
- Small bolt, nuts and washers for door
- Back-flap hinges for door

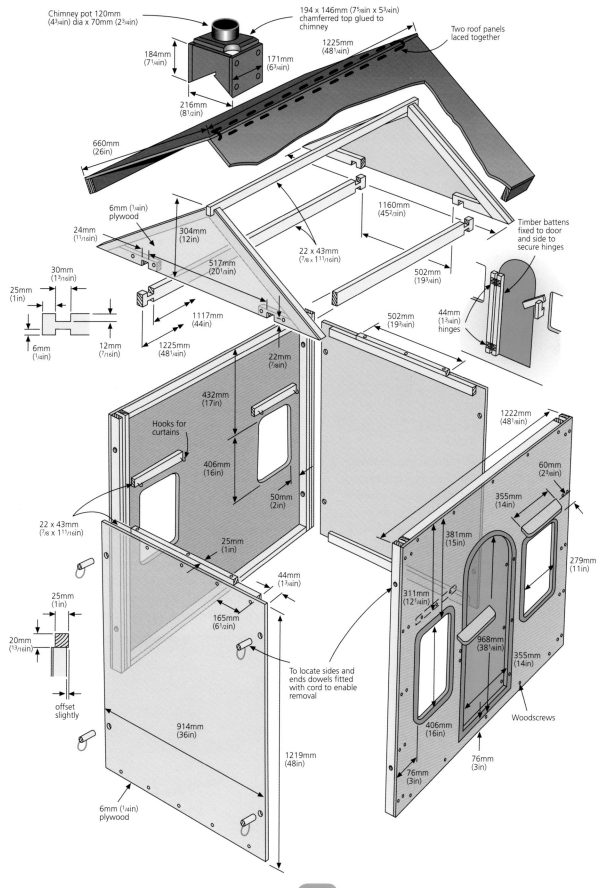

Chimney pot 120mm (4³⁄₄in) dia x 70mm (2³⁄₄in)

194 x 146mm (7⁵⁄₈in x 5³⁄₄in) chamferred top glued to chimney

Two roof panels laced together

1225mm (48¹⁄₄in)

184mm (7¹⁄₄in)

171mm (6³⁄₄in)

216mm (8¹⁄₂in)

660mm (26in)

6mm (¹⁄₄in) plywood

1160mm (45²⁄₃in)

Timber battens fixed to door and side to secure hinges

24mm (¹¹⁄₁₆in)

304mm (12in)

22 x 43mm (⁷⁄₈ x 1¹¹⁄₁₆in)

502mm (19³⁄₄in)

30mm (1³⁄₁₆in)

517mm (20¹⁄₂in)

44mm (1³⁄₄in) hinges

25mm (1in)

502mm (19³⁄₄in)

6mm (¹⁄₄in)

12mm (⁷⁄₁₆in)

1117mm (44in)

1225mm (48¹⁄₄in)

22mm (⁷⁄₈in)

432mm (17in)

1222mm (48¹⁄₈in)

Hooks for curtains

60mm (2³⁄₈in)

355mm (14in)

406mm (16in)

50mm (2in)

381mm (15in)

279mm (11in)

22 x 43mm (⁷⁄₈ x 1¹¹⁄₁₆in)

25mm (1in)

311mm (12¹⁄₄in)

44mm (1³⁄₄in)

25mm (1in)

165mm (6¹⁄₂in)

968mm (38¹⁄₈in)

355mm (14in)

20mm (¹³⁄₁₆in)

To locate sides and ends dowels fitted with cord to enable removal

offset slightly

914mm (36in)

406mm (16in)

Woodscrews

1219mm (48in)

76mm (3in)

76mm (3in)

6mm (¹⁄₄in) plywood

1 Start by cutting one of the sheets of plywood in half to form the front and back walls. Use a fine-toothed Jetcut saw for this, as it won't create as many splinters. This is a big sheet of plywood and you must support it on a table

or bench and have some help to steady the sheet while you're cutting. Once the sheet is in half glasspaper the edges to remove any splinters. Now study the drawing and familiarise yourself with the front of the house, as this is the first panel you'll work on. Pencil in where the front door and the two windows go. You'll need a straight edge or a batten offcut for this.

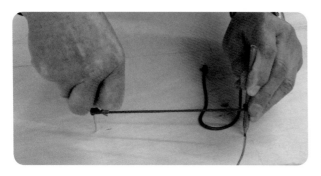

2 Work on the front door first. Pencil in the doorstep and the sides of the doorway. The curve at the top of the door has to be produced using a bradawl, a pencil and a piece of string – unless you have a giant compass! Near the top of the door, measure the distance between the vertical lines that indicate the sides and pencil in a line halfway between them. Then place the pointed bradawl on this line with the string tied to it and the pencil tied to the other end, and, stretching the string to the width of the door, draw the arch at the top (have a rubber handy!).

3 A Using a 2mm drill bit bore a hole in the bottom corner of the doorway.

B Drill a second hole and then more holes very slightly further along the outline of the door. If you carefully move the drill backwards and forwards the holes will elongate until you've created a slot.

C A fine-cut jigsaw blade can now be inserted and you can start to carefully cut out the doorway. Remember that the jigsaw blade will go right through the panel, so you need to rest the plywood on blocks

of wood to keep the blade away from the table or bench on which you're working. It's very easy to concentrate so hard on following the pencil line that you forget the blade can run into objects underneath! Once the door is cut out use glasspaper to remove any splinters. Alternatively use a random orbital sander, which will give a superb finish.

4 A Next you need to cut two windows, one on either side of the door. Refer to the drawing and use your batten and pencil to draw them on the plywood. Note that the corners are curved. These can be achieved either with a compass or with the string

and pencil you used for the doorway arch, but a much simpler solution is to choose a suitable tin lid or can and just draw round the edge.

B The method of inserting your jigsaw blade for the windows is exactly the same as for the door. You'll discover that the jigsaw cuts the semi-circular windows perfectly. While you're set up for cutting windows, it's best to take the other half-sheet of plywood and mark and cut out the windows in the back wall.

C Remember that little fingers will find any sharp edges. Ideally you should use an orbital sander to work over the door and window edges. Use glasspaper wrapped around a dowel rod to work over

the curved window corners. Once the windows are finished you need to add a small timber valance above each of them, plus battens on the inside to hold the curtain wires. The valances need to be planed up and the corners rounded off. Plane an angle of about 30° on the back of each. Then glue and screw the window valances and battens in place.

5 A Next you must hinge the door. You need two battens, to which the hinges will be attached – one is fixed to the door, the other to the wall of the house. Drill and countersink holes on the outside surface of the wall and door to take the screws that will secure the battens. Then turn the panel over.

B Slip the door into the hole from which it was cut and add two back-flap hinges. These are very simple to fit – no cutting of recesses is required, just position the knuckle of the hinge in the gap between the door batten and the wall batten.

C Start by fixing both hinges to the door batten. Use a bradawl through each screw hole in the hinge to make starting holes for the screws.

D Drive the screws into the door batten.

E Following the same procedure, drive all the screws into the wall batten.

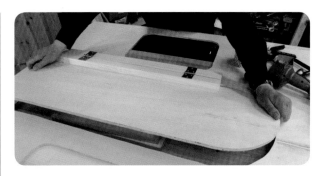

F The door is now hinged to the wall. If it doesn't open and close perfectly, take some timber off the edge with a smoothing plane. Make certain that any splinters resulting from this are removed with glasspaper.

G You need to make a simple door latch mechanism. Our door has a wooden latch secured to the door by a small nut, bolt and washer. This is much more practical than ironmongery. Ensure that the latch works smoothly and that nobody is likely to get shut in.

6 A The playhouse walls are held together using pairs of battens and dowel rods as fixing pegs. To achieve this you need to screw parallel pairs of battens to the ends of the front and back walls, and the side walls simply slot in and are held firmly in place by dowel rod pegs. See the drawing. To ensure that the side walls fit, cut two waste pieces of plywood of the same thickness and drop them in the slot between the battens before you screw these tight. If you plan to paint the house remember that paint adds thickness to the timber, so you'll need to allow a little slack.

B Now cut the two side walls to size, and attach single battens to the top and bottom of all four walls. Those on the side walls don't go the full length, but are slightly shorter to allow for the vertical 'slot' battens on the front and back walls.

7 A Slot the walls together and drill holes through the side wall and both vertical battens to accommodate the dowel rod pegs. The picture shows the drill bit emerging through the first hole.

B Drilling is complete. You need to smooth round the edges of the holes to remove any splinters.

8 To lock the walls together, use pegs made from dowel rod cut to a suitable length. Bore a small hole in the end of each and tie a loop of nylon cord through the dowel. This acts as a pull toggle.

9 Two triangular gable ends now need to be shaped up from plywood. To stiffen the plywood, battens are glued and screwed to them. This entails quite a lot of screwing and angles cut on the ends of the battens. You need to round off the corners of the gable ends – sharp edges and protrusions will always cause accidents. Saw off the ends and work over them with a block of glasspaper.

10 A Once the battens are in place, halving joints need to be cut on the underside of each gable end. Mark out the joint and cut down the edges with a tenon saw.

B Use a chisel to cut out the waste.

C Do the same at the other end and on the other gable. Then cut the three roof battens. The edges of the top one (on the ridge) have to be planed off to follow the same angle as the roof. The two lower battens aren't angled, but just fit into the halving joint slots you've cut in the gable ends.

D Just to show how it fits, this is the gable end turned upside down and the bottom fitting into the halving joint. Both these lower battens have halving joints cut on the top and bottom – one half slots over the end wall, the other into the triangular gable end. Everything should slot together firmly without fixings being necessary, but if the playhouse is likely to be used outdoors you should screw the battens to the top of the end walls.

11 **A** The battens are in place and the gable end is being fitted. The piece of timber on top of the end wall locates the gable end without the need for further halving joints

B Fit the planed-off ridge batten. This will fit into the gable ends tightly, but if you prefer you can also drive in a screw to secure it.

12 **A** Cut the roof panels from the remaining plywood and round off the lower edges. If you fit traditional hinges you'll need battens, the whole roof will become very heavy and cumbersome, and the hinges will inevitably get strained and broken. So why not lace it together with cord instead? To do this, tape both roof panels together and bore a series of holes along the top edge to take a length of nylon cord. Note the block of wood held in place behind the point where the drill will break through: this prevents nasty splinters.

B Thread the nylon cord through the holes, but don't pull it tight yet. Open the roof up and fit it in place on the playhouse, then tighten the cord and tie it off. The cord makes a good strong hinge.

13 **A** The chimney stack is really just a plywood box with the bottom missing. Make yourself a card template of the roof shape, then transfer the template shape to the chimney stack itself and cut it out with a jigsaw.

B The chimney can be made from a piece of drainpipe. Place the pipe on top of the stack, draw round it with a pencil, and then use a jigsaw to cut the hole for it. If the pipe is a good tight fit in the hole it won't need gluing.

14 Before any painting begins have a final check round for splinters and sharp edges.

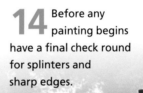

See-saw

See-saws are a great favourite with children, who never tire of playing on them. This one has a good substantial stand with legs to give it stability. Only halving joints are used: everything else is just a matter of gluing and screwing.

Cutting list

It's essential that the timber you buy is planed. Sawn timber is much cheaper, but is rough and therefore unsuitable for this project.

- Plank – cut 1 @ 2,440 x 197 x 20mm (timber)
- Strengtheners – cut 2 @ 1,730 x 98 x 20mm (timber)
- Handgrip side-plates – cut 4 @ 381 x 70 x 20mm (timber)
- Handrails – cut 2 @ 235 x 25mm diameter (dowel)
- Bump blocks – cut 2 @ 206 x 70 x 51mm (timber)
- Feet – cut 2 @ 760 x 197 x 20mm (timber)
- Foot-tie members – cut 2 @ 825 x 70 x 20mm (timber)
- Pivot side-plates – cut 2 @ 600 x 191 x 20mm (timber)
- Pivot pin – cut 1 @ 280 x 25mm (dowel)

Measurements are approximate and can be adapted to suit.

You will need:

- Battery-powered drill/screwdriver
- Drill stand and mains-powered drill
- Jigsaw
- Chisels
- Hand plane
- Drill bits
- Countersink bit
- Large flat drill bit (25mm)
- Expanding steel rule
- Carpenter's square
- Marking gauge
- Stanley knife
- Tenon saw
- Hammer
- Clamps
- Glasspaper
- Assorted screws
- Wood glue
- Timber (see cutting list)

1 Cut the two pivot side-plates to length. Mark the position for the dowel rod pivot hole (see plan) and pencil in the semi-circle at the top of the pivot plate. Clamp the pivot plate to the bench and cut to shape using a jigsaw.

2 This is what you have to cut off on both sides.

3 Use a plane to smooth the section of the shaped pivot plate that leads into the curve.

4 Do the final shaping with a piece of glasspaper wrapped around a block of wood. Work over the curve to remove any saw marks.

5 Using an electric drill mounted in a drill stand, bore a hole to take the main pivot rod. If you screw the drill stand to a scrap piece of wood, and then a batten to the underside of this, it can all be held in the vice. This makes a very stable drilling platform.

6 Use a flat bit to bore the hole. First make an indent with a bradawl, so that when you come to bore the hole you can align the drill spike accurately.

7 A good clean hole is achieved. Now repeat the operation on the other pivot plate.

8 The foot members have to be cut next. Look at the plan and identify the pieces that need to be cut. Use a clamp to fix the timber firmly to the bench and use a jigsaw to cut off the top sloping section.

9 The foot needs to have halving joints cut to take the foot-tie pieces. These not only give the see-saw stability but also strengthen the foot itself. Mark the joint out using a carpenter's square and Stanley knife.

10 Use a marking gauge to make a line to half the depth of the joint. The gauge's sharp spike leaves a good line to cut to.

11 Hatch in pencil the pieces that are to be cut out – it avoids confusion.

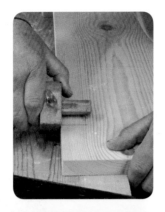

12 Turn the foot upside down in the vice and use a tenon-saw to cut down the lines.

13 Use a chisel to cut away the waste. This job has to be done on all four ends of the feet.

14 Next mark out the same joint at each end of the foot-tie members and, following the same procedure, cut out the halving joints. Matching joints having been cut in the feet and foot-tie members, they are now assembled.

15 Screw and glue the side-plates, feet and foot-tie pieces together.

16 Now work can begin on the main beam. This is made from three pieces of timber – the main plank and, beneath that, two lengths of timber that are glued and screwed to it. From the drawing you can see that the latter have to be shaped up, and holes have to be bored to take the pivot rod. This job needs to be done before fixing the timbers to the main plank. The picture shows all three timbers clamped together so that the positions for the screws can be measured out with a steel rule. Screws need to be fixed approximately every 75mm.

17 Drill and countersink the screw holes in the main beam. Before screwing and gluing the planks together check that the two pivot holes in the lower planks line up.

18 Hold the timbers together with clamps while the screws are driven in.

19 Next you need to make two handles. Bore holes to take the dowel rod handle, and round off the ends of the uprights to prevent injury.

20 Screw the handles to the main plank.

21 It's important to put bump blocks under either end of the main plank to prevent feet and/or fingers getting trapped. Use a smoothing plane to shape up the blocks. Plane an angle of approximately 30° on the bottom of each block.

22 Attach the blocks to the see-saw with screws.

23 Finally, cut the main pivot dowel rod and rub candle wax onto it to act as a lubricant. Then assemble the stand and the main beam by driving the pivot rod in. You'll find that once the see-saw has been used a few times the pivot rod will bed in and no other method of fixing is necessary.

Rope ladder

Climbing trees is as natural to an adventurous child as breathing, so there's little doubt this will be in demand – climbing a rope ladder is, after all, much easier than climbing a rope, because you have somewhere to put your feet!

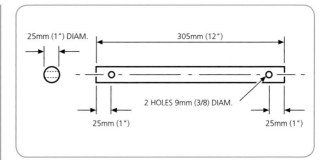

25mm (1") DIAM. 305mm (12")

2 HOLES 9mm (3/8) DIAM.

25mm (1") 25mm (1")

You will need:

- Drill stand and mains-powered drill
- 14mm Forstner drill bit
- Stanley knife
- Tenon-saw
- Marking gauge
- Expanding rule
- Carpenter's square
- Insulation tape
- Spacer rod – cut 1 @ 336 x 12mm (dowel)
- Rungs – cut 12 @ 355 x 45 x 30mm (knot-free timber)
- Polypropylene rope (max load 339kg) – 2 @ 3,660 x 12mm

1 This shows exactly what sort of timber not to buy. Knots weaken the timber and when weight is put on it the rung will eventually break. So avoid knotty timber. You'll have to pay a little extra for knot-free wood, but it's far better to be safe than sorry.

2 With the aid of an expanding rule and a carpenter's square, mark out the lengths of each rung.

IMPORTANT – SAFETY RULES

1. Make sure that an adult ties the rope ladder onto the tree, and remains on duty to supervise the first climbs.
2. It's vitally important that children are taught never to put their heads between the rungs, only their feet.
3. Only one child is allowed on the ladder at one time.
4. The ladder and the branch to which it's attached must be checked by an adult regularly.

It's advisable to buy a good polypropylene rope, which won't rot. This will come with details of its maximum recommended load – 339kg in the case of this project. It's best to be cautious and allow for the ladder having to occasionally carry really heavy individuals (parents and grandparents).

3 Cut the rungs to length with a tenon-saw. Note the cutting block, which prevents damage to the bench and holds the work steady as you saw.

4 A Mark the holes for the ropes at the end of each rung. A marking gauge makes this repetitive job much quicker. The gauge has an adjustable timber rod with a spike set in it, which you can set to scribe a short line the required distance in from each end of each rung.

B Reset the gauge to measure to the centre of the rung, and mark all the rungs.

C Pencil in the gauge lines. The point where they intersect is the centre of the hole to be drilled for the rope.

5 A Using an electric drill in a stand ensures that all the holes are at 90° in both directions. It's not essential, but when you have lots of holes to bore it does make it easier – and, of course, you get perfect holes. Don't be tempted to use a flat bit, use a Forstner bit, as this will drill a very clean hole. The Forstner bit needs to be, say, 2mm larger than the rope, otherwise you'll have problems threading the rope through.

B Once all the holes are bored put the rungs in a vice and run a smoothing plane along the edges so that the rungs are slightly rounded – plane a 'flat' strip approximately 3–4mm wide. This is a safety precaution: if the ladder catches a youngster the rung will then just bruise them rather than cut them.

6 When you cut polypropylene rope it immediately begins to unravel, and there's absolutely no way of threading it through the holes. To avoid this, bind insulating tape firmly round the end of the rope. Then leave a 2mm gap and bind a second piece of tape round the rope and, using a Stanley knife, cut the rope between the two pieces of tape. This stops the piece you want to use, and the rest of the rope on the drum, from fraying. You need to decide at this stage just how long you want the ladder to be, and cut the rope to a length that allows plenty of 'tie off' at the ends.

7 A The insulation tape binding will help you thread the rope through the holes.

B Tie a big knot on the underside of the lowermost rung to secure the rope. Allow a good 'tail' to prevent any possibility of it coming untied.

C Thread the second rung onto the rope. To avoid the fiddly job of having to measure the distance between the rungs each time, make yourself a spacer stick out of a piece of dowel or a batten offcut. Place the spacer between the rungs, put your thumb on the rope, and tie the next knot.

8 Continue tying knots and threading rungs until you've finished, checking with the spacer as you proceed. When you've finished your ladder will look like this.

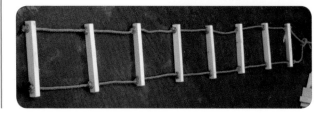

Doll's house

A three-storey town house in 1/12th scale

For many years a doll's house has been an item adored by girls of all ages. Basically it is a box, simple to make and can be as simple or elaborate as the maker (or recipient) wishes. We have chosen a easy design suitable for a beginner, but for ideas and inspiration take a look at the numerous magazines and websites available.

You will need:

- Electric jigsaw
- Hammer
- Sharp plane
- T square
- Clamps
- Sharp saw
- Sharp fine panel saw
- Stanley knife
- Drill
- Screwdriver
- Sanding block and sandpaper
- 1 sheet of 9mm MDF
- 1/2 sheet of 6mm MDF
- Piece of 800 × 500 × 4mm MDF
- PVA glue
- 'No More Nails'
- Wallpaper paste* – only use specialist doll's house paper paste; others can corrode the copper tape (if used)
- Windows*
- Front door*
- Interior doors*
- 4 × 9mm cranked hinges and screws*
- Copper tape wiring kit*
- Primer sealer
- 2 stair kits*
- Assortment of panel pins
- 4 × 19mm countersunk MDF or chipboard screws
- Wallpapers and paint
- Matt varnish
- Moisture-resistant MDF (green) is best if it's obtainable. In order to make optimum use of the sheet and avoid waste it's advisable to work out a cutting plan before cutting the individual pieces.

* Items marked with an asterisk are available by mail order from Armstrong Models 01780 444200 (email pat@patarmstrong.co.uk). For other sources of materials look at suppliers listed in specialist magazines

Cutting list

9mm MDF
- Sides – cut 2 @ 660 x 355mm
- Front door panels cut – 2 @ 648 x 302mm
- Floors – cut 4 @ 591 x 355mm
- Interior walls – cut 2 @ 355 x 203mm
- Interior wall (ground floor) – cut 1 @ 355 x 216mm
- Roof supports – cut 3 @ 615 x 76mm (cut to plan)
- House base – cut 1 @ 635 x 359mm

6mm MDF
- Roof base – cut 1 @ 635 x 388mm
- Back panel – cut 1 @ 660 x 410mm

4mm MDF
- Roof panels – cut 2 @ 400 x 336mm
- Front door overlap strip – cut 1 @ 648 x 50mm

END WALL

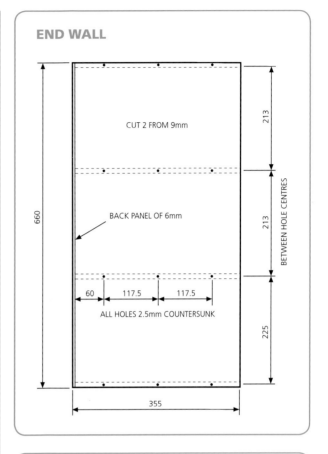

FLOOR

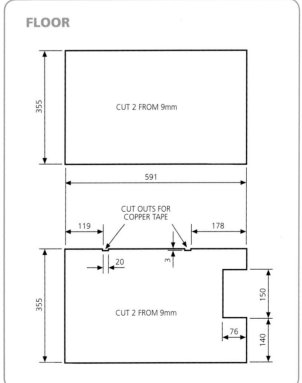

INTERIOR WALL

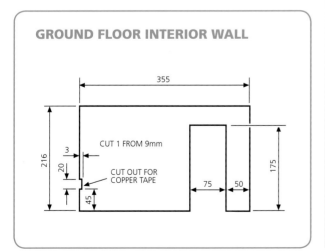

GROUND FLOOR INTERIOR WALL

LEFT-HAND FRONT

CUT 1 FROM 9mm

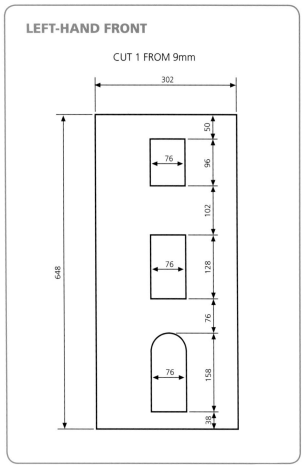

RIGHT-HAND FRONT

CUT 1 FROM 9mm

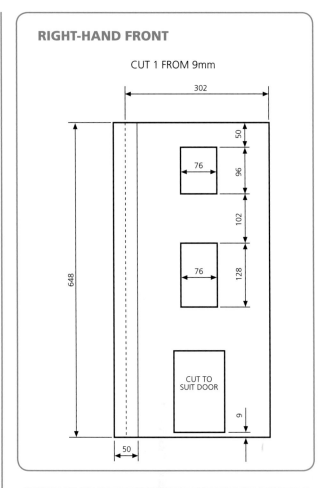

CUT TO
SUIT DOOR

FRONT PLAN

SUGGESTED COPPER
TAPE POSITION

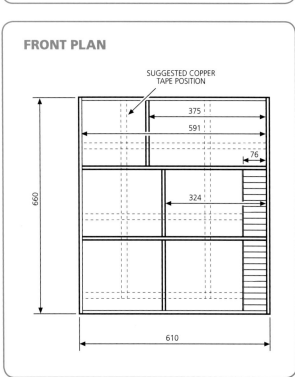

ROOF SUPPORTS

CUT 3 FROM 9mm

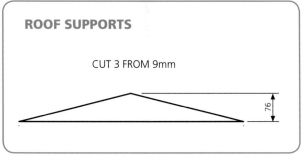

Before commencing construction study the plans, photographs and cutting list. The four floors and end walls must be exact in size and square. It would therefore be best to cut them on a table saw – your timber merchant will usually be able to do this. Cut all the other components to the measurements shown on the plans.

If the house is to be wired for electric lights, cut the necessary slots as shown on the plan.

The house must be built on a perfectly flat base. The ideal work-surface is a 40mm kitchen worktop (either a throw-out or an offcut).

Main house construction

1 Start with the four floors. Cut out the stairwell in two of them (see the first floor plan). Drill the end panel screw holes (see the end wall plans).

2 Glue and screw the end walls to the ground floor, keeping them square – drill a 1mm pilot hole to prevent the floors from splitting

3 Using the ground floor dividing wall (216mm high) as a support, glue and screw the first floor in place, making sure the stairwell is towards the front right-hand side. Using the 203mm high room walls as supports and guides, fit the third floor and roof, checking that they remain square as you proceed.

4 Cut a vertical slot 3mm wide and approximately 25mm long in the bottom left-hand corner of the back panel, 40mm from the bottom if the house is to be wired. Glue and pin the 6mm back panel in place – this will hold the house firm and square.

5 Cut door holes in the three dividing walls, and slots for the copper tape (if the house is to be wired) as shown on the plan

6 The walls can now be glued into place in the positions you've chosen for them – take care to keep them square. In this particular project the rooms are of nearly equal sizes.

7 To fit the front opening panels, begin by cutting out the door and window holes. The measurements given on the front door plans are for windows and doors suited to a town house, but if you prefer another type buy them before you cut the holes, as sizes differ.

8 Fit 9mm cranked hinges about 50mm from the top and bottom of the panels. To ensure adequate ground clearance, rest the door on a 3mm strip of wood whilst you screw the hinges to the inside wall of the house. Adjust as necessary to get a good fit. Next glue the 4mm front overlap strip onto one door panel as shown on the plan.

Roof construction

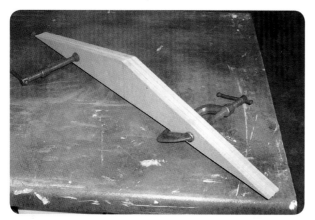

9 Cut all the components on the cutting list. For accuracy, the three angled roof supports are best clamped together and cut as one. These are then glued into place on the roof base.

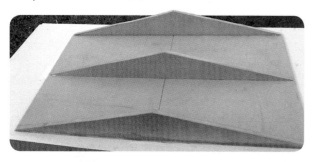

10 Chamfer the latter to follow the roof support angles. Chamfer two edges of the 4mm roof panels where they're to be joined at the ridge and glue and pin them in place. 'No More Nails' is ideal for this, as it's very strong and will fill any gaps. Clamp or tape them in place until they've set.

11 Sand the complete house to a smooth finish inside and out, removing any measuring marks and excess glue. A coat of primer sealer or PVA glue and water should also be applied inside and out at this point. When dry, lightly sand again and apply a coat of white emulsion to the interior.

Wiring your doll's house

To wire a doll's house of this type, one room deep, is easy. A suggested position for the copper tape is shown by the broken line on the plans. This is intended for wall and ceiling lights, but if fires or extra lamps are also required simply add extra tape. A copper-tape wiring kit is available that includes everything required for connections and so on.

Exterior finish

There are many finishes available, including paper, textured sheet, stone and brick. In this instance stone-textured paint was chosen, which can then be coloured to suit one's personal tastes using emulsion test pots. For added interest quoin strips can be fitted on each side of the front door panels and painted to match the centre overlap strip, usually in a natural stone colour.

- The windows and front door are now painted and fitted, and glazed if required.

- The exterior of the house should be given a coat of matt varnish to protect the paintwork.

Roof finish

Before covering the roof, paint the edges grey to blend in with the covering material. A slate-textured roof sheet was used in this instance, fixed with PVA adhesive and painted in a slate grey colour. A brick-patterned paper has been used on the gable to add interest, but it could also be finished to match the rest of the house.

Glue the roof into place, with an even overlap at each side but a larger overlap at the front to overhang the doors by about 10mm.

Interior decoration

The decoration of the individual rooms is entirely up to you. A large selection of 1/12th-scale wallpapers is readily available. Alternatively, a test pot of emulsion holds more than enough to paint a room. If you opt for paint the copper tape will need to be covered with plain paper first, otherwise it will show through the paint.

To wallpaper a room, measure the wall and cut the paper to the exact size, remembering to match the pattern at the corners. Paste the paper and carefully apply it to the wall, going over the doorways. Gently press it into place with a soft cloth or a 2in paintbrush (with its handle cut down) to remove air bubbles. Before the paper dries there'll most probably be a lot of creases and bubbles, but don't panic, these will disappear. When the paper is dry cut out the doorways and trim the edges with a scalpel. Fit the interior doors and frames when all the rooms have been decorated. Skirting boards can then be added if you so desire (paint them first).

Furniture

All styles of furniture are readily available to buy from specialist fairs or shops. *Dollshouse & Miniature* magazine also has regular features on making items of furniture.

The stairs

The stairs are fitted by screwing them in place from the outside, which allows for their removal at a later date for redecoration. They can be left open with handrails or boxed in with a piece of 4mm MDF.

Completion

Finally, the finished house should be mounted on its base, which can be painted a stone colour.

Ramps for bikes and skateboards

Ramps for skateboarding, rollerblading and BMX bike riding take a lot of punishment, and need to cope with severe stresses, sometimes in places you wouldn't expect them to. Of course, there's a huge difference between under-12s using a ramp and hulking great teenagers pounding it, but the ramps described here are designed to cope with heavy use.

A good ramp balances strength and weight – it should be strong enough to carry the kids with their bikes, blades or boards, but light enough for the kids to carry. With that in mind, you can replace parts marked * with lighter alternatives if you're building for younger riders. This will create a ramp that's easier for them to carry but will still be strong enough to ride on – but only when used by pre-teens!

No clever joints are required: the ramps just screw together, and the designs allows for easy repairs. If a cross-strut gets broken or a panel is damaged, you can usually replace it by simply taking out a few screws.

MATERIALS

For the frames, use carcassing or roofing timber that's been treated for exterior use. Avoid using pieces that have large knots in them.

For the plywood, it's important to get WPB (water and boil proof) timber, meaning exterior quality. Avoid sheets that have a lot of filler on both sides. There's no need to go to the extra expense of marine plywood: that's designed for more constant soaking and more regular immersion in water than any ramp is likely to get.

WOOD SIZES

Wood measurements can be confusing. '4 by 4', '4 by 2', and '2 by 1' are still often used as general terms. These translate approximately into 100 x 100mm, 100 x 50mm, and 50 x 25mm. However, sawn and planed wood varies in finished size. What you expect to be 50 x 25mm could be 47 x 18mm, while 50 x 100mm can end up 44 x 95mm. So check your wood carefully before cutting, and adjust your measurements if necessary. It's often easier to use direct measurement (holding the wood in position and marking the actual size), particularly when constructing a frame, rather than cutting everything in advance.

COUNTERSINKING

It's important to countersink screws properly on panels to ensure a comfortable and safe ride. It's also an excellent job for young assistants to do, as they can then see the value of doing it well.

TRANSITIONS

For skateboarders and rollerbladers, a good transition between ramp and ground is very important. BMXers aren't usually bothered, however, as the step up from ground to ramp isn't noticeable on a bike.

You can trim off the bottom edge of a ramp, so it lies closer to the ground, using a knife or sander. You can use sheet metal (about 2mm thick is good) for this, but it can be hard to find – try garden centres, pet equipment suppliers, agricultural suppliers and general engineering companies. Thick plastic or rubber sheeting can be a reasonable substitute. If you're really stumped, thick cardboard works for a while.

Whatever the material, cut it in a strip about 15–25mm wide and fix it to the bottom of the ramp with small screws. It can be helpful to cut about 30–80mm off the corners to avoid them turning up and becoming a hazard.

Building a grind box

This needs to withstand major collisions, and has to be very heavily built. It's also useful to be able to alter its height, to suit different ages and abilities. Consequently this design has legs that can be easily removed, replaced or cut down to suit to your riders' needs.

You will need:

- Circular saw
- Hand saw
- Drill with bits for wood (4mm, 5mm, 8mm) and metal (4mm)
- Countersink bit
- Angle grinder or hacksaw to cut angle iron
- Clamps or extra pairs of hands
- Screwdriver

- Extension lead
- Workbench
- RCD or safety plug
- Tape measure
- Markers
- Safety glasses
- Dust mask
- Ear defenders
- Gloves
- Try square
- Ruler

Materials

- Timber and plywood as per cutting list
- 2 x 2m lengths of angle iron
- 32 x 12g 3.5in screws for the legs
- 50 x 8g or 10g 2in screws for the panels
- 28 x 10g 2.5in screws for the cross-struts
- 12 x 10g 1.5in screws and 'penny washers' for fixing the angle iron
- 4 small screws (about 6g 0.5in)

Cutting list

12mm exterior/WPB plywood
- ☐ Top – 1 panel 600 x 1,700mm
- ☐ Sides – 2 panels 250 x 1,700mm*
  (A standard 2,440 x 1,220mm sheet provides a useful leftover for a launch-pad or small kicker.)

Carcassing softwood or roofing timber
- ☐ Sides – 4 x 1,700mm lengths of 47 x 25mm (2 x 1in)
- ☐ Cross-struts – 4 x 550mm lengths of 47 x 25mm (2 x 1in)
- ☐ Frame ends – 4 x 550mm lengths of 47 x 50mm (2 x 2in)
- ☐ Feet – 4 x 300mm* lengths of 100 x 100mm* (4 x 4in) exterior timber or fence post

* For under 13s, you can substitute 100 x 50mm (4 x 2in) for the legs; also 300mm legs may be too high to begin with, and can be reduced to 260mm. Side panels can be 6mm ply.

1 Much of the strength comes from the metal edge. You may have to search around for a suitable piece of angle iron for the top edges. For this box we've used a simple, inexpensive piece of heavy iron intended for fencing.

Using an angle grinder or hacksaw, cut the angle iron down to 1.7m, removing its pointed end. Drill and countersink a 4 or 5mm hole about 30mm from the cut end, and extra holes every 300mm or so if it doesn't already have them.

2 Mark out the top plywood panel with the position of the frames. Position the 47 x 50mm end pieces and 47 x 25mm cross-struts in place and draw round them: drill and countersink holes around the edges (about 10mm from the edge at the corners and at about 300mm intervals) and roughly in the centre of where the cross-struts will be.

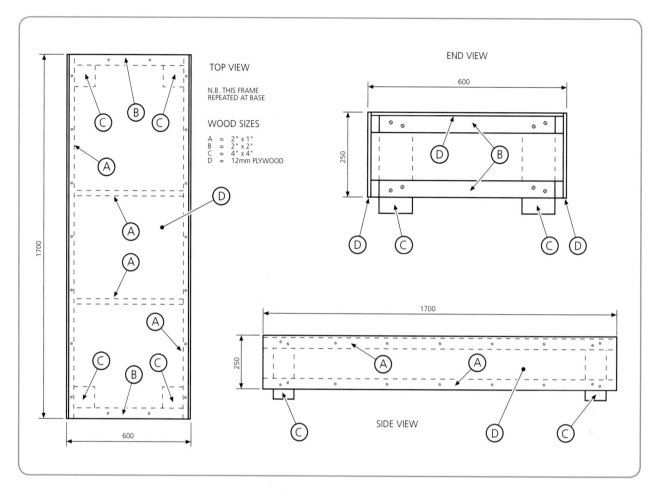

TOP VIEW

N.B. THIS FRAME
REPEATED AT BASE

WOOD SIZES

A = 2" x 1"
B = 2" x 2"
C = 4" x 4"
D = 12mm PLYWOOD

END VIEW

SIDE VIEW

3 Holding each piece of timber underneath the panel in turn, drill through and screw them in place with 2in screws.

4 Holding the cross-struts in position, drill, countersink and screw in place using 2in screws.

5 Drill and countersink holes through the sidepieces of the frame and screw in 2in screws at about 300mm intervals.

6 With the top frame constructed and attached to the top panel, start to assemble the lower frame by laying the new pieces on top of the first frame as a measuring guide.

7 Hold the pieces together, drill, countersink and screw at the corners and at the cross-struts. The new frame doesn't need to be rigid at this stage.

8 Take the side panels and screw them to the top frame, aligning the top edge of each side panel to the top edge of the top panel.

9 Put the lower frame in position at the base of the side panels. Drill, countersink and screw at about 300mm intervals.

10 Fix the legs in place using 3.5in screws, four through the end frames, four through the side of the box.

11 Put the angle iron on each edge. Screw in place using screws and penny washers.

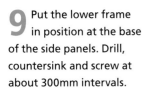

Useful cutting techniques

HOW TO CUT PLYWOOD IN A STRAIGHT LINE

Cutting plywood in a straight line with a circular saw can be tricky. It's easier if you firmly clamp a straight piece of timber to the plywood and use it as a ruler against which to rest the saw.

CUTTING METAL

Thin metal can be cut with strong metal shears.

Thicker metal is harder to cut – use an angle grinder, or a circular saw fixed with a metal-cutting blade.

Making a kicker

This is quite a large, heavy kicker, built to survive teenagers. For a more portable one for younger riders, use 6mm plywood, and scale down the design to about 500 x1,000mm.

Cutting list

12mm exterior/WPB plywood
(6mm is adequate for most under 13s' use)
■ Top – 750 x 1,500mm
Approx 100 x 50mm (4 x 2in) exterior timber
■ Feet – 2 x 400mm lengths
Approx 47 x 25mm (2 x 1in) exterior timber
■ Side-strengtheners – 2 x 1,300mm lengths
■ Cross-struts – 3 x 700mm lengths and
   1 x 650mm length (the top cross-strut)
■ Side bracers – 2 x 400mm lengths
■ Front bracers – 1 x 800mm length and
   1 x 720mm length

You will need:

- Circular saw
- Hand saw
- Drill with bits for wood (4mm, 5mm, 8mm) and metal (4mm) if using metal transition
- Countersink drill bit
- Clamps or extra pairs of hands
- Screwdriver
- Extension lead
- Workbench
- RCD or safety plug
- Tape measure
- Markers
- Safety glasses and dust mask

- Ear defenders and gloves
- Try square and ruler
- Timber and plywood as per cutting list
- 4 x 12g 3.5in screws for fixing the legs
- 25 x 8g 2in screws for fixing cross-struts to panel
- 20 x 10g 2.5in screws for fixing cross-struts through sides and for fixing bracers

The initial framework is constructed in the same way as for the grind box, with the pieces fixed directly onto the top panel.

1 Cut the two feet as in the diagram. To get roughly the right angle for the ramp, measure one side at 400mm, the other at 380mm.

2 Drill and countersink holes in the top panel for two 3.5in screws for each foot. Hold one foot in place and drill through the panel into it. Insert screws and screw in firmly, but leaving a little bit of play. Repeat for other foot.

3 Mark the side struts using direct measurement, holding them against the legs to get the correct angle.

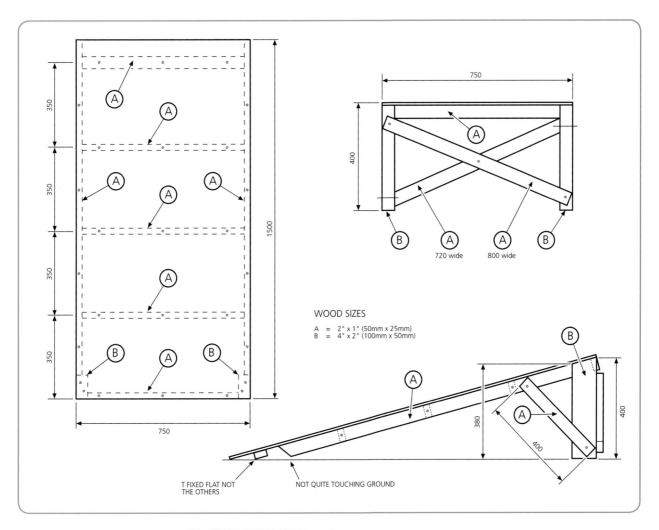

350

350

350

350

350

1500

750

750

400

WOOD SIZES

A = 2" x 1" (50mm x 25mm)
B = 4" x 2" (100mm x 50mm)

720 wide   800 wide

400

380

400

A

T FIXED FLAT NOT THE OTHERS

NOT QUITE TOUCHING GROUND

4 Cut each side strut at this end, then mark and cut the other end at an angle of about 45° so that it's about 20mm clear of the ground when fixed.

5 Clamp or hold each side-strengthener to the edge of the panel and drill and countersink holes through the panel every 300mm or so. Fix the strengtheners in place using 8g 2in screws.

6 To fix the cross-struts, drill through each end and insert 10g 2.5in screws. Add two or three countersunk screws through the top of the panel.

7 Position the lowest cross-strut so that it just touches the ground, setting it flat rather than vertical. Drill through from the top, countersink, and secure with three or four screws. This strut probably won't touch the side struts, and doesn't need reinforcing screws from the side.

8 Tighten the leg screws and fix the side bracers between the legs and the top panel using 10g 2.5in screws on each side.

9 Fix the first front bracer – find the right angle to cut by marking using direct measurement.

10 Fix the second front bracer to the legs using 10g 2.5in screws at top and bottom.

11 Fix the second front bracer, using 2.5in screws at each end and one 2in screw in the middle (into the other bracer).

12 If required, reduce the step between panel and ground by cutting or sanding off a few millimetres off the edge, and/or cut metal sheet for a smoother transition if required.

13 Use a nail punch to mark positions for drilling.

14 Cut about 30–60mm off both corners of panel.

15 Using a metal bit, drill holes for four short screws and screw in place. Countersink if necessary.

Building a quarter pipe

This design has a 2.2m radius curve, but with small adjustments you can make it 2.0m for quite a steep ramp, or 2.4m for quite a mellow one.

You will need:

- Circular saw (or hand saw) for long cuts of plywood
- Hand saws
- Drill with bits for wood (4mm, 5mm, 8mm and countersink) and metal (5mm and countersink)
- Angle grinder or hacksaw to cut coping
- Screwdrivers

- Clamps or extra pairs of hands
- Extension lead
- Workbench
- RCD or safety plug
- Tape measure
- Markers
- Safety glasses, dust mask, ear defenders, gloves
- Try square and ruler

Screws

- 12 3in x 12g to fix main frame pieces A and B
- 3 3.5in x 12g to fix scaffold pipe
- 80 1.7sin x 10g for all other framework and support blocks

- Approx 100 1.25in x 8g (or 35mm x 4mm stainless steel – making repairs easier) for fixing panels
- 6 0.5in x 6g or similar for transition

Cutting list

- A 1,220mm length of coping or scaffold pipe (some scaffold hire companies will sell small lengths), drilled with three 5mm holes and countersunk (see diagram). Standard diameter is 50mm.
- A 15-25mm x 1,220mm piece of sheet metal, 2-3mm thick, for the transition (optional).

Carcassing softwood or roofing timber
- 100mm x 50mm (4x2)
- Size A – 3 pieces x 1,190mm (2 for platform frame top and 1 for rear base strut)
- Size B – 3 pieces x 600mm (for platform frame top)
- 50mm x 25mm (2x1)
- Size C – 8 pieces x 1,180mm (for struts)
- Size D – 16 pieces (from offcuts) about 80-100mm (for strut supports)

WPB plywood
- 6mm – 2 sheets* 1,220mm x 1,440mm (for ramp surface)
- 12mm – 1 piece 1,220mm x 700mm (for the platform, piece E)
- 18mm – 1 sheet 1,220 x 2,440mm (for the walls)

* A single 6mm plywood sheet is strong enough for most under-11s.

HOW TO DRAW A LARGE CURVE
Improvise a compass either by either tying string of the right length to a pencil at one end and an old screwdriver at the other, or by taking a spare piece of 2 x 1in/50 x 27mm timber about 2.4m long and drilling two holes in it, one for the pencil and the other for the screwdriver.

HOW TO CUT PLYWOOD IN A CURVE
Cutting a curve in thick plywood is a challenge to a jigsaw and its operator. One good method is to cut a series of shallow curves just touching the line of the main curve. This produces an undulating cut that can be rounded and neatened with a sander. Slight unevenness doesn't matter, as the panels take their curve mainly from the cross-struts.

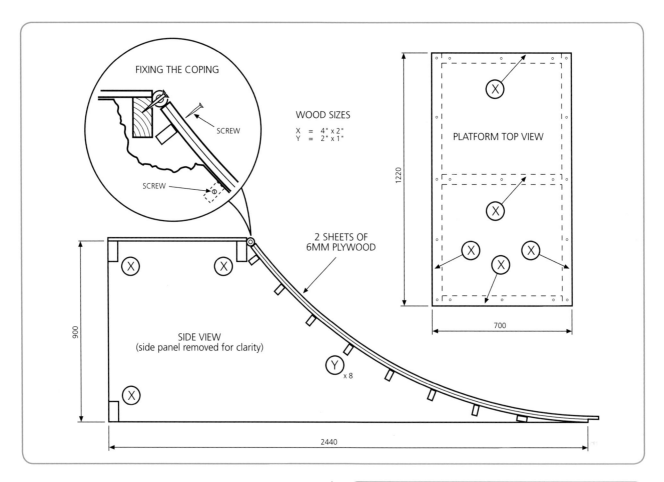

FIXING THE COPING

SCREW

SCREW

WOOD SIZES

X = 4" x 2"
Y = 2" x 1"

2 SHEETS OF
6MM PLYWOOD

PLATFORM TOP VIEW

1220

700

SIDE VIEW
(side panel removed for clarity)

900

2440

HOW TO BEND PLYWOOD

Bending 12mm plywood is very hard, so this design uses two sheets of 6mm plywood laid on top of each other, which is much easier and almost as strong. This has two advantages: 6mm plywood is fairly easily bent; and when it starts to wear or is damaged you can simply replace one sheet, at less than a 12mm sheet would cost.

You can fix the two panels on the ramp without soaking them. However, it's easier – and the panels seem to last longer – if you don't fix them while they're still very flat, so encourage them to assume a curve by resting them on the ramp, weighted down, for a day or two before you screw them in place.

FIXING TWO PANELS

It's better to fix each curved panel separately. This involves dozens more screws, but has structural advantages as well as making it easier to replace the top sheet if it becomes damaged or worn. Screws driven into the top panel need to be slightly staggered from those between the bottom panel and the frame.

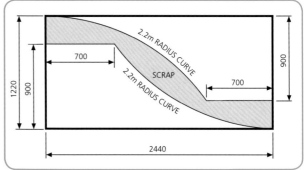

1220

900

700

2.2m RADIUS CURVE

SCRAP

2.2m RADIUS CURVE

900

700

2440

1 Mark and cut out all the wood. Clamp the two plywood side pieces together.

2 Cut a notch as shown in the photo below – this is to accommodate the scaffold pipe.

3 Drill 5mm holes at 25mm intervals along the curved edge, through both panels.

4 Lean one of the two side pieces against a workbench or hold it up, pushing one 'Size A' timber piece in the top corner.

5 Drill through and screw in place, leaving a little play. Screw to the other side piece in the same way, again leaving a little play.

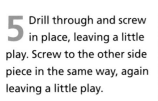

6 Hold another 'Size A' piece at the base at the rear of the ramp. Drill through, and screw at both ends.

7 Take the remaining 'Size A' piece, align it just behind the notch for the scaffold pipe, and drill and screw it in place. Tighten the screws of all three pieces, keeping the frame as square as possible.

8 Place the scaffold pipe on top of the notches, drill 4mm holes and screw it into the front frame piece.

9 Hold the 'Size B' pieces at either side, by hand or using clamps. Screw in position from the outside.

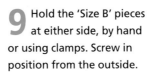

10 Complete the main frame by screwing the remaining 'Size B' piece into the middle.

11 Place piece E on top of the frame. Drill holes at about 300mm intervals round the edge, countersink and screw. Insert extra screws along the middle piece.

12 Using a spare block to measure the precise position, hold the 'Size D' blocks under the drill holes in the side panels and screw in place. These blocks will help to hold the struts at exactly the same height as the side panels.

13 Fix blocks for all the struts on both sides, except those for the top strut closest to the scaffold pipe, which can be omitted.

14 Fix the bottom strut to lie flat on the ground without any block underneath.

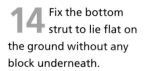

15 Screw the struts in position, resting them on the blocks and drilling through from the outside.

16 The next bit is difficult, and extra pairs of strong hands will be useful. Hold the first ramp panel exactly in position. Then, while one or two people hold it down, another needs to pin it in place with several screws, drilling holes but not countersinking at this stage. Fix screws along the top at about 300mm intervals and down both edges at about 200mm intervals. Check the panel aligns correctly all the way down. If it doesn't, unscrew it and try again.

18 Use a ruler or piece of wood to mark out where the struts lie: drill through the panel into the struts at 250–300mm intervals. Repeat the process with the second panel.

17 Pressing hard on the panel, drill, countersink and fix some of the screws. Remove, countersink and screw in again the screws you put in earlier. Work down the panel in rows, drilling, countersinking and screwing into the sides and across the panels.

19 If a transition is required, cut your metal sheet to fit the panel base. Drill through both metal and plywood, countersink and screw in position.

For additional stability, especially on uneven surfaces, you can add diagonal bracers similar to those on the kicker (page 186). Use two extra pieces of 4x2 or 2x2, and direct measurement, fixing them in between the side panels.

For skateboarding tips and tricks see pages 48-51

Model railway layout

There can be no better way to bring a Dad and his children together than to build a model railway. It can be simple or complex, large or small, permanent or temporary, and can provide an introduction to a rewarding hobby that may last a lifetime. Dad may need to do the initial woodwork, but once that's done the real fun can begin – planning the layout, laying the track, constructing the scenery and choosing the locomotives and rolling stock can involve everybody. It's a hobby almost without limits.

How to get started

Take the family to a model railway exhibition. There's always a lot to see and do at these, including demonstrations of railway modelling techniques by people who are more than happy to give advice. You'll see fine examples of layouts large and small, and there'll be trade stands displaying a wide range of new and second-hand items including locomotives, rolling stock, scenery, accessories and reference books. This in itself will provide a good few hours of entertainment, so keep an eye on the local press – and lamp-post signs – for nearby exhibitions. There's also likely to be a local club in your area, which will always be on the lookout for new members.

Model shops are worth a visit too. Many have much the same atmosphere as an exhibition and staff demonstrate the same willingness to help. And there's no shortage of shops – just look through any of the monthly hobby magazines (*Railway Modeller*, *Model Rail*, *Rail Express*, *British Railway Modelling* etc), which in addition to a wealth of practical and inspiring articles contain adverts for shops and mail order specialists. Shops and exhibitions are also listed on the very useful www.ukmodelshops. co.uk website.

At the very least such initial reconnaissance should enable you to get an idea of the different scales available. Most modellers start with either 00 or the smaller N scale, depending on the space available. A very good range of kits and rolling stock is available in both. Model scales and gauges (the distance between the inside surfaces of the running rails on the track) are explained in detail in most basic railway modelling books.

Having decided on your scale, an oval track with a siding is the traditional starting layout for many modellers. Train sets in this format are produced by companies such as Hornby or Bachmann and retail for between £100 and £200 at the time of writing, or even below £100 if Thomas the Tank Engine is your choice. For this sum you'll get the train, some track and a controller, and your children will be able to start enjoying their railway almost immediately! It's a priority to get trains running in order to hold your youngsters' interest, but a great deal more fun can yet be had, and for those children who enjoy cutting, gluing and painting the best is yet to come.

Baseboard modules

To get the most out of a railway set, your children will need a baseboard on which to set it up – it's this which transforms a simple railway set into a model railway.

Taking a modular approach to baseboard construction will enable the layout to begin in a modest way and then develop as time and money permit. A useful size for modules is 48 x 24in (1,220 x 610mm). Modules of this size can then be used in multiples to construct a baseboard of the size that your track occupies.

The following principles of baseboard construction are fine for a stand-alone layout, one that's attached to a wall, or as part of a larger modular layout that has to be dismantled for transport or stored in a limited space.

Begin by getting your children to lay the track out in the formation they want, and then measure its overall dimensions. Remember to allow some extra space outside the track area to accommodate trackside scenery and backdrop scenes.

The usual material for the framework is 2 x 1in (50 x 25mm) planed softwood. The top should be of 12mm Sundeala, 15mm chipboard or 9mm plywood. Sundeala is easier to cut, but chipboard or plywood provide greater overall rigidity. Many large DIY product suppliers will cut large sheets of wood to size for easy transportation, but a

You will need:

- Hammer
- Cross-cut or tenon-saw
- Screwdrivers
- Power- or hand-drill
- Tape measure
- Engineer's square
- Bradawl
- G-clamps
- Sanding block
- Pencil
- Portable workbench

Materials per baseboard:

- 1 sheet Sundeala, chipboard or plywood cut to size
- 3 9ft (2,700mm) pieces of 2" x 1" (50mm x 25mm) minimum dimensions, planed softwood
- 20 1/2 in No.8 steel countersunk woodscrews
- 24 1in No.8 steel countersunk woodscrews
- White PVA glue
- Red Dog baseboard alignment dowels (two pairs per joint)
- 75 x 8mm hexagonal-head bolts for connecting multiple baseboards
- Wing nuts and 38mm diameter washers (two sets per joint)
- 50 x 5mm pan-head screws for each demountable joint
- 5mm pronged T-nuts and 25mm washers for each demountable joint

The specialised baseboard fittings can be found in the advertisement pages of model railway magazines.

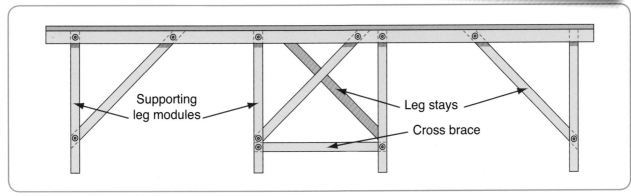

Supporting leg modules

Leg stays

Cross brace

builders' merchant might offer a better deal on the whole purchase. Support legs, if fitted, would need to be thicker: they must be solid and yet capable of being dismantled when necessary.

Since the principles used to construct the baseboard frames are equally applicable to the support framework, step-by-step guidance isn't necessary.

The structure described here has a rigid frame for the middle board, which could also be used for a smaller stand-alone layout. Additional frames for extended layouts are attached 'piggy-back' fashion to the central unit, and therefore only need legs at one end. The schematic diagram illustrates the principle. This system makes it possible to accommodate a huge range of layout configurations

The rigidity of the main board gives the whole layout its stability. The bolt-together system of main board and extension pieces means that the layout is portable and can be dismantled easily for storage or transport.

Use screwed and glued butt joints throughout. Check the measurements frequently as construction proceeds, since the dimensions of planed wood from different suppliers can vary noticeably.

To add extra rigidity to the structure, you can fit two 6mm ply triangular reinforcing pieces to the top joints.

The leg modules, which are the same width as the baseboard frames, require two noggins inside which the legs fit. Noggins are small bracing pieces that allow the legs to be attached to the boards with screws and T-nuts.

All the connecting joints on the support framework and board couplings are identical and use standard fittings.

There are many ways to make a system that can be dismantled; this one uses 5mm pan-head machine screws, 'penny washers' and matching 5mm pronged T-nuts. The prongs on the T-nuts hold them in the wood and obviate the need for extra washers and wing nuts. Fit these with care to ensure that the nuts and the holes in the wood are perpendicular to the wood. This will prevent cross-threading.

Use G-clamps to hold the two parts together and drill a 6mm hole through both pieces. The hole can be widened with a 7mm drill to accommodate the T-nut.

Finally, it's worth giving consideration to the overall height of the baseboard. Kitchen worktop level is common and convenient for modelling and operating whilst seated. However, if it can be raised a little higher the visual effect at eye-level is enhanced and can be spectacular for younger family members – though you'll need to ensure it isn't too high for them to see or play with!

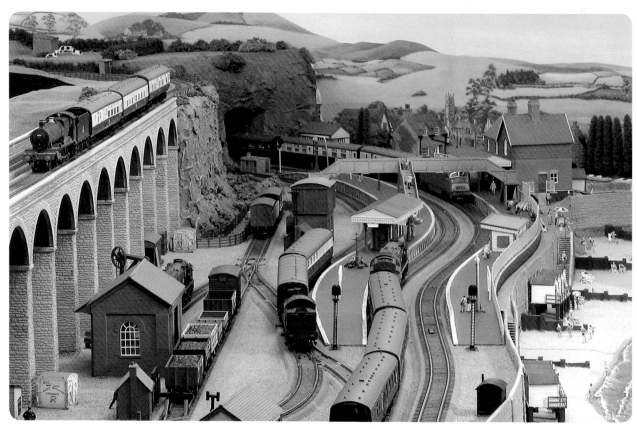

Buildings and scenery

Once a good baseboard has been built and the track has been satisfactorily laid it's time to transform your layout into an image of the location you want to depict. This could be a faithful representation of a real-life railway setting, either historical or contemporary, or an entirely imaginary scene. Either way, there are a number of scenic techniques that will make a layout effective and personal to the builder.

At its simplest, the addition of some ready-made buildings, track ballast and ground cover will make an initial difference. Then there are roads, rivers, fields and trees. A good look through the modelling magazines and accessory catalogues will provide plenty of ideas! Hornby produce complete 00 buildings in their Skaledale series and N scale buildings in their Lyddle End series.

If you're modelling an actual location, a good source of reference material will be invaluable. Libraries, photographs, magazines and the Internet can help greatly. Look at the Hornby, Bachmann, Peco, and Dapol websites, plus any others given in magazine adverts.

The range of kits on the market for N and 00 scales is vast, and increasing numbers of ready-made buildings are also becoming available for those who require more instant results. Plastic kits remain popular – all children love them – and cardboard building kits can be very effective too. Apart from adding scenic items to an existing layout, kits of viaducts and bridges can be used as integral components of its overall design. You and your children can enjoy building the kits together; they range from very simple to quite complex, so each of you can enjoy them in your own way.

The Ratio & Wills catalogue gives a very good idea of the extent and possibilities open to plastic kit constructors. You should also visit the www.peco-uk.co.uk website, which is a mine of information and advice.

Ideally a few tools are required to build plastic kits – hobby cutters, scalpel or craft knife, razor saw, tweezers, jeweller's pliers, pin chuck and drill bits, a set of needle files, an engineering ruler and a cutting mat – but much of this equipment will last for years, so the initial expense will set your family up in the hobby for a long time.

Remember to ensure that your children work in a well-ventilated area when they're cementing plastic parts together. Also, it's better to use liquid polystyrene cement applied with a small brush rather than squeezed out of a tube, since it's much easier and cleaner to handle. A tube of cyanoacrylate (superglue) will come in handy for attaching metal parts to plastic or other metal parts, but you need to be sure that children know how to use it safely.

Difficult though it will probably be, try to encourage

your children to take plenty of time building kits: the experience can be very enjoyable in itself, and the end results will be so much better than if they rush. And make sure that they obey all the safety instructions when they're using cutting tools, glue and solvents.

The kit parts should be cut out on a cutting mat placed on a firm flat surface. Carefully trim or file off moulding flashes with a scalpel or needle file and do a dry assembly first to see how the components go together. Incidentally, it's often a wise idea to paint the smallest parts while they're still on the sprue.

Before applying the cement, it's best to hold the two parts firmly together. Then use a brush to run a small amount of cement into the unseen side of the joint; capillary action will draw it along the joint surfaces. Wait for a few seconds, and the joint will be solvent welded. At the end of the gluing session, use thinners to clean the glue brush.

Painting

Kits are often produced in a colour of plastic that's acceptable for its intended purpose. However, the slightly shiny and perhaps unrealistically perfect surface might eventually become irritating. The solution is to give it a matt paint finish and apply 'weathering' (see below). Children can get thoroughly involved with painting.

Some equipment and materials will be required, such as good quality sable brushes Nos. 000–1 with pointed round tips for detail work and Nos. 0–2 with wide round and flat tips for washes and large areas. Then, of course, you need paint. Cellulose/acrylic undercoat in the form of a car spray aerosol is best. Use white, grey, red-oxide or black, depending on which colour is nearest to the finish of the final model. Only a very thin undercoat is needed.

Matt enamel paint can be bought in very small tins that are convenient to store and provide enough paint to use on a number of small models. Several layers of thinned paint will produce a finer result because unthinned paint doesn't flow so easily into the smaller crevices of intricate mouldings. Use the correct paint thinner, but observe the ventilation and safety instructions supplied.

Make sure children don't rush the painting process, and allow plenty of time for each layer to dry before they apply the next. If the previous layer isn't fully dry, the next brush stroke will drag it off!

It's best to start with the lighter colours and use masking tape where relevant. The difficult corners and smallest details need to be done first, and then the larger areas.

Weathering? What's that?

Once the kit is painted with enamels and has a pristine appearance, it will look slightly too good to be true. No outside structure is in perfect condition. Roofs are stained by birds, walls have uneven patches, and the weather takes its toll on paintwork. So, many modellers like to slightly 'spoil' the finish to add realism; this is called 'weathering'. Many books and articles have been written on the subject, but the principles are fundamentally simple.

Use a wide, flat-ended brush and matt plastic enamel paint in shades such as light grey, dark grey and brown to replicate the staining and dirt caused by pollution, industrial activity and bad weather; almost any dull colour can be used to create the desired effect. Drain out most of the oily liquid in the top of the paint tin before you mix it. When you apply the paint your brush must be almost dry, so wipe it on scrap paper to remove most of the paint and try it on an unseen part of the model or a piece of scrap plastic. Brush in a downwards direction to imitate the effect of rain washing the dirt down the surface. The more localised effect of moss requires finer brushwork using green and yellow acrylic. Encourage your children to look at actual buildings to get a realistic idea of colours and stain patterns.

Variants of these techniques can be used for rural, industrial and lineside buildings such as the locomotive smoke stains over the mouth of a tunnel or the white residue on buildings at a cement works. White 'concrete cancer' or the dark rust stains on ferro-concrete buildings offer further possibilities. Your children will enjoy experimenting on scrap plastic to get the best weathering effects! You can even buy them a cheap 'sacrificial' kit on which to try out new weathering experiments.

Why are you all still sitting there?

As you can see, railway modelling has limitless possibilities beyond simply running trains round and round an undecorated layout.

Railway Modelling by Iain Rice (published by Haynes) describes in readable detail exactly how to approach every aspect of building a model railway. Note that special attention should always be paid to good track-laying and wiring, which are absolutely vital to a successful layout and will permanently affect its reliability and smooth running and ensure that it remains fun to play with for many years to come. Your local club and the various magazines can provide plenty of help regarding track wiring and DCC (Digital Command Control), which is the modern way to control trains, but none of the technical stuff is very difficult, and it will give you as well as your children something new to think about!

How things work

Car engine 202

Aeroplane 204

Electricity 206

Telephone 208

Radio 210

Television 212

Computer 214

Car engine

A car engine is actually quite a simple machine that converts chemical energy – stored in the fuel – into mechanical energy in the form of motion.

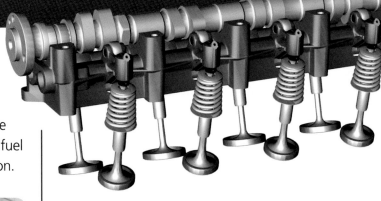

Above: A typical camshaft and valve arrangement. As the camshaft turns it pushes on rockers, which push the valves open against the springs which normally hold them shut. (Ford)

The engine consists of a number of cylinders – anything from two (quite rare) to 16 (the most advanced high-performance cars). The most common number for everyday cars is four. Each cylinder has a piston inside, and is sealed at the top by the cylinder head. The cylinders are located in the cylinder block, the largest single component of the engine.

The cylinder head contains inlet and exhaust valves. The valves allow the air/fuel mixture into the cylinder, and burnt gases out into the exhaust system. The valves are opened and closed by a camshaft, which is driven from the crankshaft, usually by a belt (the 'cam belt' or 'timing belt') or sometimes a chain.

The fuel needs to be mixed with air to enable it to burn, and the air/fuel mixture is burnt inside a 'combustion chamber' at the top of the cylinder. The air and fuel are mixed together either in the inlet tract, which is separated from the combustion chamber by the inlet valve(s), or in the combustion chamber itself.

Almost all engines produced since the early 1990s (both petrol and diesel) use fuel injection, which means that the fuel is injected under pressure into the engine. The fuel is injected either into the inlet tract, where it's mixed with the air; or, on the latest direct injection (DI) engines, directly into the combustion chamber.

As each piston moves up its cylinder it compresses the air/fuel mixture, and when the mixture ignites and burns it expands very quickly and pushes the piston back down the cylinder. The bottom of each piston is fastened to a connecting rod, which is in turn fastened to the crankshaft. As the pistons move up and down, the connecting rods push the crankshaft round. The crankshaft carries all the power from the engine to the transmission, which drives the car's wheels.

Most car engines are four-stroke, which means that each piston moves up and down twice (two up-strokes, and two down-strokes) to produce one pulse of power.

Left: A cutaway view of a Ford 1.8 litre engine. (Ford)

Below: The air/fuel mixture is mixed together in the combustion chamber and, in a petrol engine, is then ignited by a spark plug. (Ford)

Various systems are fitted to keep the engine running smoothly, including an oil system, cooling system and engine management system.

Oil system

An engine needs oil to reduce the friction between its moving parts and to help to keep it cool.

When the engine is stopped, the oil is stored in a tray called the sump, at the bottom of the cylinder block. When the engine is running, oil is pumped from the sump to all the moving parts. The oil passes through an oil filter, which catches small particles of dirt. Eventually this filter will clog up, so it must be changed whenever the engine oil is changed during servicing.

Cooling system

The cooling system stops the engine overheating and keeps it at the best temperature for it to work efficiently.

The coolant is pumped around the engine by the coolant (water) pump, collecting heat from the engine components as if flows through. The hot coolant passes from the engine to the radiator (mounted at the front of the car, under the bonnet), where it's cooled by the air forced through the radiator as the car moves forward.

Engine management system

The engine management system is controlled by an electronic control unit (ECU) connected to various sensors and actuators fitted around the engine. These sensors monitor the engine and send information back to the ECU. The ECU then processes all the information and sends signals to the ignition, fuel injection and emission control systems in order to manage the engine efficiently.

Four-stroke cycle

In a four-stroke engine the four strokes are:

1 Intake stroke ('suck') – the piston moves down, sucking air/fuel mixture into the cylinder through the inlet valve.

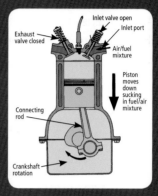

2 Compression stroke ('squeeze') – the valves are closed and the piston moves up, compressing (squashing) the mixture until it's ignited by a spark (petrol engines) or the heat and pressure (diesel engines) at the top of the stroke.

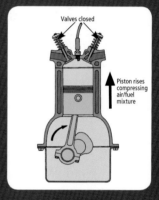

3 Power stroke ('bang') – the piston is pushed down by the force of the controlled explosion as the burning mixture expands.

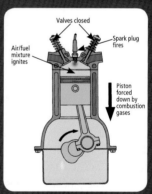

4 Exhaust stroke ('blow') – the piston moves back up the cylinder (because of the momentum produced during the power stroke), and the burnt gases are pushed out through the open exhaust valve. The cycle then starts again, with another intake stroke.

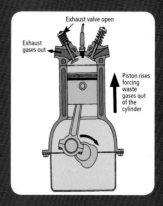

Crown Copyright RAF

Aeroplane

Aeroplanes fly by harnessing the forces of nature, so let's take a look at what's involved.

An aeroplane has four forces acting on it:

The four forces that act on an aeroplane when it's flying

LIFT

DRAG

THRUST   GRAVITY

- ■ Gravity – the weight of the aeroplane.
- ■ Lift – an 'aerodynamic' force produced by the wings, which depends on the shape of the wing and the speed of the air flowing over it.
- ■ Drag – an 'aerodynamic' force caused by air resistance, which depends on the shape of the aeroplane.
- ■ Thrust – generated by the aeroplane's propeller or jet engine.

Lift and drag are called 'aerodynamic' forces because they exist due to the aeroplane's movement through the air.

The four forces work in pairs – lift opposes gravity, and thrust opposes drag. The forces have to be controlled to allow the aeroplane to fly. For an aeroplane to take off, thrust must overcome drag to allow the aircraft to move forwards, and lift must overcome the aeroplane's weight before it can become airborne. When an aeroplane is flying straight-and-level at a constant speed, thrust exactly equals drag, and lift exactly equals the aeroplane's weight. For the aeroplane to land, thrust must be less than drag, and lift must be less than the aeroplane's weight.

Gravity, drag and thrust are fairly easy to understand, but lift needs a little more explanation. It's produced by an aeroplane's wings. To see how this happens, hold a piece of paper in one hand, with your hand resting under your chin, then blow over the top of the paper: the paper will rise into the air. If you slide a paperclip onto the end of the paper, the paper will still rise – the harder you blow, the more paperclips can be lifted. The same thing happens if you pull the paper through the air instead of blowing over it.

This effect can be explained using a principle discovered by a Swiss scientist called Daniel Bernoulli in the mid-1700s. Bernoulli found that an increase in the speed of any fluid (air is a fluid) always goes hand-in-hand with a decrease in its pressure. When you blow over the paper, you're increasing the speed – and so lowering the pressure – of the air on top of the paper, so that the higher pressure under the paper pushes it up. This is exactly how a wing works.

A wing has a special shape, with a curved upper surface. When air hits the front edge of the wing some of it travels underneath and some goes over the top. To reach the back edge of the wing, the air passing over the curved top must travel further (and so faster) than the air passing underneath. Because the speed of the air going over the top is increased its pressure is reduced, so the pressure underneath is higher than the pressure above, which pushes the wing up.

An aeroplane therefore flies because its wings are designed to produce enough lift to overcome its weight.

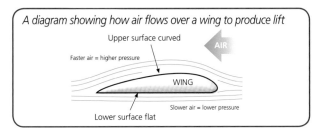

A diagram showing how air flows over a wing to produce lift

Controlling an aeroplane

An aeroplane changes direction by moving around one or more of three axes of rotation:

■ Lateral axis – a horizontal line between the wing tips; movement around this axis is called 'pitch'.

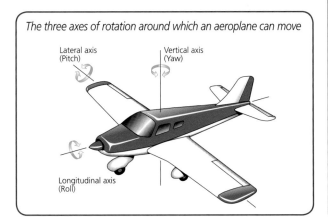

The three axes of rotation around which an aeroplane can move

■ Vertical axis – a vertical line through the middle of the fuselage; movement about this axis is called 'yaw'.
■ Longitudinal axis – a horizontal line running through the nose and tail; movement about this axis is called 'roll'.

The pilot controls the aeroplane using two main controls – the control column (or 'stick') and the rudder pedals, which operate movable control surfaces fitted to the aeroplane's wings and tail to control pitch, yaw and roll:

■ Pitch is controlled by the elevator, fitted to the aeroplane's horizontal tail surface.

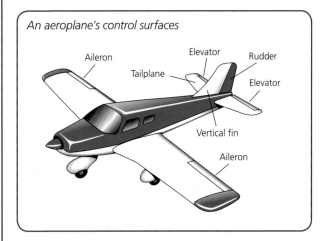

An aeroplane's control surfaces

■ Yaw is controlled by the rudder, fitted to the aeroplane's vertical tail surface.
■ Roll is controlled by the ailerons fitted to each wing.

When the pilot pulls the 'stick' back towards him it moves the elevator up, to point the nose upwards and make the aeroplane climb. The opposite happens when the 'stick' is pushed forwards, making the aeroplane descend.

When the pilot moves the 'stick' to the left, the left-hand aileron moves up, lowering the left-hand wing, and the right-hand aileron moves down, raising the right-hand wing. This makes the aeroplane roll to the left. When he moves the 'stick' to the right, the opposite happens.

When the pilot pushes the left-hand rudder pedal the rudder moves to the left, making the aeroplane yaw in that direction. The opposite happens when the right-hand rudder pedal is pushed.

To turn an aeroplane, the pilot uses both the 'stick' and rudder pedals to operate the ailerons and the rudder. This keeps the forces on the aeroplane balanced, and helps it to turn more easily.

And that's how an aeroplane flies!

Electricity

Electricity is actually a flow of tiny particles called electrons. An electron is one of the minute particles that make up an atom. To give an idea of just how small an electron is, to make a torch bulb stay lit for just one second takes a flow of about one million million million electrons!

Before we can explain how electricity flows, you need to know a little about how molecules and atoms work. Molecules are the basic building blocks of materials, and molecules are made up from groups of atoms (two or more) joined together. A single atom has a 'nucleus' (at the middle of the atom) with a number of electrons moving around it – if our solar system was an atom, then the sun would be the nucleus, and the various planets would be the electrons orbiting around it.

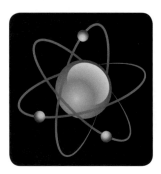

LEFT: Electrons orbiting round the nucleus of an atom.

All materials are either 'conductors' or 'insulators' – conductors allow electricity to flow through them, and insulators don't. The best conductors are metals, and they conduct electricity because when the atoms in a metal combine together to make molecules, the electrons near the outside of the atoms can wander freely around from one atom to another in the metal. These electrons are called 'free' electrons, and they make it easy for electricity to flow through the metal because they carry electrical energy from one atom to another.

So, electricity can flow easily through a metal, but it still needs something to make it flow from one point to another in the first place. The easiest way to get electricity flowing is to use a 'generator'. This uses the relationship between magnetism and electricity to make electricity flow, so now we need to explain a little about electricity and magnetism to show how a generator works.

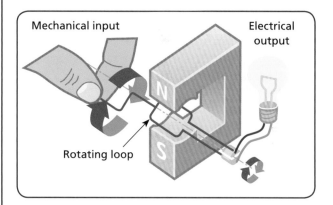

Mechanical input

Electrical output

Rotating loop

When electricity flows through a wire a magnetic field is created around the wire. Similarly, if a magnet is moved near a wire the magnetic field will cause electricity (electrons) to flow through the wire. A generator is a device that moves (spins) a magnet near a wire (or a wire near a magnet) to create a steady flow of electricity through the wire. A generator moves electricity rather like a pump pushing water through a pipe. A water pump can pump a certain amount of water, but it can also pump the water at a certain pressure; and a generator can pump a certain amount of electricity (the 'current', measured in 'amps'), but it can also pump it at a certain pressure (the 'voltage', measured in 'volts').

Another way to get electricity moving is to use a battery. A battery uses a chemical reaction to produce a flow of electrons, and electrons must flow from the negative terminal of the battery to the positive terminal for the chemical reaction to take place. This means that a battery will only produce a flow of electricity when an electrical circuit is connected between the two terminals.

Regardless of the method used to produce electricity, the source of the electricity (generator, battery, etc) will always have two terminals, one positive and one negative, and the flow of electrons will always be from the negative terminal through a wire or electrical circuit back to the positive terminal.

In an electrical circuit, a 'load' can be connected, and a load can be any device such as a light bulb, a TV, a cooker, a fridge, and so on.

So, now that you know where electricity comes from and how it flows, let's follow its journey from a power station to your home.

Electricity is produced at a power station by a generator, which works very much like the generator described previously. Most power stations use a generator driven by a water-powered (hydroelectric power station) or steam-powered turbine, although wind-powered generators are also becoming more common. A steam-powered turbine can be driven by burning coal or oil, or by a nuclear reactor.

The electricity flows from the generator to a 'substation' at the power station, where transformers convert the electricity to produce a very high voltage that will help it travel through wires over long distances. The electricity then passes into thick wires, often suspended by large pylons, which form the 'distribution grid'. When the electricity reaches a town or village, it runs into another substation, which lowers the voltage again to a safe level for use in the home. The electricity then passes from this substation through more wires to homes and businesses, ready to work its magic when a switch is pressed.

ABOVE LEFT: An ageing coal-fired power station produces a lot of pollution...

LEFT: ...but modern power generating systems, such as wind farms, are kinder to the environment.

RIGHT: Large pylons carry high-voltage electricity through wires over long distances.

BELOW: A typical electricity substation.

Telephone

A telephone is a remarkable simple device, which has very few components.

An ordinary telephone consists of the following basic parts:

- Microphone – changes the sound waves made by your voice into a varying electric current.
- Loudspeaker – changes electrical signals received from another telephone back into sound waves.
- Switch – connects the telephone to the telephone network.
- 'Duplex' coil – stops the sound of your own voice reaching your ear through the loudspeaker.
- Keypad and frequency generator – produces electrical signals to dial a number.
- Bell or electronic circuit to generate a ringing tone – tells you when your 'phone is ringing.

When you lift the handset, a switch connects your telephone to the 'phone network. When you dial a number, the keypad creates a number of electrical pulses that correspond to the number being called. These pulses are sent down the telephone line to an exchange, where electronic equipment automatically reads the signal so that it can route the call to the 'phone you're calling. The exchange can route calls to other national or international exchanges, which can transmit the signals by wire, fibre-optic cable, radio, or even satellite.

The exchange then sends a ring signal to the number being called so that the 'phone rings. When the person being called picks up their 'phone, the network connects the 'phones so that the people can talk to each other.

Now let's take a look at how a telephone sends your voice through the wires to the 'phone at the other end. When you speak into the mouthpiece its microphone converts the sound waves from your voice into electrical signals. Inside the microphone is a diaphragm, a thin metal disc which vibrates when sound waves hit it. Under this disc is a small cup-shaped container full of tiny carbon particles. A loud sound moves the metal disc a lot, which squashes the carbon particles together hard, but a quiet sound squashes them less. An electrical voltage – supplied either through the 'phone line, or from a battery in your 'phone – runs through the carbon particles to produce a current. The amount of current that can pass through them depends on how tightly the particles are squashed together – when they're tightly squashed (loud sound), more current can flow – so as you speak the electrical current flowing into the wires connecting your telephone to the network varies. These electrical signals are sent through the wires to the 'phone at the other end of the line.

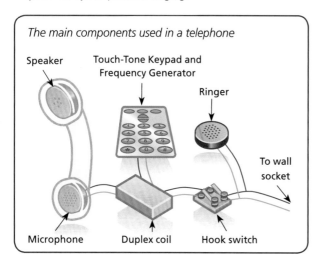

The main components used in a telephone

Speaker

Touch-Tone Keypad and Frequency Generator

Ringer

To wall socket

Microphone   Duplex coil   Hook switch

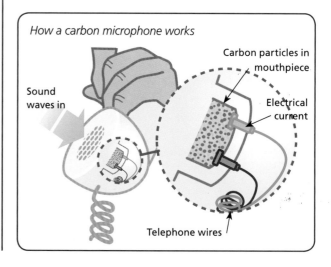

How a carbon microphone works

Carbon particles in mouthpiece

Sound waves in

Electrical current

Telephone wires

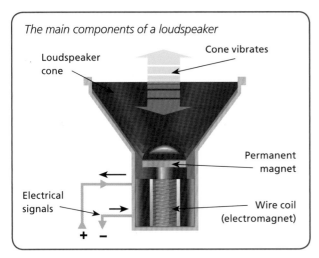

The main components of a loudspeaker

Loudspeaker cone

Cone vibrates

Permanent magnet

Electrical signals

Wire coil (electromagnet)

+ −

When the signals arrive at the 'phone you're calling they flow through an electromagnet in the earpiece, creating a magnetic field that pulls on a thin metal disc (another diaphragm). The amount that the diaphragm moves depends on the electrical current flowing through the electromagnet. As the diaphragm moves it moves the air around it, creating sound waves. The movement of the diaphragm turns the electrical signals back into sound waves almost the same as the ones that went into the microphone at the other end of the line. Because electrical signals travel extremely fast you can have a conversation with the person at the other end of the line just as if you were both in the same room.

Cordless telephone

A cordless 'phone works using radio signals, the handset having a built-in transmitter and receiver. The system works in exactly the same way as a normal 'phone, but all the electrical signals travelling to and from the handset are converted into radio signals and sent to and from a 'base unit'. The base unit also has a radio transmitter and receiver, and is connected to the 'phone line. The base unit connects the handset to the 'phone network, making it possible to hold a conversation as long as the handset is within radio range of the base station.

Mobile telephone

With a mobile 'phone, all the signals are sent via a radio network instead of through a network of wires.

The 'phone sends signals to a base station which has an aerial mast and a small unit containing radio equipment. There are a huge number of base stations, which divide the country up into small zones. When you make a call, your 'phone communicates with the nearest base station, which sends signals to the mobile 'phone company's exchange. This exchange is connected to the rest of the mobile network and also to the normal landline 'phone system. As you move around, your mobile 'phone is switched to communicate with the nearest base station, and as long as you're within range of a base station you'll always be able to use your 'phone.

Radio

The sound produced by a radio is carried by invisible waves travelling through the air. Thousands of radio waves are travelling around us all the time, and since they travel at the speed of light it's possible to transmit and receive information instantly. They can be used to transmit many different types of information, including sounds, TV pictures and signals used by satellite navigation systems and radio control models.

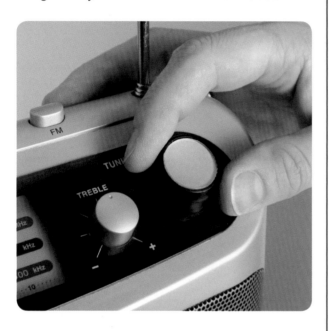

Radio systems work by turning signals (such as sound or TV pictures) into electrical signals. These signals are used to control a radio wave, and the wave itself is produced by continuously varying an electrical current in a wire. The wave produced is called a 'sine' wave – a wave which varies smoothly. When a sine wave passes through a wire it produces a radio signal, which, when it's passed to a transmitter aerial, can be sent through the air or even into space.

A normal sine wave doesn't contain any information itself, but it can be added by varying or 'modulating' the wave. There are three different ways of doing this:

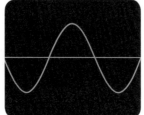

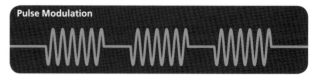

Pulse Modulation

■ Pulse modulation (PM) varies the wave by simply turning it on and off. This is the system used in simple Morse code transmitters. The first radio signal sent across the Atlantic in 1901 was a simple Morse code message.

Amplitude Modulation

■ Amplitude modulation (AM) varies the 'amplitude' of the wave. The amplitude relates to the height of the wave's peaks, and depends on the voltage used to make the wave. AM is used for AM radio stations and for TV picture signals.

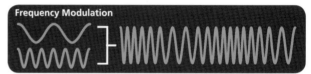

Frequency Modulation

■ Frequency modulation (FM) varies the 'frequency' of the sine wave. The frequency of the wave relates to the distance between the wave's peaks. Peaks close together give a high frequency, and peaks further apart give a low frequency. FM is used for FM radio, TV sound signals and mobile 'phones.

So the information that needs to be sent, such as a voice or music, is used to modulate the radio (sine) wave, and when the radio wave is sent into the atmosphere it transmits the information. The work of changing the information into an electrical signal, using the electrical signal to modulate the radio wave and sending the radio wave into the atmosphere is done by a 'transmitter'.

To be able to read the information that the radio wave carries, a 'receiver' is needed. Radios and TVs are receivers, and a mobile 'phone contains both a transmitter and a receiver.

A receiver has an aerial to allow it to find radio waves in the air. Because there are thousands of radio waves passing through the air at any one time, the radio waves picked up by the aerial are sent to a tuner, which separates the signal that's wanted from all those that aren't. If you're listening to a programme on the radio you'll have tuned the radio to the station you want to listen to. The station you're listening to is transmitted on one particular frequency, and by tuning the radio you tell the tuner to allow that frequency through but to ignore all the others picked up by the aerial. The tuner sends the signal to a 'detector', which turns the information carried by the radio wave back into an electrical signal. The electrical signal is sent to an amplifier, and the amplifier sends the signal to a loudspeaker to produce the sound.

Because a huge number of devices use radio waves and there are thousands of radio waves passing through the air at any one time, all the signals need to be different so that they don't get confused and interfere with each other. Each signal therefore has a different 'frequency', meaning

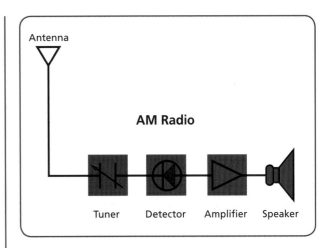

the distance between the peaks of the waves. If you get fed up with listening to one frequency (station) you can tune in to another.

To avoid interference and confusion, there are rules about radio frequencies to make sure that a certain frequency can only be used by one device in a particular area.

Television

TV pictures and sounds, whether they're recorded or are being transmitted live, are transformed into electrical signals – usually by a TV camera or a video recorder/player – before they're transmitted by radio waves or cables.

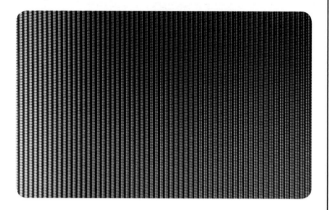

The electrical signals needed for a TV programme are transmitted in exactly the same way as radio signals, although two separate signals are transmitted (the picture signal and the sound signal). A TV set has a receiver, similar to a radio receiver, which decodes the radio signals and turns them back into electrical signals.

TV sound works in exactly the same way as in a radio, and the sound signals are sent to loudspeakers. The sound is synchronised with the picture signal so that the scene on the TV appears realistic.

Television pictures work by making use of the way the human brain pieces together information. A TV picture is made up of thousands of tiny coloured dots, and because the dots are tiny the human brain can piece them together to make an image. These tiny dots are called pixels.

The movement on the screen is actually made up of a rapid sequence of still pictures. Each picture is very slightly different, because something – or several things – will have moved. When these pictures are shown in sequence, rapidly, one after the other, the brain puts them together to produce movement. How realistic the movement looks depends on how many pictures (frames) per second are shown on the screen. If any less than around 15 frames per second are shown, the movement starts to look jerky.

There are three common types of TV screen: CRT (cathode ray tube – the traditional type of TV set), plasma display and LCD (liquid crystal display).

CRT display

This has a large vacuum-filled tube, with a screen (which is what you see) at one end. Behind the screen is an electron gun, which fires three separate beams of electrons at the screen. (See the section on how electricity works for an explanation of what an electron is.) The three beams of electrons correspond to the three colours used to make up TV pictures – red, green and blue.

To move across the screen and make up the picture these electron beams need to be controlled. This is done using 'steering coils', which steer them by means of a magnetic field. Varying the magnetic field deflects the beams.

The screen is coated with thousands of tiny dots of phosphor, a chemical which glows when hit by electrons. Three different types of phosphor are used. One glows red, one green and one blue, and they're grouped together in threes – one dot of each colour – to form pixels. How brightly each dot glows depends on the intensity of the electron beam that hits it. Using the three coloured dots, each pixel can be made to show any colour.

To fill the screen with a picture, the electron beams move rapidly across the screen to 'paint' lines across it. In the UK the picture is made up of 625 lines, and the whole screen is filled around 25–30 times per second, so the electron beams move across the screen over 15,000 times per second!

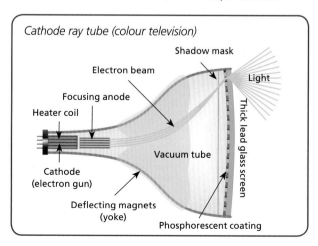

Cathode ray tube (colour television)

- Shadow mask
- Electron beam
- Light
- Focusing anode
- Heater coil
- Thick lead glass screen
- Cathode (electron gun)
- Vacuum tube
- Deflecting magnets (yoke)
- Phosphorescent coating

Plasma display

A plasma display works using a similar principle to the CRT display, by illuminating tiny dots of phosphor (grouped to form pixels) to form a picture. But instead of using electron beams to light up the phosphor dots, plasma is used. The plasma used in TV screens is a gas which gives off light when electricity flows through it.

The screen is made up of thousands of dots of phosphor, each of them in its own tiny sealed cell containing plasma. A network of electrodes (wires) run across the screen, and by carefully controlling the electricity supply to the electrodes the amount of light produced by each cell can be controlled, in turn controlling the colour of each pixel. A computer controls the electricity supply to the electrodes according on the picture signals received from the TV tuner, and the electricity supply to each individual cell can be varied many thousands of times in a fraction of a second to change the picture on the screen.

An LCD display

This uses 'liquid crystals' of a substance part-way between a crystal (solid) and a liquid. The display is made up of a thousands of cells like a plasma display, and again the cells are grouped in threes to form pixels. However, instead of plasma and a dot of phosphor each cell contains a liquid crystal substance with a coloured filter, either red, green or blue.

The liquid crystal doesn't actually produce light, but the amount of light allowed to pass through it can be varied depending on the electrical current going through. LCD displays therefore need to have a source of light, usually provided by fluorescent tubes fitted behind the display.

Again, a computer controls the supply of electricity to each cell, to vary the amount of light passing through, which in turn changes the picture on the screen.

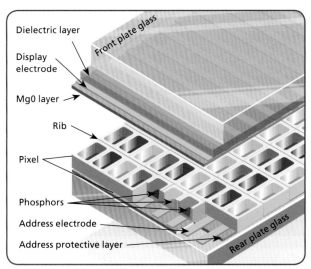

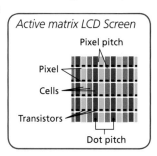

Active matrix LCD Screen

Computer

A computer is a machine which can carry out millions of calculations per second. For a computer to do its job, three things are needed – hardware, software and an input.

- ■ Hardware includes the computer itself and its internal components, and peripherals such as keyboard, monitor, mouse, printer, etc.
- ■ Software is the programs that the computer uses to perform the jobs it's asked to do.
- ■ Input is supplied by the person operating the computer when they type a command on the keyboard or click on the mouse.

The heart of any computer is it's central processing unit (CPU), a microprocessor which carries out all the main calculations and information processing necessary for the computer to complete the jobs it's asked to do.

A microprocessor carries out calculations using a 'binary' number system – a system of counting where just two digits, '0' and '1', are used to represent all numbers. (The numbers we use in everyday life are 'decimal' numbers.) To understand how binary numbers work, let's look at how decimal numbers work first.

A decimal number such as 3,568 is made up of three thousands (3,000, or 3 x 10 x 10 x 10), five hundreds (500, or 5 x 10 x 10), six tens (60, or 6 x 10) and eight ones (8, or 8 x 1). Now for the most important part – 1,000 (10 x 10 x 10) can also be written as 10^3 or '10 to the power of three', and 100 (10 x 10) can also be written as 10^2 or '10 to the power of two', whilst 10 (1 x 10) can also be written as 10^1 and 1 can also be written as 10^0. So, working from the right-hand end of the number, the first digit corresponds to 10^0, the next digit to 10^1, the next digit to 10^2, the next digit to 10^3, and so on. So, the number 3,568 is:

$$(8 \times 1) + (6 \times 10) + (5 \times 100) + (3 \times 1,000) = 3,568.$$

Just as the number we looked at previously is made up from 'powers of 10', so a binary number is made up from 'powers of 2'. Let's take the binary number 10010 as an example. If we work from the right-hand end, the first digit in the number 10010 represents 2^0, or '1', the second digit represents 2^1, or '2', the third digit represents 2^2, or 4, the fourth digit represents 2^3, or 8, and the final digit represents 2^4, or 16. So, the number 10010 is:

$$(0 \times 1) + (1 \times 2) + (0 \times 4) + (0 \times 8) + (1 \times 16) = 18.$$

This shows how any number can be represented using '0s' and '1s'.

A microprocessor is really a very complex system of thousands and thousands of switches, and the microprocessor processes information by turning switches on and off. A switch operates when a certain voltage is passed through it, so the voltage determines whether the switch is on or off. So, if two different voltages are used in the circuit that contains the switch, the two voltages can be used to represent two different numbers, '0' and '1' ('on' or 'off'). This is how a microprocessor can carry out millions of calculations per second by using binary numbers.

Let's look at the other main components of a computer, and how they work with the CPU:

- Power supply – supplies electricity to the computer's circuits.
- Operating system – the software that allows the computer to function.
- Memory – allows the computer to 'remember' information. Various different memory systems are used, but the two most important are RAM (Random Access Memory), used to store temporary information that the computer is currently working with, and ROM (Read Only Memory), a permanent memory used to store information that doesn't change.
- Motherboard – the main circuit board, which usually contains the CPU, memory and various other systems.
- Hard disk – a permanent storage area, used to store large chunks of information such as programs and working files, etc.
- Modem – translates the digital signals produced by a computer into signals which can be transmitted via a 'phone line.
- Mouse – translates the movement of your hand into signals the computer can understand.
- Keyboard – translates keystrokes into signals that can be recognised by the computer.
- Monitor – allows the data being input and output to be viewed.
- Ports – allow various peripherals, such as printers, scanners, cameras, etc, to be connected to the computer.
- Removable storage devices – allow data to be read from, or stored on ('written to') discs, such as CDs, DVDs and memory sticks.
- Sounds card, graphics card, etc – convert the digital signals produced by the computer into sounds, signals that can be displayed by the monitor, etc.

All the above components are linked together – the hard disc is connected to the various peripherals via interfaces, so that data can be input and output. Interfaces are electronic circuits that allow the hard disk and the CPU to communicate with the various peripherals.

Internet

The internet is basically a network of networks. When your computer connects to the internet through your service provider (ISP) you become part of their network, and their network connects to tens of thousands of others through the internet.

The millions of signals travelling through the internet are passed to their correct destinations using 'routers'. A router joins two networks, passing information from one to another.

Every computer connected to the internet has an IP (Internet Protocol) address, which identifies it. By using the IP addresses two computers that are communicating can make sure that the information being sent is routed to the correct receiving computer.

Managing editor	Louise McIntyre	
Copy editor	Ian Heath	
Design and layout	Richard Parsons and James Robertson	
Colour illustrations	Rob Loxston	
Line illustrations	Matthew Marke	

SUBJECT	AUTHORS	PHOTOS
INTRODUCTION How to be a brilliant father	Andrew Parkinson	istockphoto.com
MAKING TOYS Stilts All other projects	 Richard Blizzard Andrew Parkinson	 R J Coleman James Mann
SIMPLE FUN All projects	Andrew Parkinson	James Mann and istockphoto.com
SKILLS Riding a bike Skateboarding Tying knots Juggling	 Pete Shoemark Andrew Parkinson Andrew Parkinson Andrew Parkinson	 istockphoto.com, Paul Buckland James Mann istockphoto.com istockphoto.com
SPORTS BASICS All subjects	Martin Sayers	istockphoto.com
GAMES All subjects	Andrew Parkinson	James Mann, istockphoto.com, alamy.com (page 82)
TRICKS All subjects	Andrew Parkinson	James Mann, istockphoto.com
OUT AND ABOUT All subjects	Andrew Parkinson	istockphoto.com
KITCHEN FUN All subjects	Maggie Pannell	istockphoto.com, foodanddrinkphotos.com
GROWING FUN THINGS All subjects	Zia Allaway	Brian North
BUILDING THINGS Go-kart Playhouse See-saw Rope ladder Doll's house Ramps Model railway	 Steve Rendle Richard Blizzard Richard Blizzard Richard Blizzard Charles Armstrong Andrew Parkinson Robert Iles	 Steve Rendle, Paul Buckland R J Coleman R J Coleman R J Coleman Charles Armstrong James Mann Peco publications and publicity
HOW THINGS WORK All subjects	Steve Rendle	istockphoto.com, Ford

The publishers would like to thank all contributors to the *Dad Manual*, in particular Andrew Parkinson, for his ideas, time and commitment to the projects (helped by the fact that he's obviously a great dad!)

Richard Blizzard would like to thank:

Robert Coleman, Robin and Claire Birchill, Patricia Blizzard, David Ward, David Barlow, Robert Amor and Mr McCrudden of J.B. Nedia Ltd.

Andrew Parkinson would like to thank the following for their contribution:

Ellie Rowles, Jacob Rowles, Roy Williams, John Parkinson, Edd [sic] Stoneman, Mark Gale, Rosie Morrison, Norman Reed, Rose Reed, Stephen Biggs, Tom Butterworth, Bill Keen, Roy Williams, Gareth Soden, Marie Parkinson